Library Co-Operation in a Networked World

Library Co-Operation in a Networked World

Neelesh Kashyap

RANDOM PUBLICATIONS
NEW DELHI (INDIA)

Library Co-Operation in a Networked World

ISBN 978-93-5111-852-7

Published in 2016 in India by

RANDOM PUBLICATIONS

4376-A/4B, Gali Murari Lal, Ansari Road
New Delhi-110 002
Phone : +9111-43580356, 011-23289044, 011-43142548
e-mail: sales@randompublications.com,
info@randompublications.com, randomexports@gmail.com

Type Setting by : Friends Media, Delhi-110089
Digitally Printed at : Replika Press Pvt. Ltd.

Preface

Libraries have been cooperating and collaborating on collection building and resource sharing for many years. The cooperation was based on inter-library loan and preparation and publication of union catalogue. But the ways of cooperation in building resources and access to information resources was not easy and effective. Library cooperation for access to information resources was limited to the formation of networking among the libraries having homogeneous interest. To ascertain the status of collection of information resources, networking, resource sharing and automation of libraries, a questionnaire based survey has been conducted. The library surveyed fall into the following categories (a) academic libraries (b) research / special libraries. It is found that in terms of collection of information resources, the efforts of most of the libraries are confined to acquiring books only. Majority of libraries are not subscribing to current titles of journal.

Many libraries have not taken part in resource sharing network and library cooperation programme. However, a large number of libraries surveyed subscribe to online journals through a library consortium and they already initiated library automation programme. But a great chunk of the libraries developed library software to provide database service to its institution members only. Very few libraries developed software to provide database service to serve world wide. The establishment of digital library by majority of libraries to provide full text information resources is still a far cry. This study delineates the ways of web-based library cooperation with the conclusion that the automation of libraries and effective formation of country consortium can only promote the effective library cooperation for access to world wide information and global resource s haring. Current study also recommends that government should take up development project to provide appropriate ICT training at global standard.

–Author

Contents

1

National Information Policy Issues in the Networked Environment with References to Library Co-operation

NATIONAL POLICY ON PUBLIC LIBRARIES IN INDIA

Pre–Five-Year Plan Period

The programmes executed by provincial and central governments since 1910 for the social and adult education of the populace have paved the way for the enactment of library laws and rules for grants-in-aid in the country. Hence, public library finance is part of the education budget. The level of literacy in 1941 being as low as 16 per cent, universalization of elementary education and eradication of illiteracy in the nation were the aims of the education policy of the government. To fulfil this goal, a variety of programmes were undertaken such as extension services, continuing education, social education, part-time education, refresher courses, non-formal education, and adult education.

In order to accelerate the pace of socio–economic development, the government considered public libraries to be an integral part of development projects. In 1948, the first public library bill was passed in the state of Madras, mainly due to the efforts of the eminent librarian S.R. Ranganathan. One of the earliest Advisory Committees-the Sinha Committee, appointed in 1957-recommended that public libraries be developed on the basis of a hierarchical network. The hierarchy should have the national central library at the apex, followed by state central libraries, district libraries, block libraries and panchayat libraries. This is the foundation upon which the public library system has been built.

First Five-Year Plan (1951–1956)

The first plan provision was ₹ 140 million for social education, physical education, and youth welfare, out of the total budget for education of ₹ 1.33

billion. Libraries were considered to be part of social education. ₹ 5 million was set aside for establishment of the national central library, but this sum was not used.Improvement of library services was mentioned in this plan for educational development. The essence of the scheme was to establish district libraries in each state, which were to be supplemented by a state central library. The government of India also initiated a scheme, "Integrated Library Service," with the support of the state government. The scheme targeted units in every area selected by the governments for intensive educational development.

The experimental project was meant to monitor the impact of a number of educational institutions in areas covering 100 villages. Each area was to have five model community centers, plus a main library with branches to distribute books to 20 villages. This pilot project was implemented in 29 areas in the country. Nine states made plans to open state central libraries, and some others were in the process of setting up district libraries in about 100 districts. This cost approximately ₹ 10 million, of which nearly two–thirds was contributed by the government of India. Thus, libraries were considered to be an essential part of the Community Development Programme that was launched during the first plan period.

Other important developments included establishment of the Delhi Public Library in 1951. The Central Reference Library in Calcutta was established in 1955. Connemara Public Library, in Madras became the State Central Library in 1950 under the provisions of the Madras Public Libraries Act of 1948; in 1955, it became one of the three depository libraries. At the end of March 1954, the country had 32,000 libraries with a book stock of about 7.1 million volumes; an amount of ₹ 9 million was spent on library services. By 1951, the level of literacy had risen to 18.33 per cent.

In 1954, the Delivery of Books Act was passed to include newspapers. The act obligated every publisher in India to deposit a copy of its publication with the National Library in Calcutta; the Asiatic Society Library, Bombay; Connemara Public Library, Madras; and the Delhi Public Library. On the basis of books received under this act, India has a national bibliography which is published by the Central Reference Library, Calcutta. The bibliography, however, does not include textbooks, musical scores, maps, and atlases.

Second Five-Year Plan, (1956–1961)

Of the ₹ 2.040 billion budgeted for education, ₹ 100 million was proposed for social education, physical education, and youth welfare. This plan contained the same provisions as the first plan, plus additional provisions for establishing integrated library service. There were three objectives. First, state and district libraries were to be set up in each state. Second, the library services were to be organized on the basis of legislation. Finally, district libraries were to form the link between the state central library and village libraries. As a result, nine states in India established state central libraries and 254 district libraries. But the national central library was still not established. In 1960, the state of Andhra Pradesh enacted library legislation.

During this plan period, a total of ₹ 2.040 billion was spent on educational development, of which ₹ 9 million was spent on library development. Even though ₹ 18.6 million was provided, the states only used 48.6 per cent of this amount. Thus, the number of libraries nearly doubled in 1964 as compared to 1951, and the expenditure on public libraries in this period increased three–fold. A UNESCO report published on the occasion of the Public Library Seminar held at Delhi in 1955, India had 24,086 public library service points at the time. The level of literacy in 1961 increased to 28.31 per cent.

The Advisory Committee for Libraries was appointed in 1957 by the Government of India, with K.P. Sinha as the chairman.

The committee drafted a Model Library Bill and drew up a 25-year plan. In 1959, the committee submitted a report with recommendations, some of which follow:

- Enact library legislation, in all constituent states, to establish public libraries;
- Build nationwide library service with detailed suggestions for financing through the state and central governments;
- Extend public library service to the blocks, panchayats, and villages; and,
- Create an independent Department of Social Education and Libraries.

Third Five-Year Plan, (1962–1967)

The amount of ₹ 5.6 billion was budgeted for education in this plan period, but the amount to be spent on libraries was not clearly indicated in the plan. Of this amount, ₹ 620 million was expected to be available for social education. During this plan period, the system of central government assistance to the states was changed, and funding for libraries was kept to a bare minimum.

Thus, it was up to the individual states to take the initiative and develop their public libraries. With the beginning of this plan period, the scheme to assist state governments in establishing state central libraries, district central libraries, and block development libraries was abandoned. The central government decided to let the states decide on the development; the decision was a major setback that hindered the development of public libraries.

During this plan period, four national libraries were to be established at Delhi, Calcutta, Bombay, and Madras. District–level libraries were to be established in all the states. A sum of ₹ 32.3 million was made available to the states for this purpose.

In 1962 the central government sent a model Public Libraries Bill to those state governments which had not adopted any library legislation, hoping to persuade these states to show an interest in passing the legislation. A Working Group on Libraries was appointed by the Planning Commission in 1964. Group recommendations included:

- By the end of the Fifth Five Year Plan, set up libraries at block headquarters and in every village having a population of 5,000;
- Encourage the Programme of Adult Education to use the services of the public libraries to eradicate illiteracy.

As of January 1, 1965, according to the information received from the states by the Working Group:

- Twelve of 18 states/UT had state central libraries;
- 205 of 327 districts had district central libraries;
- 1,394 blocks of 5,223 had block development libraries;
- 28,317 villages out of 566,878 had village libraries.

Library legislation was passed in two states during this period: Karnataka in 1965, and Maharashtra in 1967.

Fourth Five-Year Plan, (1969–1974)

The education budget was estimated at ₹ 7.120 billion of which the social education component was ₹ 100 million. Thus, the tempo that had built for the development of library services slowed. However, ₹ 130 million was provided in this plan period for provision of information services, which included information centers, radio transmitters, film production, mobile cine vans, and other media.

The literacy level rose to 34.45 per cent in 1971.In 1972, the Working Group on Development of Public Libraries was constituted by the Government of India Planning Commission to make recommendations for library development. These recommendations were to be included in the Fifth Five Year Plan.

The group submitted detailed proposals for:

- Allotment of ₹ 310 million for the development of public libraries; but the amount actually provided was a meager ₹ 20 million;
- A network of libraries to cover the whole country, and other recommendations similar to those made earlier by the Advisory Committee.

Figures provided in 1973 concerned the number of public libraries, and read as follows:

- Fifteen of 21 states/UT had state central libraries;
- 235 of 376 districts had district central libraries;
- 1,500 of 3,100 sub–districts had sub–district central libraries;
- 50,000 villages of 566,878 had village libraries;
- 1,800 of 2,641 towns had town libraries.

In 1972, during this plan period, the central government established the Raja Rammohun Roy Library Foundation. The foundation was created as an autonomous body under the Department of Culture, controlled by the Ministry of Education, for the development of public libraries in India. This foundation matches the funds of the states for purchasing furniture and books, organizing conferences and seminars, and providing mobile library service to the rural areas. It also advises the central government on all matters relating to library development in the country.

Fifth Five-Year Plan, (1974–1979)

An adult education programme was the emphasis of this plan. The programme was to be supported by a network of libraries at the village and block levels, and various community centers. Thus, steps were taken to strengthen not only the village and block libraries, but also the central and state libraries, and the district libraries. The states were assisted by the Raja Rammohun Roy Library Foundation, which was established in 1972. During this plan period, the amount of ₹ 15.620 billion was allocated for general education, and ₹ 350 million was budgeted for social education.

The only state that enacted a public library law during this plan period was West Bengal, in 1979. In 1978, the government adopted the National Adult Education Programme, but it did not recognize the public library as an agency that could be assigned a role in solving the literacy problem. Rather, the public library was relegated to the role of post–literacy work. This view was also promulgated by the Draft National Policy on Education (NPE), 1979. However, the need for the rural public library system to play a role in continuing education in the villages and rural areas was recognized.

In 1979, the Ministry of Education in the Department of Culture established a library section under the charge of an under secretary. The goal: to promote development of public libraries in India. Since then, libraries have not been part of the social education budget. Instead, they have been included in the art and culture component of the budget.

Sub–Sixth Five-Year Plan, (1980–1985)

This plan emphasized minimum essential education of all adults, to be achieved by inter-sectoral cooperation and interand150; agency coordination. These efforts were to be supported by post–literacy, continuing education through a network of rural libraries as well as instructional programmes conducted through mass communication media. The amount allocated for general education was ₹ 21.622 billion. The art and culture component was ₹ 839 million.

During this period:

- Twenty–six states/UT out of 31 existing in 1982 had established/ designated state central libraries;
- Out of 401 districts, 291 had district central libraries;
- Out of 5,027 blocks, 1,798 development blocks had block libraries;

- Out of 575,936 villages, 41,828 had village libraries;
- Out of 2,643 towns, 1,280 had town libraries.

Of the 29 metropolitan cities with a population of 400,000 and above, only four — Madras, Hyderabad, Bangalore, and Delhi — have city public library systems with central libraries, branches, and deposit stations. Thus, it is estimated that approximately 20 per cent of the literate population has access to public library service.

A Working Group on Modernization of Library Services and Informatics in the Seventh Plan was appointed by the Planning Commission in 1983. In its 1984 report, the group recommended formulation of a National Policy on Library Services and Informatics in support of similar recommendations made earlier by other committees.

From its establishment in 1972, to 1982, the Raja Rammohun Roy Foundation provided funds of ₹ 250 million to assist 15,000 rural libraries. In 1982, the Delhi Public Library became a copyright library. The level of literacy increased to 43.56 per cent in 1981.

Seventh Five-Year Plan, (1985–1990)

During this Plan period, the Planning Commission's objective was to address the needs of 90 million people, ages 15–35, in the Adult Education Programme. The network of libraries was to play a role in the development of literature for neoliterates. Library systems were to be strengthened with specific attention given to improvement of facilities at the national-level institutions. The general education budget was ₹ 47,753 million; ₹ 4.821 billion constituted the art and culture component.

An important development during this period was the 1986 adoption of the National Literacy Mission, which emphasized the education of women and also the establishment of rural libraries.

In 1989, there were 7,180 main libraries and 18,000 service points. The collections of the National Library of Calcutta were increased significantly. The Central Secretariat Library started creating a database on the epic "Mahabharata." The Raja Rammohun Roy Foundation set up an "Integrated Research Cell-cum-Computer Unit" for promoting research in librarianship, and also started a database of public libraries in the country. A Committee on National Policy on Library and Information System was appointed in 1985 by the Government of India, Department of Culture. The resulting final report was submitted in 1986. This policy stressed the need to establish strong links between a village's community library and primary school. If the school lacked a library, the community library was to provide the children with adequate resources. Furthermore, a children's section was to be organized in every public library. The National Policy on Education, 1986 barely mentions libraries. It states that a nationwide movement for improvement of existing libraries and the establishment of new ones will be taken up, provision will be made in all educational institutions for library facilities, and the status of librarians improved. The school library programme, "Operation Blackboard," was initiated with the provision of essential teaching and learning materials.

The National Book Policy–1986 also had an impact on libraries, as it recommended:

- Provision of reading material for children by all the agencies involved;
- That 10 per cent of the annual education budget of the governments be used to purchase books for libraries.

During this plan period, these states passed library acts: Manipur in 1988, Assam in 1989, Haryana in 1989, and Kerala in 1989.

Eighth Five-Year Plan, (1992–1997)

The money allocated for this period for general education is ₹ 168.133 billion; for art and culture, ₹ 7.276 billion has been allocated. Universalization of elementary education, eradication of illiteracy in the 15-35-year age group, and strengthening of vocational education in relation to emerging needs in urban and rural settings are the major thrusts of the plan. These goals are to be achieved by using formal, non-formal, and open channels of learning. The plan states that in those states with an advanced library system, rural libraries should become the focal points for post–literacy and continuing education programmes.

Book promotion is also emphasized in this plan, to be promoted by the organization of a National Centre for Children's Literature, which should produce 3,000 titles annually. Important books are to be translated into the various Indian languages, and books for neoliterates published. Publishers and voluntary agencies will be given assistance, and the school library programme, undertaken as part of the "Operation Blackboard" scheme of the National Policy on Education-1986, will continue.

Public libraries of national importance are to be provided funds for improvements/innovations such as the following:

- The Khuda Baksh Public Library proposed establishment of an Institute of Oriental Studies and open regional units for research on Indo-Islamic and comparative religion;
- The Rampur Raza Library would acquire sophisticated equipment for preservation of its collections;
- The Asiatic Society, Calcutta, is to open an art gallery, introduce a desktop publishing system, and construct a new building;
- The National Library proposed making microfilms available, producing a national union catalogue, and providing book production statistics;
- The Central Reference Library is to be reorganized into a National Bibliographical and Documentation Center with a computer center; and,

- The Delhi Public Library is to open two new libraries within its service area.

The Raja Rammohun Roy Foundation proposes assisting state central libraries in their quest to obtain reprographic equipment. The Foundation also hopes to assist certain libraries in the processing of rare books, and to provide assistance to rural libraries, and to those public libraries that have completed 100 years of service.

The Model Public Libraries Act is based on the national seminar on this subject, which was held February 14, 1990, in New Delhi. The seminar was organized by the Indian Library Association in collaboration with the Raja Rammohun Roy Library Foundation. This excellent document encompasses all aspects of legislation important to the establishment of public libraries.

The National Cultural Policy, 1993 is the new policy designed by the Government of India. It was created by merging the National Policy of Library and Information Science, the National Book Policy, and other related policies dealt with by the Department of Culture of the Ministry of Human Resource Development.

LIBRARY LEGISLATION

The Nature of the Problem

It would appear at first sight that provision and public maintenance of a system of public libraries would be an obvious step in any country where education and the promotion of literacy were considered important. Education, after all, is not an end in itself; the individual must not only have access to the printed word during his period of formal education, he must have the means of enlarging his experience after school and university, and this necessarily implies organized collections of printed materials. If a library is an essential adjunct to school or college, it is an essential adjunct in the world outside.

One would also think that the legislative base for such a system of public libraries would be a comparatively simple matter, and that those libraries would automatically be free for all to use. It is almost universally recognized that education should be compulsory, and that it should be free up to a certain level. True, cost can be a limiting factor but few countries today do not devote a large proportion of their resources to educational provision. Neither of these assumptions is in fact correct. Systems of public libraries, as against individual public libraries, have only recently been recognized as essential, even in advanced countries, and many countries, some with a secure basis of culture and education, do not have generally applicable public library legislation. Examples are France, Belgium, the Netherlands and Italy. Even where public library legislation has been long established, it can be seen from the examples studied here that, in the framework of the modern State, public library law is noticeably defective. The development of public libraries has probably been hampered by the paradox that they were in fact recognized as instruments of popular education and social welfare long before the conception of compulsory education and before the legal framework of the modern State was established. The concept of the public library has been essentially that of a local community project.

All countries have public libraries, buildings where books are provided for general reading, either free of charge or for a small subscription. They have been provided in thousands all over the world by charitable bodies, educational, social and religious organizations, by philanthropic individuals, as memorials to a person or to commemorate an occasion.

The public libraries in England and the United States in the early nineteenth century were typical, but they are not always a passing phase of development. The traveller interested in the phenomenon will come across examples almost anywhere: in Asia, for example, the Hardinge Library in Delhi, the Connemara Library in Madras, the Raffles Library in Singapore; in Africa, the King George VI Memorial Library in Tanga, the Connaught Library in Nairobi. Some become moribund.

Some are being or have been incorporated by good fortune into a national or local public library system. Some operate even today with some success. But they are not public libraries in the modern accepted sense, nor were they, for that matter, in the nineteenth century.

Edward Edwards, pioneer of the public library in Great Britain, summed up their built-in failure over a hundred years ago, in evidence to the Select Committee on Public Libraries of the House of Commons in 1849:

- Without some assured provision of the means of continued increase, as well as simple preservation-no man ever secured to posterity the true advantage of a public library. To those persons, therefore, who took thought of such matters, two principles to start with seemed plain. The one that new libraries should be formed in a catholic spirit. The other, that they should be freed from all dependence either in gifts or in current 'subscriptions', for their permanent support. The first principle involved the corollary that the new institutions and their management should stand entirely aloof from party influences in politics or religion. The second principle involved the corollary that the maintenance must be by rate, levied on the whole tax-paying community, and administered by its elective and responsible functionaries.

This statement quite obviously implied that a legal basis was necessary, if the public library was to be a permanent institution and on the implications of this statement most of the public library legislation of the nineteenth century and early twentieth century was founded. In 1949, Unesco issued the first international declaration on the need and the functions of the public library, and in it was contained the same principle:

- This manifesto, by describing the potentialities of the public library, proclaims Unesco's belief in the public library as a living force for popular education and for the growth of international understanding and thereby for the promotion of peace.
- The public library is a product of modern democracy and a practical demonstration of democracy's faith in universal education as a lifelong process.
- Though primarily intended to serve the educational needs of adults, the public library should also supplement the work of schools in developing the reading tastes of children and young people, helping them to become adults who can use books with appreciation and profit.
- As a democratic institution operated by the people for the people, the public library should be: established and maintained under clear authority of law: supported wholly or mainly from public funds: open for free use on equal terms to all members of the community, regardless of occupa-tion, creed, class, or race.

The manifesto goes on to define the purposes and list some of the services of the public library. It did not, however, attempt to deal with a problem that was already engaging the attention of public librarians and those concerned with the spread of education and literacy, that there must not only be a legal base, but that that base must give equal opportunity to all citizens to use the services of public libraries. In other words, the legislation must be mandatory and cover the whole of the area falling within the scope of the legislation. The legislation must also provide for something more than opportunities for voluntary co-operation between libraries-it must provide for a nation-wide service, even though the public library remains a locally rooted institution. In 1953, Unesco organized its first seminar on public libraries in developing countries, at Ibadan, in Nigeria. Eighteen countries were represented, mostly in West Africa. Legislation was one of the primary subjects discussed, and in the general report of the seminar, the following statement of principles was included:

- Only legislation can empower the appropriate authorities to provide the service and ensure adequate financial support and efficient administration according to a national standard. Only legislation can define the functions of the providing authority, create the conditions in which it may fulfil those functions, and ensure development.

Library law for national schemes should include the following elements:

- General authorization of expenditure without fixing a maximum.
- Compulsory implementation whenever conditions become favourable. The basis of favourable conditions, it is suggested, is the possession

of necessary finance and all requisite material by the providing authority, the existence of a tested organization and the presence of trained and experienced personnel. Compulsory provision is never likely to precede compulsory primary education.

- The obligation to employ only qualified and trained personnel as librarians, and to authorize development only when professional librarians are available to administer the service.
- Service for the entire population in some form or other.
- The inter-lending of books between libraries so that the book resources of the whole territory shall be available to all.
- The book stock shall embrace every shade of opinion, without prejudice to anyone.
- The national scheme in all its parts shall aim at free service.

An addendum to this statement pointed out that there was great difficulty in arriving at a conclusion regarding compulsory legislation, since it was recognized that permissive legislation might well allow for a high standard to be set by enthusiastic authorities, which would act as an inspiration to others. This, and other proposals of the Ibadan seminar, were an act of faith at the time they were published, in view of the conditions of West Africa at the time, just beginning to emerge from colonial rule, with very few African librarians. But the statement was the beginning from which can be traced the rapid development of public library services in Ghana, Eastern Nigeria and Sierra Leone, based on simple but mandatory legislation. In 1955, the Public Libraries Section of the International Federation of Library Associations published a memorandum on the development of public library services, of which one section was devoted to legislation:

Each State should adopt library laws which will include the following provisions:

- Appropriate local authorities must be empowered to expend public funds for public library purposes.
- The amount of local expenditure should not be limited: local authorities should be able to expend as much as they are willing and able.
- The public library purposes for which funds may be expended shall be so defined as not to restrict development.
- Local authorities should be empowered to enter into arrangements with other local authorities for joint schemes for providing the whole or any part of the service, and to contribute to the cost of schemes for cooperation and mutual assistance.
- Each local authority should appoint a library committee directly responsible to the local council.
- Each local authority should have power to appoint staff who shall be

employed in accordance with the conditions and regulations applicable to other local government officers.

- The use of all the services provided must be available to all inhabitants free of any charge whatsoever.
- Though each local authority provides services primarily for the use of its own inhabitants and those who work or study in its area, other persons living outside that area should be able to use those services if they wish... when adequate library services are provided generally in a country or region, however, they should be available to all, regardless of place of residence, without payment.

As soon as practicable, all appropriate local authorities should be legally obliged to maintain adequate public library services. The document was adopted as a statement of policy, with the recommendation that it be sent for study to all governments and appropriate agencies concerned. One further example may be given of the continuing concern with the importance of library legislation. In October 1955, Unesco organized a further seminar on public libraries, this time at Delhi, India, where a successful demonstration project had been founded. The seminar was held in the Delhi Public Library and twelve Asian countries were represented by forty-six librarians and educators. Again, public library legislation and its nature were under discussion, and the following proposals were accepted:

Over-all control and co-operation of development, to provide for a permanent and progressive national public library service, can be obtained only by legislation, which should provide for the following:

- Opportunity for the development of public library service which will be available to all people on the basis of free and equal access.
- An independent service, and not one attached to another department.
- The constitution of a governing body, to be referred to in this report as the central library board, or in a federal state a number of such bodies, subject to a national body with advisory functions.
- Provision for adequate public finance.
- The constitution of district library boards responsible for administration of units of public library service.

Other parts of the report pay tribute to the work done by private bodies in founding and maintaining public library services, but affirm that planned direction and control are now required, and that these cannot be achieved by subsidy to private organizations. On finance the report states: It is of fundamental importance that finance should be by public funds, whether national, state or local, or a combination of these... differences in the structure, powers and financial resources of government at local, state, and national level are such that a simple statement of general applicability cannot be made. It can be said however that sources of finance must be adequate for the support of the service established. The proportion of local funds to national or state funds is a matter for decision by individual governments.

On the unit of service:

- At an early stage in the establishment of a national public library service, the question arises of the convenient administrative unit. This may be defined as the smallest autonomous unit of public library service... the selection of this unit as the real basis for the development of public library service, is a matter of some importance. It should be a viable area as regards finance and administration, and should conform as for as possible to existing local government boundaries... for ideal development, the area chosen should contain both rural and urban districts.

It is illustrative of the complexity of the problem that these four authoritative statements on public library development, issued over a short period of time, should vary so greatly in their emphasis. The Unesco Manifesto concentrated on the value and use of the public library, but said nothing about its financial or legislative base. The Ibadan seminar defined as a first principle that only legislation could provide the necessary secure and permanent foundations. It said nothing about the administrative unit on which implementation must depend, or financial problems, but it did prescribe mandatory legislation under favourable conditions.

The IFLA statement, though it defined the nature of public library service, proposed what was in fact permissive legislation, and it did not make any proposals about central control, the size of the administrative area, or financial viability of local authority areas. Although it said there should be no upper limit on expenditure, it did not mention the vital problem of minimum expenditure. The Delhi seminar proposals, with the previous statements before it, went much further, and proposed legislation which would provide for over-all control, viable areas and financial support at national and local level. But it found itself in difficulties when it attempted to define the nature of the viable area. Any acceptable general statement must be vitiated by the enormous differences between countries in national administrative and executive structure, local government and its relationship to central government, the powers existing at different levels of government, and above all, the financial capacity of these different levels.

The stage of educational and technical development of a country must also be taken into account, but this is possibly not quite as important as it may appear. While literacy is obviously a primary requirement of public library use, most countries now have an extensive programme of primary and secondary education, and in many countries, too, advanced technology exists side by side with primitive standards of living in some areas. It should also be remembered that in the last century, in some countries, notably the United Kingdom, public library legislation actually preceded general legislation on education. It would be a mistake, also, to assume that the problems of public library legislation are confined to the developing countries. If there is one thing that emerges quite clearly from this study of public library law, it is that the problems of an adequate and effective library law are just as great in the more advanced countries as in the developing ones, apart from the fact that some advanced countries do not yet have a general public library law.

In some countries, such as the United Kingdom, the United States and Canada, the problem is primarily one of reshaping law which is defective and inadequate to meet the need of the user of the public library in the twentieth century, who requires access to the enormous and increasing flood of printed material, numbered in books by the hundred thousand, and periodicals by the thousand. These requirements create in their turn a need for more and more specialized and trained personnel. The search is for a legislative base for viable units which can meet the readers' needs, and provide not only the material, but the technical services, equipment and staff required.

In other advanced countries, such as Norway and Denmark, the problem is not one of the viable unit, which in fact cannot be provided, but of compulsory co-operation to give the same results. The problems facing the developing countries may be different, but not so very different. It has often been stated that in social legislation, some African and Asian countries are at the stage others had reached in the nineteenth century. This is only superficially true. We are all living in the twentieth century. If the legislation of the nineteenth century is to be repeated, there is a long road to travel. Not only long, but unnecessary. The example of the past is to be learned from, not repeated.

Basic Principles and Practical Considerations in the Framing of Legislation

Assuming for the purpose of this chapter that new legislation is being considered, the first consideration in the framing of legislation is, of course, the nature of the State itself and the place that legislation takes in its structure. Particularly in social legislation such as the establishment of public libraries, which has primarily a local impact, account must be taken of the nature of the authority by which national government passes on its responsibilities, the basis of taxation at local and national level and in a federal State, the constitutional rights of established organisms within the State. Even where there is no general legislation, in countries where the doctrine of ultra quires does not apply and organs of local government may establish any service they are not specifically forbidden to do, public libraries may exist perfectly legally by local legislation, and this in turn will cause difficulties in framing a general law.

This is the case in the Federal Republic of Germany, and to some extent in the Netherlands and Belgium. Apart from this, there are patterns in the relationship of local government to national government which must be taken into account. H. F. Alderferl in his study of local government in developing countries, identifies four basic patterns, which are established in developing countries either through adoption or by passing on of previous colonial development. The French pattern, which exists in a large part of Africa, carries the doctrine of ultra vires much further than in England or the United States. Local government has no powers not granted to it by constituted authority.

Local government also is subject to executive jurisdiction which is independent of the administrative and legislative branch to a great extent. Generally, he states, French local government is characterized by centralization, chain of command, hierarchical structure, executive domination and legislative subordination. The English pattern, as defined by Alderfer, is characterized by decentralization, with local decision-making bodies with more or less independent powers, as against concentration, in the French pattern, where all power lies with the central government with local units acting as agents.

The English pattern generally implies also legislative dominance, the committee system and voluntary citizen participation. The Soviet system is one of 'democratic centralism', with all organs as links in one continuous chain of governmental power. Communist Party direction and leadership exist at all levels, and local agencies are not law-making or executive bodies in their own right, but subject to correction not only at the next higher level but at other levels. The 'traditional' form of local government is non-Western, though in Western forms there are traditional residues. The pattern is one of a chief or local leader, or a group of people, having jurisdiction over a village or group of villages. Essentially the form is non-urban, but it has deep roots and cannot be ignored as a working unity.

The Indian panchayat system of local government is an example of a traditional form being incorporated into the local government system of a modern State, organized generally on the English system. The clash between two systems, and the different types of law that may be produced, was illustrated in Africa when, at a UNESCO seminar at Enugu in I961, the question of a model Act for African countries was discussed. The Act proposed was on the English model. This was simple and mandatory, giving almost unlimited authority to an independent board, subject to central government control. It was this type of legislation which has been successful in practice in Ghana, Eastern Nigeria and Tanzania.

The delegates from the French-speaking countries could not accept this since it was not an acceptable type of legislation for their countries, and they proposed a different model Act for their purposes. Without quoting this in full, it can be said that it was at once more detailed and less specific. Though it set up a directorate attached to the Ministry of Education, and advisory bodies, it could be said to be rather a statement of intention than a legislative instrument. Subsequent decrees in the various territories have similar structure. Thus, the decree for the Ivory Coast goes into some detail on expenditures and staff required, but does not provide for means of raising the necessary funds or an organization charged with continuous development.

The differences may be more apparent than real, given a determination to create a public library service, but it does seem that in Europe, the Scandinavian countries, the United Kingdom and Ireland have been more successful, through planned co-operation between local and national government, than for instance, in France. A recent survey in Le Monde of the public libraries of Paris showed enormous variations in expenditure on libraries in the various communes, with seemingly no co-operation or standards imposed centrally. A generous system of subsidies for building is offered by the central government, but there does not appear to be any way of forcing local authorities to take advantage of them if they do not wish to provide their share.

There are other, important factors to consider in pre-consideration of legislation. Some investigation must be made of the practical problems, and a body of facts built up. While the survey is important, it must be a practical move towards action, and not an end in itself or a means of delaying action. One of the most successful librarians in charge of a library service in a developing country has said that until a service is provided it is impossible to say what sort of service is needed. A careful analysis at grass roots level involves a detailed statistical examination of a community-its growth rate, its educational levels, its literacy rates; it involves the testing of different types of reading materials and a survey of existing places for reading and studying.

Such an approach overlooks the complete lack of basic statistics on which to base the survey. And above all, it ignores the sense of urgency which permeates any developing country trying to pull itself into the twentieth century by its bootstraps. I am sure that these critics would produce a magnificent report... and that report would probably conclude that the contemplation of any form of library service was premature. By the time it appeared it would have been overtaken by events, such is the speed of development of Africa today. This may be overstating the case against survey, but it is true that a survey should be made after decision-to discover specific problems and how they might be overcome.

These problems can be summarized as follows:

- *Educational Situation:* The provision of libraries depends on adult literacy, and is also concerned with the provision of primary education. Literacy rates based on averages are deceptive-for instance, the adult literacy rate in India is less than 20 per cent, but in Delhi in 1954 it was nearly 40 per cent and is now over 50 per cent. The Government of India report of 1959 did not consider that a literacy rate of 20 per cent was any barrier to a nationally organized public library service, but of course one would assume that a low average literacy rate would suggest concentration on urban areas. In terms of cost relative to use, there would be no point in providing for an elaborate system of mobile libraries to serve rural areas.

- *Language and Book Production:* The number of languages in use and their relative importance is a factor in pre-consideration. Allied to this is the matter of book production. Lack of book production in the national language is an extreme limiting factor, though the establishment of public libraries may well stimulate production and in fact has done so in some countries. But it must be observed that the success of public library development in some African countries has been due largely to the fact that English is the established language of communication, thus giving immediate access to an abundant source of material.
- *Population Density and Concentration:* It goes without saying that a rural and scattered population is more difficult to provide for than an urban one. The problem therefore is not one so much of over-all density as of concentration, and this can well affect the unit of administration
- *Communications:* This also affects the matter of the unit, and administrative arrangements. Decentrali-zation may well be necessary. This may be a problem of organization rather than legislation, but it must be considered.
- *Income and tax structure:* This affects the time factor during which legislation can be expected to come into effect, and also the proportion of cost to be met from various sources.
- *Existing Legislation:* This may exist nationally or locally, and consideration must be given to its possible incorporation in new legislation. In some countries, Ceylon is an example, effective public libraries exist in some areas through local legislation, and a new library law must take into account their existence and their legislative base.
- *'Trained Librarians and Training Facilities:* While most countries will have trained librarians, though not in public libraries, pre-consideration must take into account the availability of trained librarians to implement legislation. Opportunities for training abroad must also be considered. While it is an important consideration, the availability of trained librarians is no more than a temporary limiting factor, since there is little point in training unless there are opportunities for employment. In India and Pakistan, facilities for training and qualification are in advance of employment possibilities in the public sector-not only bad planning but wasteful public policy.

These are some of the major items For pre-consideration and survey. The objective is to determine what a country can afford, how great is the need, what structure is required, and how legislation can assist rapid development, without placing too great a burden on financial ability or the administrative structure. None of them should be over-emphasized. The objective remains the same; the limiting factors affect how it is to be attained and at what speed. In this connation, the object by E. M. Broome repays careful study. Nearly all these limiting factors were present, but none of them deterred the Government of Tanzania from passing legislation and implementing it with determination and success.

As was reported at the Delhi seminar:

- In all countries represented at the seminar, public library service is already being provided in some degree, and the time is ripe for further development. In no country do the material difficulties appear to be unsurmountable, nor is a low literacy rate a decisive adverse factor. The rate of development may vary with the speed of overcoming these problems, but the basis for public library services should be laid now. The major deficiencies in present provisions are: lack of over-all control, and the existence of small unco-ordinated units; lack of, or deficiencies in, existing legislation; lack of sufficient funds and government interest; and lack of trained and experienced librarians.

Practical Considerations in Framing Legislation

It has been said that it is easier to pass a law than it is to change it, and this is a lesson to be learned from existing legislation. In the United Kingdom, for nearly seventy years only minor amendments were made to the enabling legislation, despite the fact that under the existing law there was no means by which county councils could set up public library services for rural populations.

Legislation should therefore be flexible and allow for changes in social conditions, in local-government structure and in the tax base. It should be capable of immediate application, but with progressive application. Study is made of the comparative merits and defects of existing legislation, but certain basic problems can be enumerated for primary consideration.

The Public Library as an Independent Service or Part of a National Library Service

In any country which can even consider the foundation of a public library service, there will already be in existence many libraries of high standard: university libraries, libraries of institutions, government departmental libraries, technical libraries and almost certainly a national and probably state libraries. It is tempting to think that there is an advantage in creating an integrated library service of which such libraries are a part. But it must be remembered that public libraries are for the whole community, whereas all other libraries are designed to serve a section of the community for a special purpose, and that purpose must be their prime consideration. Techniques are similar, but basic purposes are different. Uniting all libraries in one piece of legislation at an early stage is hardly practical, since not only would it tend to stifle the growth of the public library, but it would also entail bringing independent libraries under the legislation, and this would undoubtedly be resisted. At the same time, there is an obvious need for provision for cooperation and some co-ordination, probably best organized around the national library. Bibliographical and interloan functions should be of value to all libraries. The national library could therefore be usefully linked to the central public library authority.

The Central Authority

The need for a central authority charged with carrying out the provisions of legislation is clear. Should it be an independent body or one linked to, or subordinate to, a government department? This is a matter for decision at governmental level. There are advantages in making the central authority part of the department of education, with a department for libraries and controlling body, which should have more than advisory functions. The central board or authority is a modern device of government much used in developing countries, and experience of its past success in other circumstances will affect legislation for public libraries. But the implementation of legislation should not be left to any other body but education, and if education is chosen as the implementing and organizing department, then a section including trained librarians is essential, with advisory and inspecting functions.

Permissive or Mandatory Legislation

It has been shown that permissive legislation is of limited effectiveness, even when accompanied by financial inducements. Legislation should therefore require action to be taken, wherever the ultimate source of action. But provision should be made for progressive implementation at a rate to be determined by resources.

Relationship Between Local and Central Authority

It is generally accepted that the public library is a local community service. In fact, this becomes less and less true with the explosive growth in production of information material and technical developments in library organization. The answer must be sought in the local government structure of the country concerned. In some countries, a nationally controlled public library service has been created, with provision for some devolution to local government at later stages. The existence of federally organized states also presents some problems. But it must be stated that local interest is desirable and must be stimulated. This implies the passing over of some authority, or the creation of local advisory bodies.

The Size of' the Unit

Assuming that local authority interest is essential, the question then arises: what unit, what size and with what authority? The lbadan seminar, speaking for the situation in Africa, concluded that since recognition of local authority was only beginning, the sole public authority should be the national or state agency. At the same time, the appropriate local authority must eventually be given a responsible place in any national scheme of book service. The roots of the service must be in the local community rather than in the state, regional or national headquarters.

The size and authority of the local unit are important questions, even when there is a suitable urban authority. An urban authority should never be the sole local unit, since its economic and social catchment area is equally important for public library purposes. The requirements for a viable unit, as we have seen, were well stated in the report of the Delhi seminar, but it is already clear, fifteen years later, that they are expanding. In developed countries for example, much larger units than previously thought necessary are now postulated, and the basing of a service on too small a unit can be disastrously hampering in later development. Apart from size, there are other considerations. Whatever the attachment at national level, it is generally conceded that at local level the public library service should be executively independent of other agencies, whether education or other departments such as cultural affairs or social education.

The public library serves all, but is not solely a part of any, SO it should remain independently governed and administered. The question of policy control is a matter of the form local government takes. There is much to be said for the board system, independent but responsible to the local-government system, but this is not always legally possible. But it should be possible at all times to bring into consultation persons of knowledge and goodwill.

Finance

It is generally now accepted that financial support for public libraries should come from public funds, that is, taxation. It is also generally recognized that the service should be free to the user, though this is not always the case in practice. In most developing countries, this means major support at national level, with assistance at local level so far as practicable, having regard to the limitations of local taxation in most developing countries. The acceptance of this principle has been a major limiting factor in public library progress, even in advanced countries, as will be demonstrated in study of existing legislation. It follows, therefore, that any unit at local level must be a tax-raising body, and provision for funds from taxation at a national level must be written in to any legislation. In a federal system, of course, another stage of financial support will be introduced.

Various calculations of the cost of a public library service have been made, but they are of little value in view of changing needs, and could not sensibly be included in basic legislation. No one would expect a public library service to spring armed and ready from the ground, like Jason's dragons' teeth, and financial provision must depend on the rate of implementation of legislation. The Government of India report of 1959 postulated a period of twenty-five years for the creation of a full service, but its calculations as to cost are already completely out of date. Given progressive implementation, standards of service required are also a matter for progressive regulation, and not a suitable one for inclusion in legislation. The power to make regulations on standards and other matters should, however, be given.

Other Considerations

There are several other considerations which may have to be taken into account in framing legislation, but their importance will vary according to country. In some countries, there will be a problem of fitting in private or subscription libraries to the system. There must also be some provision for co-operation between libraries, but this again will vary with the primary decisions already taken. If a linkage with the national library, for instance, is envisaged, or if the unit of service is the whole country, then these provisions can be taken care of automatically under regulation. But if existing resources, as provided by various agencies, are to be fully utilized, then some provision for co-operation and inter-lending must be made. Although university and institutional libraries may not be fully integrated, their resources, after their first priorities are met, should be circulated generally. Whether library education, or the encouragement of library associations, should be incorporated in legislation is a moot point.

It could be fairly argued that if opportunity for employment of qualified people is given by the provision of a public library service, then educational institutions will provide the necessary further education facilities for training librarians and technicians, without any legal requirement to do so. Library associations, also, should not be too dependent on legislative assistance. Again, the provision of a service will itself exert the necessary stimulus for the creation of an active body of professional librarians. And if such associations are to encourage further progress and technical improvement, they should be independent. All these problems and others applying to particular countries will need to be closely considered before framing suitable legislation in terms which will create a permanent, expanding public library service available to all people, whatever their age, status or geographical situation.

The way in which the problems have already been approached and the answers embodied in legislation is the subject of the next stage. There are many lessons to be learned, and the gap between intentions and results is often a depressing commentary on how the goodwill of legislators can be frustrated by circumstances unforeseen or unsuspected. Government and legislation are, alas, by no means an exact science. But in the framework of the modern State, legislation as an instrument of authority is necessary. In the case of public libraries it can truthfully be said that no successful public library system can exist without legal authority, but that many devices have been necessary to get round defective legislation. Public libraries happen to be the subject of this study, but no doubt authorities on law and government could produce better examples of problems caused by legislation rather than solved by it.

The Pattern of Legislation Comparative Solutions

The main body of this study consists of summaries of the existing legislation in fourteen countries, and taking into account the federal countries, twenty Acts are considered, with others mentioned in passing. More could have been chosen, but in fact, not more than thirty countries have effective general library legislation, less than a quarter of the independent nations of the world. Of the countries chosen, four are developing countries, two are countries with centrally planned economies and three are federally organized.

This, therefore can be considered a reasonably representative sample, ranging from the most advanced countries, where coverage is complete and basic standards established, to a country which has only just become independent, Botswana. They all have one thing in common; in none of them is legislation, even now, entirely satisfactory and effective, in that it encourages development to the point of greatest efficiency and maximum results. All have problems to some degree, despite the fact that in most of the countries considered there has been revision of law in the last ten years. The advanced countries, most of which have had public library legislation in some form for many years, but with varying effectiveness, have no great problem of financial ability to provide a nationwide system of public libraries, if that ability can be brought to bear.

The problem is rather one of an inadequate and unsuitable local-government structure, and the supplementation of local resources, or in some examples, replacement of local initiative, by central-government intervention. A pattern clearly emerges in nearly all recent legislation, first of a search for a larger and more viable unit of service, which must be both geographically and financially able to deploy larger resources for public library service, and second of the creation of a central advisory body to encourage improvement of public library service. One can see similarities in the solutions adopted, but there are also wide variations.

It is proposed in this chapter to show by comparison the major similarities and variations of the law as it stands in advanced countries. There are important lessons to be learned by the developing countries in framing their own legislation, and it appears that the advanced countries could also learn from their neighbours. In making these comparisons, it must of course be borne in mind that though public library law is evolutionary in character, it cannot be separated from the general body of law of a country, and it must be set in the executive, social and geopolitical structure of the country concerned.The fact that some countries with a high educational and cultural standard have not so far been able to enact general mandatory legislation on public libraries proves this to be the case. Permissive legislation has been replaced by mandatory legislation in most countries. The appropriate local authorities are now required rather than permitted to provide a public library service.

In some countries, notably the United Kingdom, Finland and Sweden, mandatory provision is not necessary, since coverage is already complete. In Norway, obligatory provision is laid down in the Act, and in Denmark a date is set for all communes to provide public libraries. In Canada and the United States, though provision is not mandatory, the problem is no longer one of provision but of viability, and this could be said generally of all the countries considered, except the countries having centrally planned economies, where the law has nothing to say on this. But it would appear that in Hungary, at any rate, there is complete coverage.

Central Government and Advisory Bodies

In all countries, the intervention of the central government, either at state or federal level, or both, has led to the setting up of a central body to guide future progress, and this is the most common feature in all recent legislation. These central bodies may take many forms, either advisory or executive. They may be independent, or responsible to a department of State. Their membership may be drawn from organizations or individuals. Their constitution and powers can be summarized as follows:

Czechoslovakia

The Central Library Council is an advisory body in the Ministry of Education and Culture. There are two bodies, one for Bohemia-Moravia and one for Slovakia. Membership consists of representatives of authorities and expert librarians. All proposals concerning libraries are submitted to them, and they have the right to initiate proposals themselves.

Denmark

The Library Council consists of sixteen members representing all sections of the Danish Library Service. They are appointed by the Minister of Cultural Affairs, are consulted in all matters of importance to the working of the Libraries Act, and have the right to initiate representations. The chairman is the Library Director, head of the State inspectorate.

Finland

The library delegation is an advisory body responsible to the Central Board of Schools. There are twelve delegates, representing the Department of Education, local authorities, library training and other organizations working for libraries and adult education. The delegation can take the initiative in submitting proposals to the Central Board of Schools.

Hungary

The National Council for Library Activity, responsible to the Ministry of Culture, has a section for public libraries. It has also a working organization, the State Institute of Libraries, similar in some respects to the State inspectorates of Scandinavian library systems. The functions of the National Council are advisory and technical, but being a direct organ of central government, it obviously has great prestige.

Ireland

The Library Council has as its main purpose the operation and supervision of the Irish Central library, and a secondary purpose of assisting local library authorities to improve their services. Its membership is by nomination, and a majority of the members are nominated by universities or the National Library. The powers of the Library Council are considerable, since it considers applications for grants from local authorities and its functions are much more than advisory. In view of the form of local government in Ireland, it can be said to be an executive body with potentially great powers. In fact, the original secondary function has become the primary one.

Qntario

The Provincial Library Council is an advisory body responsible to the Minister for Education, and it consists of nine members appointed by the minister, and one for each regional system. It has certain functions under the Act and may also make recommendations regarding development and co-ordination of library service.

Quebec

The Quebec Public Libraries Commission is responsible to the Minister for Cultural Affairs. Its membership is six persons nominated by the minister, whose qualifications shall be their interest in the development of public libraries, and the Director of Public Libraries of the Province. The powers and duties of the commission are wide, in that it is generally charged with the study of the best means of developing public library services, and it must report every three months on its findings regarding the working of the Public Libraries Act.

United Kingdom

The Library Advisory Councils, set up by the Minister of Education under the 1964 Act, one for England and one for Wales, have no set number of members, nor any stated qualifications for membership. They are nominated directly by the minister, and actually the representatives are drawn from local authority members, university and public librarians representing all the major interests of local government and various sizes and types of library. The function of the councils is purely advisory, and their main work is in connexion with the achievement of standards and the general working of the Act. But by their existence, they have become the advisory bodies for libraries in general, and on such matters as librarianship training.

Washington State

The State Library Commission is an executive commission appointed by the Governor, and responsible for administration of federal and state funds for improvement of public library services. It operates through the state library and appoints the state librarian, who acts as secretary to the commission. Though its main functions are executive, it also has advisory responsibilities. The functions of these bodies are mainly advisory, and as will be seen generally from their constitutions, are intended as a source of expert opinion on public library development.

They are useful bodies, but equally important, their existence creates a secretariat, and that secretariat, whether clearly laid down in legislation as in Quebec, or not, as in England and Wales, inevitably assumes supervisory functions. Those functions can be of inspection and control, as in Finland and Denmark, or they can be limited to advice to the appropriate minister and the right to ask for regular reports and give advice to individual library authorities. Even where there is no central coordinating body, there is invariably a central coordinating government department.

In Norway, the State inspectorate is recognized by the Act, and the State Inspector is a direct appointment of the Crown, though responsible to the Ministry of Church and Education. In Sweden, there is a Library Section of the Central Board of Education, and its functions include supervision of State grants, approval of building plans, and supervision of the School of Librarianship. With the change in local government law, its functions are now more limited, being more advisory than supervisory.

In the United States, in addition to the state departments concerned with public libraries, now established in most states, there is an office in the Department of Education in Washington charged with supervision of the very substantial grants under the Library Services and Construction Act. Except in Scandinavia, where they have been in existence for many years, the emergence of these bodies and the departments attached to them is comparatively recent, and their influence on public library development is bound to increase. It will be noted that the usual attachment of the library councils and their civil-service bureaux is to the Ministry of Education, in some cases to the Minister of Culture. But this attachment at central-government levels does not necessarily imply any attachment of public libraries at lower levels of government to any particular department.

Provision for Co-Operation

In most countries, legislation shows a marked preference for the provision of public library services within the existing local-government framework, and an equal reluctance to interfere with those existing agencies, even when they are clearly not viable. The only exception to this in recent legislation, where smaller authorities are required to give up their powers, is in England and Wales, where there is provision for the compulsory surrender of library powers by authorities of less than 40,000 population.

Even here, the clauses have not so far been used, since a major local-government reform is expected to make them unnecessary. Local-government reform in Sweden and Denmark is also making the problem less urgent, though it will still exist.

Failing the forcible creation of larger public library authorities, the search for the larger unit must take the form of co-operation, and recent legislation is characterized by the creation of a superstructure of co-ordination, often at two or three levels, either mandatory or permissive. Library authorities are either to be persuaded to join with others in a library system, or a superstructure of co-operation is created above them, in which they have the opportunity, or are compelled, to take part. Financial assistance is usually given. Some examples of this kind of provision are as follows:

Denmark

A number of suitable libraries are designated as county libraries, serving a district. Their functions are to assist the local libraries in the district by lending or obtaining for them books and other suitable materials they cannot provide themselves, and by giving advice and technical assistance. In the present legislation, the Library Director recommends which libraries shall be recognized as county libraries, and the minister shall ensure that the district served is of a suitable size and that the county library is able to carry out its functions. In the past, it is thought, too many county libraries were designated, and the districts were too small.

The provision is mandatory, that is to say, all libraries must join a district, and an advisory committee is formed to direct the work. National grants are made to the county libraries, and the county or counties must also contribute at rates laid down. The communes themselves do not contribute directly.

Norway

The system of regional central libraries is similar, except that the designated libraries have wider functions in super-vision of their local libraries. The problems of establishment, and suitable areas, are very great in Norway, and though nineteen regional libraries have now been established, they vary greatly in resources. Again the inclusion in an area is mandatory, and grants are made to meet the cost, with supplementary grants from the areas covered.

Sweden

In addition to the establishment of county libraries on similar lines to Denmark and Norway, a further superstructure has been added of three inter-library loan centres, which lend to the county libraries and receive grants for their services from the State. It must be emphasized that in the Scandinavian countries, the aid-giving libraries are the larger libraries in their area, and though they may establish special departments for their additional functions, in no sense, except in a limited way in Norway, do they administer or supervise the other libraries in their area.

Quebec

The regional libraries in Quebec are quite different from others, and serve a different purpose. They are intended, not to superimpose an additional system, but to encourage the provision of public library service in those sparsely populated areas which cannot provide for themselves, even with grant aid. The system is fully described in the appropriate section, but briefly, when a minimum area containing 25,000 inhabitants can be defined, an ad hoc committee is formed. The kind of service depends on the size of the area and other factors, but generally, grant is 85 per cent of the total cost. Such a system is only required under extreme adverse conditions, but the similarity to the Norwegian system in its northern area is obvious.

Ontario

The Ontario method of creating larger areas is in effect a three-tier system. In a county, a combined library system can be formed at the request of 75 per cent of the authorities in the county, then a county library service is formed, and a separate public library board set up. But it is only responsible for that part of the county which has asked for inclusion. The system has obvious defects, but it does have the effect of helping some at least of the smaller authorities to combine. Superimposed on this system of county libraries and independent libraries is provision for regional library systems, working roughly on the Scandinavian pattern, and having similar responsibilities. Substantial grants are available from state funds, but regions are not necessarily inclusive of all the libraries in their area since, throughout the legislation of Ontario, there are no mandatory powers.

United States of America

There are no mandatory powers in the United States, and most recent legislation, both federal and state, has written into it an injunction that the independence of the community library is to be respected and preserved.

The creation of the larger unit therefore is by the voluntary amalgamation of independent libraries into 'systems', in which service is often provided by contract between one library and another. It is interesting to note that current thinking puts the minimum viability of a system at 150,000 population.

United Kingdom

A voluntary system of co-operation has existed for many years, with member libraries paying subscriptions usually on a per capita basis. The country is divided into fourteen regions for this purpose. The 1964 Act legally recognizes this system, and provides for compulsory membership by all library authorities, and for amalgamation of the regions where necessary.

Two of the largest regions, comprising London and the south-east of England, have already amalgamated, with the authority of the Ministry of Education. The purpose of the regions is principally inter-library co-operation, and for this purpose provision is made in legislation for bringing into the system other than public libraries.

LIBRARY LEGISLATION IN INDIA

India became an independent republic in January 1950. It is a federal union of states, there being seventeen states and ten union territories. The form of government is democratic, with a president and two Houses of Parliament. The Upper House, or Council of States, is indirectly elected, the members being elected by the legislative assembly of each state. The Lower House, or House of the People, consists of 500 members directly elected by adult suffrage. Each state has its own legislature, directly elected.

Certain legislative powers are retained by the central government, but education, the most important function so far as libraries are concerned, is reserved to the states, though there is a central Ministry of Education with co-ordinating powers, including that of making grants for specific purposes.

These powers have been increased by the very large sums made available under successive Five-year Plans. The area of India is 1,262,275 square miles, and its population approxi-mately 5II million.

Local Government

Local government is in the hands of some 2700 municipal authorities which have primary functions relating to their own areas and frame their own budgets, though usually, however, these require approval at state level. For rural areas there is a three-tier system of panchayats, or local councils-at village, block and district levels.

Generally speaking, the block panchayats consist of groupings of village panchayats, but this does not apply to the whole of India, There are nearly 4000 block panchayats, and some 212,000 village panchayats. The district is the taxing authority below the state. The system is virtually complete and one can therefore say that local administration proceeds from state to city, district or municipality, and right down to its roots in the villages.

Education

The literacy percentage is approximately 24 - men 34.5, women 13. Despite this very low rate of literacy, very great progress has been made in education, and the rate has been improved by 8 per cent since 1951. Over ₹5,000 million were spent on education in 1964 and over 750,000 primary and secondary schools were in operation. The official national language under the Constitution is Hindi, but under the Official Language Act of 1963, English will continue to be used as an official language for an indefinite period alongside Hindi. The regional language of the state is also taught at various levels. There are fourteen officially recognized regional languages.

Library Provision

In the light of the facts the problems of public library provision are very great. India is a very large country with a predominantly rural population, a small per capita income and a number of recognized languages. There are other problems, arising from the local-government system and the relations of the central government to the states. India is a federal State and, as in Canada and the United States, provision of public libraries is reserved to the states and is their sole responsibility. Even grants under the Five-year Plans, given specifically in the past for public library development, were changed under the third plan to block grants to be spent at the discretion of the states. The central government has therefore no coercive powers to enforce legislation by the states, or to dictate the form of such legislation.

The legal powers to take over the many private or association libraries are also limited. To bring them into the public sector would require separate legislation which is unlikely to be voted. In view of the numbers of such libraries, this is important. Given a government determined enough to create a nation-wide public library system, the position could, of course, be changed.

There is a national Ministry of Education, and it could be given coordinating functions. In fact, the Advisory Committee of I 959 proposed this in the form of an All-India Library Advisory Council, with an executive committee nominated by the Minister of Education, and a secretariat consisting of a division of libraries in the Ministry of Education. It also suggested that the Government of India should contribute to the library funds of the state an amount equal to funds raised by property tax. Presumably, these proposals would require legislation at national level. Despite many obstacles, India has a strong and continuing literary tradition, and there is a thirst for knowledge which is evidenced by the fact that over 10,000 periodicals and newspapers are published in India. Book production, although its organization is chaotic, flourishes and there is not in fact, any shortage of libraries. Very few Indian towns or even large villages are without a library of some sort, provided by a charitable foundation, by an educational organization or by executive action on the part of state, municipal or district authority.

Very few of these institutions are well endowed, many are little more than reading-rooms. In this connexion, the statement by the Advisory Committee on Libraries, which reported in 1959, is of value in estimating the true position:

- In India the phrase 'public libraries' is used in a very loose sense. It is used to denote any library which permits members of the public to use its material for reference or borrowing on payment of fees or rent. In this sense, all kinds of libraries, national, university, schools and subscription libraries, etc., would be public libraries. Because of the loose connotation of the term, it would appear from the statistics published by Unesco in 1956 that India leads the world in the number of public libraries, which is given as 24,086. The statistics are flattering; they express the aspiration rather than the achievement of the country. The internationally accepted definition of a public library is that it is a library which is:
  - Is financed out of public funds;
  - Charges no fees from readers and yet is open for full use by the public without distinction of caste, creed or sex;
  - Is intended as an auxiliary educational institution providing a means of self education which is endless;
  - Houses learning materials giving reliable information freely and without partiality or prejudice on as wide a variety of subjects as will satisfy the interests of readers. Were such a definition adopted, the number of public libraries in India could not be counted by tens, let alone by hundreds or thousands.

A framework of library provision does, however, exist, and it has been expanded by grants under successive five-year plans, at national level. In the first five-year plan, 1951-56, a scheme of improvement of library service was included calling for a network of libraries to be spread over the whole country. The kernel of the scheme was the establishment of district libraries, which would circulate books throughout the district. These were to be supplemented and supported by a central library for the whole state, or for a whole linguistic region. A supplementary scheme to set up integrated library units was also commended to state governments in connexion with the areas selected for intensive educational development. Under successive Five-year Plans, the schemes have been developed but have not so far been backed up generally by a legislative base, despite strong recommendations by the Advisory Committee in 1959. These recommendations were for a comprehensive state library law, which would provide for free library service for all. Funds would be provided by a library rate on property tax, the income to be covered by a matching State grant. The unit of library service would be the district. Proposals were also made for legislative action by the Government of India to collate the various Copyright and Book Deposit Acts and to make them viable for a national library service. The Act should also provide for assistance to state governments for public library service. Since provision of public libraries by executive action is an important feature in public library provision in developing countries, a typical example in India, that of West Bengal, is worthy of brief examination.

West Bengal Library System

West Bengal not only contains the largest city in India, Calcutta, but also India's National Library. Its population is over 65 million, and the principal language is Bengali. The literacy rate is 30 per cent. The first public library was opened in Calcutta in 1836 and it was followed during the nineteenth century by the founding of many other libraries on a subscription basis. After independence, small grants were made by local authorities and from state funds, and in 1950, about 1,000 subscription libraries were receiving small grants. In 1956, a coordinated scheme was sponsored by the state government, with financial assistance on a 50 per cent basis from the Government of India.

In 1969-70 a sum of ₹4,313,000 was given in annual grants. All the districts of West Bengal now have a district library and much progress has been made in the provision of buildings, furniture and equipment. A reasonably coherent library system has now been established, with a state central library in Calcutta, over 68 district and area libraries and 579 rural libraries, with total staffs of over 1500. Many of the libraries are still subscription libraries, and grants in fact are still given to many subscription libraries outside the system. While it is a source of satisfaction that public library service has been created, it cannot be denied that it is far from ideal. Since the entire service is under the Department of Social Education, district librarians have no real executive powers, and there appears to be little co-ordination of book stocks. Above all, the lack of a legislative and tax base necessarily makes for uncertainty in future planning.

The Delhi Public Library

Another example of executive action is the Delhi Public Library. This was founded by joint action of the Government of India and Unesco as a demonstration project applying Western concepts of book provision, furniture and equipment in a developing country.

In the final terms of agreement between Unesco and the Indian Government, the terms of reference for the project were set out:

> "It shall provide a public library service for the people of the City of Delhi and shall be a model for all public library development in India, and in all other countries where similar development of public libraries can be undertaken. The library shall be designed to carry out the policy of the Unesco Public Libraries Manifesto and to serve the needs of popular education."

The organizers of the library had, therefore, to plan for a library which would have complete open access to the shelves, which would make no direct charge to readers, and would be organized not for preservation, but for use by readers of all ages and all levels of education. These concepts were not new to India. They had been propagated by the devoted work of Dr. Ranganathan and his disciples. But between concept and execution there was still a wide gap, and the Delhi Public Library was the first in India, and probably the first in Asia, to apply these principles. The library was opened in 1951 by the Prime Minister, Mr. Nehru, and the present author was consultant to the project during the first year of its life. The government of the library is by the Delhi Library Board, an autonomous body acting on behalf of the Ministry of Education.

It is a well-balanced body, now with fifteen members. The Ministry of Education, the Finance Ministry, the Delhi Municipal Corporation, the Delhi Administration and the New Delhi Municipal Committee are all represented and four experts with technical qualifications or library experience are co-opted.

The director of the library is secretary of the board and ex oficio member of it. Finance was jointly from the two sponsoring bodies in the first two years, but is now the sole responsibility of the Indian Government, with small grants from the municipal bodies. The story of the Delhi Public Library has been told many times, and it is not proposed to repeat it here. From its inception it was an enormous success, enrolling over 10,000 members in the first few months and lending over 70,000 books.

In 1966-67, membership had increased to 136,000 and annual issue of books to nearly 2 million volumes. Book stocks have increased from 14,000 to 350,000. It is still, in the words of a recent Indian writer, 'the only public library in India worth the name.' In 1955, the author was invited by Unesco to make a detailed evaluation of the project. This was published by Unesco in 1957. In 1956, the Government of India notified its acceptance of this evaluation, the preamble of which began with the statement: 'During this period of five years the library has made gratifying progress and it has, therefore, been decided to place it on a permanent basis. ' After twenty years of existence, this statement is still the only basis on which the library operates.

Its functions have never been more clearly defined than in the original terms of reference as a pilot project, and it is still not a statutory body. More curious still, though it spends over I million rupees a year, by far the greatest expenditure of a single Indian public library unit, it still has not been given over-all responsibility for providing public library service in Delhi.

In 1964, a further evaluation of the library was made by the board itself, which has this to say about the area of the library's responsibility:

> "A rather peculiar feature of the situation regarding public library service in Delhi is that in addition to the Delhi Library Board, three other bodies, *viz.*, the Delhi Administration, the Delhi Municipal Corporation and the New Delhi Municipal Committee operate a few libraries and reading rooms, and the New Delhi Municipal Committee proposes to open small lending libraries in the area within its jurisdiction. There is no co-operation at all between the several authorities administering these libraries. The fact is stated here because of a possible wasteful duplication of effort and money."

The fact that Delhi is the seat of government and has no state administration possibly accounts for the perpetuation of this rather odd situation. But one would have thought that a short enabling Act would have been possible giving the Delhi Public Library responsibility for providing all public reference and lending services in the Delhi area. Nevertheless, the Delhi Public Library has shown and continues to show that a modern public library can exist and can flourish in India.

Model Libraries Bill

In 1960, following the recommendations of the Advisory Committee on Libraries, the Government of India appointed a committee for drafting a library bill. This was submitted to the Ministry of Education in 1963 and in 1964 the ministry circulated the bill for comments to the various state governments and professional organizations. No further action has yet been taken. The bill is intended for adoption on a nation-wide basis. It would therefore need to be adopted by each state and presumably general legislation by the Government of India would be necessary to define the rights of the citizen to access to libraries, similar to those he has to education, to provide for some form of co-ordination of the various state library services and to provide for financial assistance for the state public library services as envisaged in the Model Bill.The exact form of such legislation, in view of the states' rights, is difficult to foresee, but a similar problem was solved in the United States with the Library Services Act. A long process of legislation is therefore obviously involved, and an equally long process of organization. The integration of the present systems of public libraries provided by executive action will in itself present certain problems.

State Legislation

The Model Bill has been discussed at length because it is presumably the basis on which future legislation will be founded for all the states. But four Indian states have already passed legislation: two, Madras and Andhra Pradesh, before the publication of the Advisory Committee Report and the Model Bill, and two, Mysore and Maharashtra, after the publication of the Model Bill.

Madras Act

Madras State (capital: Madras) has a population of 37 million. The literacy rate is 30 per cent. Tamil is the principal language. Madras was the first state to pass legislation to create a public library system, in 1948. This was largely due to the unremitting efforts of Dr. Ranganathan, but the bill was watered down in its various stages to make it acceptable and it is generally agreed that in its present form not only is the Act defective but that its implementation has been unsound.

In the words of S. K. Mookerjee:

> "The Madras Act and its implementation in the sphere of library organization have taught us all a very good lesson. It has shown how completely the intentions of the legislature can be flouted and the public needs neglected when such implementation is entrusted to the wrong agency."

The main provisions of the Madras Act are as follows: A state library committee is formed for the purpose of advising the government. Its membership includes the Minister in Charge of Education, who is to be president of the board, representatives of universities and local library authorities and three persons nominated by library associations in the state. But the Director of Public Instruction is named as being ex officio Director of Public Libraries and a 'Special Officer' assisting the director in the administration of the Act is secretary of the committee. It is quite clear that it is not intended that the special officer shall be a librarian and there is no place in fact in the Act for a state librarian with technical qualifications.

It has been stated that the 'Special Officer', not a librarian, was in fact appointed with some haste. The Director of Public Libraries is charged with managing the State Central Library, superintending the work of local library authorities and superintending and directing all matters relating to public libraries in the state. The Act creates local library authorities, one for the City of Madras and one for each district, each district authority being given full powers of management of libraries within the district.

This is a much more sensible arrangement than the one in the Model Bill, in that it creates, in theory at any rate, more viable authorities. There are thirteen districts in Madras, so the average effective literate population of a district is around I million. The powers and duties of district library authorities do not, however, include provision for the appointment of a librarian, and there is no provision for a librarian on the committee.

The power to make regulations also includes clauses: to 'provide for the admission of the public to public libraries in its area on such conditions and on payment of such fees as it may specify'; and 'requiring from persons desiring to use such libraries any guarantee or security against injury to, misuse, destruction or loss of the property of such libraries'.

These sections of the Act do, of course, nullify the whole function of public libraries if acted on, although they are permissive. Each local library authority is empowered to levy a library cess in its area, of six paise per rupee. This can be increased by an authority with sanction. The principal defects of the Act, apart from the omission of a requirement for trained staff with some status and the out-of-date provisions for access to the libraries, are that the Act does not in any way create a system of libraries. The State Central Library has no duties in relation to the district libraries and the district libraries have no duties in relation to each other. A parallel system of libraries is also created under the Act, since one of the duties of the director is to declare what libraries are eligible for government aid. In the rules made under the Act, the director is to maintain a register of such libraries and conditions are laid down for eligibility for grant. There appear to be no provisions, as in the Model Bill, for eventual merging of these libraries within the public libraries administered by district authorities. Despite the defects of the Act, and its slow implementation, in recent years the public library service has obviously made some impression.

In 1965, total expenditure reached over 7 million rupees as against I,685,000 in 1957, and of this sum I,897,000 was raised in library cess. Over half the total expenditure in 1965, however, was by special grant, under the five-year plan, and it is not known whether this has been maintained since. Book stocks are reported as being nearly 2,500,000, visitors to the libraries nearly 18 million.

But one notes with surprise that there are in the whole state only 15,000 registered borrowers and only 143 trained library staff, of whom only I have full library qualifications. But however suspect some of the statistics, and it must be noted that criticism of the Madras library service by Indian librarians has been very severe, it is undoubtedly true that some progress has been made which would not have been made without a legislative base.

It is to be hoped that the efforts of Dr. Ranganathan and others to improve the Act will eventually bear fruit and that Madras may then emerge as not only the first, but also the foremost, Indian state with a tax-based, legally founded, public library service.

Andhra Pradesh

Andhra Pradesh was a linguistic state formed from Hyderabad and parts of Madras State. A Telugu-speaking area, it has always had a strong library and literary tradition. In the words of an Indian librarian, 'the library movement has had a vast influence on the social and political life in Telugu land'. The population is over 40 million. When the new state was formed, there was already an Act in force for Hyderabad, while the parts of Madras taken over were covered by the Madras Act. In 1960 an integrated Act was passed for the entire state. In many ways the Act is similar to the Madras Act, in the provision of a state library committee, the constitution of local library authorities, the levying of library cess and the matching of the funds raised in this way by grants from the state government. But generally the Act is a great improvement on the Madras Act, and corrects many of its defects.

The Act creates a separate department of public libraries, although the Director of Public Instruction may be the director in charge of the department. But the librarian of the State Central Library has a place on the State Library Committee. In the provisions for the district authorities and the city authority it is laid down that the District Librarian and the City Central Librarian shall each be secretary of the respective committee. The amount of library cess is fixed at four paise, which may be increased to eight paise at the discretion of the district authority. It is prescribed in the Act that no fees for admission to any public library shall be charged, but it is not clear whether a fee can be charged for borrowing of books. Again, a parallel system of libraries is formed, since under the definitions, a public library can be 'a library established or maintained by any local body or co-operative society and declared open to the public', or 'a library declared to be eligible for aid and receiving aid from the Government or from the Library Fund'.

The duties of the Director of Public Libraries also include a declaration of what libraries are eligible for aid and under the rules of the Act conditions for such aid are laid down. It is clear that these are libraries outside those provided directly by the library authority, but there are no provisions, as in the Model Bill, for taking them over. The Act has been rapidly implemented, and appears to be working fairly satisfactorily.

Mysore Act, 1965

This Act has taken features from the Madras Act, the Andhra Pradesh Act, and the Model Bill and is a great improvement on all of them. Mysore is a Kannada-speaking State formed under the States Reorganization Act. The capital is Bangalore and the population is approximately 27 million. The literacy rate is 25 per cent (36 % males). The preamble of the Act states that it is:

'To provide for the establishment and maintenance of public libraries and the organization of a comprehensive rural and urban library service for the State of Mysore.'

The State Library Authority includes a member representing the State Library Association, but the State Librarian, though *ex officion* secretary of the authority, is not a member. A department of public libraries is formed under the Act, with the State Librarian at its head. This clause takes the administration of the public library out of the province of the Department of Education. The State Librarian is also specifically stated to be a whole-time officer with qualifications to practise as a librarian. All posts in the Department of Public Libraries are to be filled by appointment of persons employed by the state library service. This may seem supererogatory, but is obviously intended to prevent appointment of persons already in other departments of the civil service. It is one of the grievances of Indian librarians that posts are often filled by people without library qualifications, coming by promotion from such departments as social education and community development.

Local library authorities are specified for cities and urban areas with populations of more than 100,000, and for each district authority. The chief librarian of the city or district is *ex officion* secretary of the local library authority. Development plans are to be prepared for each district and advisory committees formed by branch libraries and mobile libraries under the plan. The library cess is not confined to a levy on property, but is also levied on other taxes in city areas. It is limited to three paise in the rupee, subject to increase at discretion, with an upper limit of six paise. It will, of course, raise much more money, though the rate is the same, than property tax.

The grant from the state to districts is met from land revenue tax, at the rate of three per cent. In addition the whole of staff salaries in the library authority is met by the state. The State Central Library has, among other functions, the task of providing facilities for the blind. This is not mentioned in any other Act. The Act also specifies a number of public libraries owned by societies which are to be taken over under the Act. Whether this is by prior agreement or not, it is an immense step forward. The Mysore Act, it will be seen, is in many respects an improvement of the Model Bill, particularly in its creation of an independent library service and the widening of the tax base for urban libraries. The provision that all staff are employees of the state library service and paid by the state creates, for the first time in any of the Indian legislation, an integrated library system with the State Central Library at its head.

Maharashtra, 1967

Maharashtra, a Marathi-speaking State has a population of 46 million. Literacy is 30 per cent (males 42%). The Maharashtra Act, passed in 1967, has some of the features of the Mysore Act in that it creates a state library council, with a director of libraries who is a member of the council, acts as its secretary and must be a qualified librarian. A department of libraries is established and a state library service with staff salaries to be paid from state funds. There the resemblance to the Mysore Act stops. A state library is to be established and a divisional library for every division. But provision for library service in a local area can only be made if the director is not satisfied that a local authority, society or trust is willing or competent to provide a public library service. No such library however shall be established without an opportunity being given to the local authority, society or trust to show because why the state authority should not establish a library. The Act gives no powers of taxation; the Library Fund is made up solely from general and special grants, and central government grants. The general state grant is to be not less than 2,500,000 rupees, not a large sum. It is difficult to see from this how the Act can work satisfactorily, even though a functioning department and qualified staff are provided for.

SUMMARY

The Indian position has been dealt with at some length because of the variety of existing legislation and the fact that for the greater part of India there still is no legislation. This is not for want of trying. There must be few countries where there has been so much effort, so many reports, such unremitting lobbying of politicians. Dr. Ranganathan has devoted a lifetime to the problem, as well as gaining an international reputation for his contributions to librarianship, and nearly every Indian state has been in consultation with him at one time or another over legislation.

All states have active and persistent library associations, hampered by lack of funds it is true, but making up for it in publications and conferences. The will is there, the sympathy is there, but results have been more than disappointing. The main problem is, of course, one of taxation. The states' governments are reluctant to pass mandatory legislation that will increase the tax burden; the rural and urban areas have not sufficient potential revenue to provide library services; and the states themselves have a limited amount of revenue to disburse.

Finally, the central government, although it has distributed large sums for libraries under successive five-year plans, is reluctant to make permanent commitments. But eventually the problem must be solved by central government contributions to make up the deficiency in the states. It has been suggested that 5 per cent of the amount spent on education should be aimed at as the total. This would not provide expensive buildings and equipment, but it would provide a basic public library service. The difficulty is that the longer the central government hesitates to insist on mandatory state legislation, the more difficult it will be to provide this basic service.

A start must sometime be made on bringing the many semi-public libraries into a system and possibly channeling and consolidating the small sums they spend. Grant-in-aid to them altogether must amount to a respectable sum and a large part of it is wasted so long as these libraries are independent, using untrained staff and decrepit premises. The attitude is that they are better than nothing, but this is not true if they give the impression that they are a library service. There is also a danger that more states will pass defective legislation, and the more that do, the longer it will take to bring them into line.

The only Act which is reasonably acceptable so far is the Mysore Act and it is the only one to create a state-wide service. It is now nearly ten years since the Advisory Committee reported and gave a comprehensive view of the situation. It is surely time for the Government of India to make a definite move, if only because otherwise they may be faced with a series of defective and conflicting Acts by the states.

2

Network Models for Library Co-operation

INTRODUCTION

Digital Library systems are the computerized information storage and retrieval systems connected to computer networks and have maximum flexibility, durability, immunity, stability, scalability, accessibility and compatibility with other media at minimum cost, space and maintenance. Library network provides transmission of information dissemination of catalogues; abstract and full text formats as well as various basic functions of libraries like acquiring, digitizing and archiving of contents. The networking of library resources means that users or patrons can access the information from their desktops irrespective of their physical location. The library networks provides library without walls.

TRADITIONAL LIBRARY NETWORK MODEL

Traditional library network setup was established with Ethernet technology and fewer clients and server machines. Ethernet has become the most commonly used LAN (Local Area Network) technology worldwide. More than 85% of all installed network connections are using Ethernet technology, according to International Data Corporation. As a transport protocol, Ethernet operates at 10Mbps data transmission speed and Layers 1 and 2 of the 7-layer OSI networking model, delivering its data packets to any device connected to the network cable. This type of network have very limited infrastructure.

The hardware and software is used make library network it includes one server machine and 5 to 10 client machines connected to gather. The server is responsible for all library related activities and like storage and retrievals. The same server runs library management software like SOUL and provides resources to the clients. The other hardware requires is hub/switch, network interface card (NIC) etc. while software need is generally network client software and network card drives. The figure shows the typical library network. This setup has only one server, which provides library management information, database storing and retrieving, running library software for library with limited support for services.

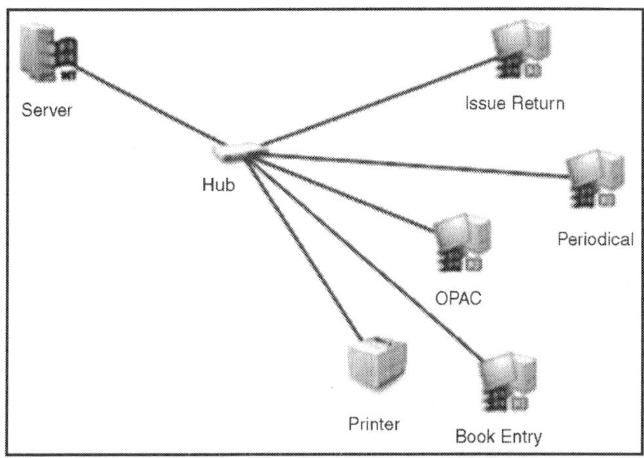

Fig 7.1. Traditional Library Network Setup with one Server and Four Client Machines

GENERAL NETWORK MODEL

Traditional library networks model operate at 10Mbps speed. At these speed libraries that use extremely large files such as transferring audiovisual contents to desktop, can experience long delays when sending such data across the network.

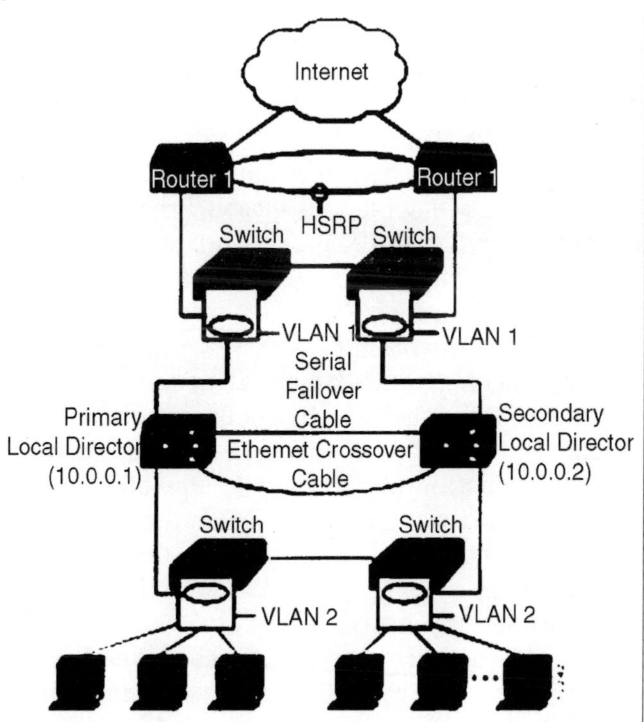

This model uses the extended version of Ethernet called fast Ethernet, which is simply, an extension of existing Ethernet technology, running 10 times faster at 100 Mbps. The general network setup for libraries is shown in figure. This setup model has two servers one for library applications and the other is for Internet access through remote location. These two servers provide information to switch, which is of 100Mbps.

Both the server NIC are of 100Mbps, which is little, bit higher then the traditional network setup. The figure shows four machines like issue return, periodical, OPAC and Admin machine are directly connected to switch with 100Mbps NIC installed on each machines, giving total bandwidth of 100Mbps. The Windows NT server provides user authen-tication and library management services to the various clients connected to it. While Internet server provides Internet services with remote online librarics, and Internet services (Fig. 7.2).

HIGH SPEED NETWORK MODEL

Traditional and general setup model operates at 10/100Mbps speed, while high speed network operates at gigabit 1000Mbps speed. Easy and straightforward migration to higher performance level without disruption, low cost of ownership including purchase and support cost and flexibility in network design are prime criteria for the high speed network model. This model is 100 times faster than regular 10 Mbps Ethernet and 10 times faster than 100Mbps fast Ethernet. The high-speed model as shown in figure shows the server farm to switch connection is of 1000Mbps gigabit Ethernet.

This also employs the same protocol, same frame format and same frame size as its predecessors like 100Mbps fast Ethernet. This model setup has three main server connected to central switch with 1000Mbps gigabit data transmission speed. All three-server has gigabit Ethernet card Installed. The high speed network switch has 1000Mbps network link and distributes network traffic to four hub/switch segments like Internet services, digital content reading room, audiovisual learning and finally library management. Out of four hub/ switch segments three are working at 100Mbps speed with 100Mbps fast Ethernet cards installed on each desktop machines.

The hub connection has also 100Mbps link support. The fourth segment named audiovisual self-learning as shown in figure needs more than 100Mbps because the data transmission is of high-end audio and video graphics files. Transferring this high bandwidth intensive file on the shared Ethernet makes network busy or low so that this segment must of 1000Mbps. This high-speed network segment provides simultaneous access to all the clients with streaming audio and video without any hustle form network speed. The high-speed performance is possible because the traffic is segmented. The figure shows library management, user authentication etc. services from windows-NT sever while NAS (Network Attached Storage) server provides database, digital books, thesis, journals audio and video learning material storage. The NAS server has very large capacity storage with 1000Mpbs gigabit card installed on it. This server provides automatic storing and transfer of data on network with supporting domain server. IIS server provides Internet access and web services of any other digital library from Internet.

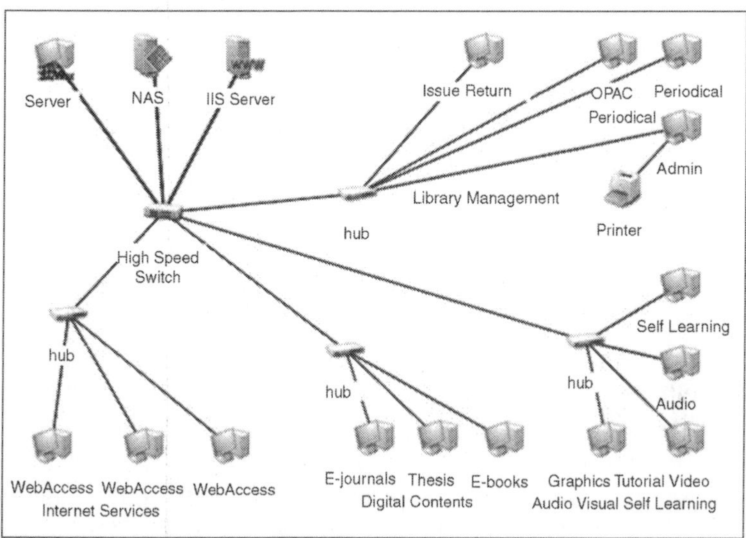

Fig. High Speed Library Network Model with Three Servers and One High Speed Layer-2 Switch Supporting Four Subnets

NETWORK SECURITY

The process of securing your library network begins with realizing what the library stands to lose if security is not pursued. Network security is not just "another thing to do." Its importance lies in protecting the library's network resources. Network resource means the equipment, software, and data that make up a networking system, including the user data that is shared over the network.

In terms of network communication, this includes the servers, workstations, hubs, switches, routers, firewalls, and telecommunications links that make up a network. In terms of usage, this includes shared printers, database systems, shared software, user accounts, the shared or user-specific files stored on a central server, and the keystrokes and form information that travel across the network.

IMPLEMENTING NETWORK SECURITY

We divide the realm of network security in libraries into seven main categories: physical security, password security, hardware security, server security, workstation security, perimeter security, and financial security These areas are expanded in the *Checklist* by separating out specific configuration issues related to web servers and general administrative issues related to budgeting, planning, and policy development.

There are many sections in the security checklist:

- General security.
- Physical security of computers and network equipment.
- Password security.
- Hardware security.
- Workstation security.
- Network server security.
- Network equipment security.
- Switch/Router/Hub security.
- Web server security.

LOCAL AREA NETWORK SECURITY

Securing any computer in a library must be achieved without any compromise to these three basic concepts: public service, user privacy and legal access. In an office or business environment, security is a matter of making sure those documents and transactions haven't been tampered with, corporate information is protected, personal employee information is kept private, and data is available when the business wants it to be. Network and computer security in a library setting faces these same challenges and a few additional ones. The major local area network security points are: Password Security, Hardware Security, Workstation Security, LAN/Domain Server Security, and Network Equipment Security. As a librarian we have to protect these levels of security in the network.

PASSWORD SECURITY

The least expensive and most important aspect of network security is the use of appropriate passwords.

Password protection is inherent in various aspects of the network:

- Administrative access to server functions
- Workstation access to various files and services (such as the Internet)
- Administrative access to network hubs, switches, routers, and firewalls
- Access to administrative files, such as confidential personnel files or reports

Here are the checklist items related to password security:

- Develop written password policy and provide to all staff and patrons using specific user logons
- Develop written instructions in creating strong passwords and provide to all staff and patrons using specific user logons
- Document passwords for all network equipment, servers, and workstations

- Store password documentation in secure location known only by library director and one other person

HARDWARE SECURITY

Hardware security is a convenient category used to classify miscellaneous items related to your computer and network hardware. The first set of items relate to the BIOS (the Basic Input/Output System) of your servers and workstations. The BIOS is a well-known feature on all Intel/AMD PCcompatible servers and workstations. It performs basic tests of internal components to be sure they are working satisfac-torily. It also stores and manages the configuration of many of the parts inside the CPU case.

WORKSTATION SECURITY

Properly securing workstations is a very important part of the overall network security in a library. There are a large number of configuration issues to address when securing workstations. Using the Windows NT Workstation/2000 Professional operating system provides a better security foundation than does Windows 98.

Those libraries using Windows 98 on public workstations are highly encouraged to install special software to secure many of the workstation functions:

- Configure NT Workstation/2000 Professional partitions with NTFS file systems.
- Windows NT/2000, unlike Windows 98, includes a feature known as file system security.

LAN/DOMAIN SERVER SECURITY

This paper assumes the use of Windows NT/2000 as the library's server operating system. In most small library local area networks, there will be one or two servers: a main server, usually a *domain controller* under Windows NT/2000, which verifies the logins of all users, and a file server used with the library automation system. In some libraries, these two services are combined on one server. It is possible to operate in a very small environment with just Windows NT Workstation/2000 Professional-based computers and no server at all, but it is more difficult to maintain security in this environment. So this base level of security assumes the presence of at least one server.

The following items are needed to secure the local area network servers in the library:

- Configure all NT Server partitions with NTFS file systems.
- Configure separate operating system and data partitions (both NTFS).
- Mirror server drives (or implement RAID), if funding allows, for redundancy.

- Configure servers with private IP addresses (LAN-wide recommendation).
- Remove unnecessary services.
- Remove unnecessary files/programmes.
- Configure file system with proper file/folder access permissions.
- Restrict access to the Network Monitor Agent.
- Disable anonymous user logons.
- Disable caching of user logons.
- Configure account policy to restrict unauthorized logon attempts.
- Create logon-warning message (a warning against unauthorized logon or access and use of restricted resources).
- Create alternative Administrators group and restrict membership.
- Restrict privileges of default Administrators group
- Create alternative Administrator account (with new name) with full privileges.
- Disable default Administrator account.
- Configure auditing of Administrator account logon attempts (to track hacking attempts).
- Set a strong password for current administrator account.
- Use different passwords for domain/server accounts than for local workstation accounts, or use different account names.
- Restrict access permissions for the everyone group.
- Disable Guest account if enabled.
- Create appropriate user and group accounts (minimum of three groups: Patrons, Staff, and Administrators).
- Set appropriate group access permissions.
- Implement procedures for file backups according to backup plan.
- Restrict access to backup programme.
- Create and maintain current Emergency Repair Disks, and store in a controlled location.
- File all server component documentation (papers/manuals/disks) for use by service technicians.

NETWORK EQUIPMENT SECURITY

Network equipment refers to all the devices required to get data signals from one computer to another. Generally, these include hubs, switches, routers, and firewalls. Libraries should be purchasing network equipment that provides management capabilities. This provides the possibility of remote management of the network even if the library does not contract for that service initially:

- Set appropriate network management protocol (SNMP) passwords/ community strings

- Record and secure any password settings created by staff or contractors

These two items minimize the risk of network equipment configurations being altered by unauthorized personnel. When the library hires a vendor to install and configure network equipment, be sure to document all passwords used to secure the equipment. It is the library's responsibility to secure these passwords by documenting them and storing the documen-tation in a secure (preferably locked) location.

- Configure audit logs properly, if available
- Implement procedure for monitoring audit logs
- Schedule periodic installation of firmware updates
- Document equipment settings for future use in reconfiguring equipment
- File all network equipment documentation (papers/manuals/disks) for use by service technicians.

CONCLUSION

A Library network service is an assemblage of digital computing, storage and communication machinery together with the software needed to reproduce, emulate and extend the services provided by the conventional libraries.

The analysis of depicted models indicates that scalability in the increasing processing capabilities of digital computing of workstations and servers providing services to the clients, larger and larger storage needs and effective management of storage and increasing requirements of network bandwidth and high speed data transfer are the prime issues of infor-mation technologies. The library network once established is not secured from the administrators' point of view but must provide network security policy for servers, clients and other connectivity devices to provide satisfactory level of network security.

LIBRARY AND INFORMATION NETWORKS IN INDIA

The explosion in the amount of literature that is available, increases among the number of users and their different needs, and the application of electronic media are forcing libraries to construct and participate in networks. Magnetic tapes, floppy disks, and CD-ROMs provide enough data storage capacity. Retrieval through telecommunications networks and access to international databases are available for searching for information on various subjects. With the advent of networks, remote transmission of texts and graphics, video clips and animated clips are also possible.

DEFINITIONS

- A library network is broadly described as a group of libraries coming together with some agreement of understanding to help each other with a view to satisfying the information needs of their clientele.

- UNISIST II working document defines Information Network as
  - A set of inter-related information systems associated with communication facilities, which are cooperating through more or less formal agreements in order to implement information handling operations to offer better services to the users.
- The National Commission on Libraries and Infor-mation Science in its National Programme Document defines a network as
  - Two or more libraries engaged in a common pattern of information exchange, through commu-nications for some functional purpose.

OBJECTIVES

- To promote and support adoption of standards in library operations.
- To create databases for projects, specialists and institutions to provide online information services
- To improve the efficiency of housekeeping opera-tions
- To coordinate with other regional, national and international network for exchange of information and documents
- To generate new services and to improve the efficiency of existing ones

NETWORK DEVELOPMENT IN INDIA

Some factors that are responsible for the development of library and information networks in India are:

- The report of the working group of the planning commission on modernization of library services and informatics for the seventh five year plan, 1985-90
- The National Policy on Library and Information systems document accepted by the ministry of HRD, Government of India.
- The report on national policy on university libraries prepared by the Association of Indian Universities
- The UGC report on information systems for science and technology under the Department of Science and Industrial Research (DSIR) Government of India has been vigourously promoting an integrated approach to library automation and networking.

LIMITATIONS IN NETWORK DEVELOPMENT

A network may fail in the early stages if there is not proper planning or if adequate funds are not available. Moreover, a common memorandum of agreement signed by the partici-pating libraries at the institutional level is essential for the success of a network venture. On a more practical level, catalogue data must be in a standard, machine readable form for it to be shared and exchanged. And, finally, a continuous flow of external assistance is crucial for the network's survival.

TYPES OF NETWORKS

Presently, there are three types of computer networks:

- LAN;
- MAN and
- WAN.

Local Area Network (LAN)

A LAN is a number of related computers and electronic devices that share information over a transmission media. A typical use of LAN is to tie together personal computers in an office so that they can all use a single printer and a file server. The LAN can be within a building or a campus wide network.

Metropolitan Area Network (MAN)

Attempts are being made to develop this type of network in metropolitan areas such Delhi, Calcutta, Bangalore, Madras, etc.

Wide Area Network (WAN)

A large-scale network, involving offices in different cities and countries is referred to as WAN, which is specially designed to interconnect data transmission devices over wide geographical areas.

CATEGORIES OF NETWORK

Library networks have been divided into two categories: general network and specialized network. The latter can further be divided into metropolitan network and countrywide network.

GENERAL NETWORKS IN INDIA

NICNET:

- *Title:* National Information Center Network
- *Sponsor:* Planning Commission, Govt. of India.
- *Membership:* Four national and regional nodes, 32 state and union territory nodes; seventy cities and towns
- *Services:* Bulk file transfer; teleconferencing; full text and bibliographic retrieval services
- *Application:* ICMRNIC Center; MEDLARS in India; Chemical Abstracts database

INDONET:

- *Title:* INDONET data Network
- *Sponsor:* CMC Ltd = Informatics India Ltd

- *Membership:* Commercial computer network
- *Services:* Database services such as DIALOG, COMPUSERVE; IP; SHARP
- *Applications:* ACME; file transfer; international gateway

I–NET (VIKRAM):

- *Title:* I–NET
- Sponsor: Dept. of Telecommunications, Govt. of India
- *Connectivity:* Packet switched public data network covering nine cities
- *Services:* Information exchange through e-mail/FTP; Bibliographic databases

SPECIALIZED NETWORKS

Metropolitan Networks

CALIBNET:

- *Title:* Calcutta Libraries Network
- *Sponsor:* NISSAT–Govt. of India
- *Applications:* Cataloguing; serials control; acquisitions; circulationediting and retrieval of records;delivery; library automation; CALIBNET INFO Services

BONET:

- *Title:* Bombay Library Network
- *Sponsor:* NISSAT & NCST
- *Objective:* To promote cooperation among libraries in Bombay
- *Services:* online catalogue; online document delivery; IRS; interlibrary loan; dissemination of information

DELNET:

- *Title:* Developing Library Network
- *Sponsor:* NISSAT & NIC
- *Objective:* To promote resource sharing; develop a network of libraries; collect, store, disseminate information
- *Members:* 165 Institutions, 600 Libraries, 15 States in India, 5 from outside India
- *Services:* resource sharing; free Software; ICE online facility; books database; thesis database; Indian specialists; database

ADINET:

- *Title:* Ahmedabad Library Network
- *Sponsor:* NISSAT, DSIR & INFLIBNET
- *Objective:* To bring cooperation among its regional libraries; to develop databases; to integrate scientific and technical information systems
- Members: nine libraries
- *Services:* library automation; library holdings; database in progress

MYLIBNET:

- *Title:* Mysore Library Network
- *Sponsor:* NISSAT
- *Objective:* Developing software tools; conducting seminar; workshops/ training programmes; conduct surveys
- *Host Site:* CFTRI, Mysore
- *Members:* 116 Institutions
- *Services:* MYLIB Database; E-journals; food patents; CFTRI Library Bulletin; public services.

Countrywide Area Network

DESINET:

- *Title:* Defence Science Information Network
- *Sponsor:* DESIDOC, Delhi
- *Activity:* Focus on scientific, research and defence communities

ERNET:

- *Title:* Educational and Research Network
- *Sponsor:* Dept. of Electronics, Govt. of India; UNESCO
- *Members:* eight institutions
- *Services:* Communication services such as e-mail, file transfer, remote log on, database access, bulletin board etc.,

SIRNET:

- *Title:* Scientific and Industrial Research Network
- *Sponsor:* CSIR (Commissioned Agency-NCST, Bombay)
- *Members:* 40 labs and R&D Institutions
- *Applications:* scientific communication; leather technology; natural products; food technology; medicinal Plants

VIDYANET:

- *Title:* VIDYANET (Dedicated Communication Computer Net)
- *Sponsor:* TATA Institute of Fundamental Research, Bombay
- *Objectives:* To provide rapid means of communi-cations by linking computers at various institutions in India to similar networks outside the country; to stimulate corporate research, the day-to-day exchange of research information and the execution of joint projects and publications
- *Services:* File transfer facility; sharing of computer resources and access to remote applications, data-bases, libraries, etc.

BTISNET:

- *Title:* BTISNET (Specialized Information Network)
- *Sponsor:* Dept. of Biotechnology, Govt. of India.

- *Connectivity:* 10 Specialized Information Centres in genetic engineering, plant tissue culture; photosynthesis and plant molecular biology; cell transformation; bio-process engineering.
- *Services:* Data processing using applications software; online communication access; facsimile facility

INFLIBNET:

- *Title:* Information Library Network
- *Sponsor:* UGC
- *Connectivity:* computer communication network of universities and R&D; libraries and bibliographic information centers throughout the country
- *Members:* 200 Universities; 400 College libraries; 200 R&D libraries
- *Services:* catalogue service; database Scrvices; document supply services; e-mail; BBS: audio and video conferencing, etc.

BALNET:

- *Title:* Bangalore Library Network
- *Sponsor:* JRD;. Tata Memorial Library
- *Members:* 100 Libraries

MALIBNET:

- *Title:* Madras Library Network
- *Sponsor:* INSDOC and NISSAT
- *Members:* 15 Libraries
- *Activity:* Two important databases, a directory database of current serials in Madras and a contents database covering articles published in 300 journals available in Madras libraries.

DIGITIZATION PERSPECTIVE OF MEDIEVAL MANUSCRIPTS

Medieval Manuscripts are rich sources of tradition, history and culture. These ought to be preserved, organized and disse-minated to make them available to the world at large. The western countries have taken a lead in starting digital initiatives to preserve the manuscripts but such initiatives in India are either poorly organized or in primitive stage of development.These rich treasures of our country are distributed in private and public institutions in variety of media (parchment, vellum, palm leaves, paper etc.), languages, scripts, collection sizes and in different conditions. Hence there is a scope to address the problem and focus it from different dimensions to suggest solutions. The information technology has come with a promise to develop digital initiatives for manuscripts for preservation, dissemination and delivery.

It is further desirable to initiate digital libraries for medieval manuscripts (DLMM) to achieve following goals:

- A cost effective bibliographic control of manuscripts.

- An unhindered access to contents over computer and communication network without any barrier (political, geographical, social etc).
- The effective retrieval is possible in digital format because surveying and cataloguing them manually has not been carried out in a scientific, systematic and uniform way and that has resulted in their poor recall and precision etc.
- The medium, generally paper, used in these manuscripts is old and not of superior quality. Most of the manuscripts are moth eaten, torn out, water stained etc. Thus digitization is a viable alternative to enhance the longevity of its life and preserve them from different hazards.
- The digital format can serve as an electronic archival copy accessible in the network from where users can make multiple copies at different points.
- Modern times witness new weapons of warfare and destruction coupled with escalating terrorism having inbuilt tendency to devastate treasures of culture and scholarship. Therefore, it is significant to address the problem and use image technology advances to preserve the manuscripts from such hazards.
- Manuscripts are not fully exploited by the scholars and researchers and to make them available in digital form around the globe via internet and fully searchable through search engines will make their diffusion much wider and give more visibility to cultural heritage of ancient and medieval scholarship.
- The revival of culture, moral values and traditions eroded by technological and industrial developments is desired these days. Hence, MMDL may help to rediscover it by making manuscripts (containing rich culture and traditions) more transparent, accessible to one and all. The attention of world towards rich past will help to have better understanding of each others values and traditions and will generate a fresh quest for knowledge among scholars who are already well set for making increasing use of computers and communication networks.

DIGITIZATION PROCESS

The main focus of digitization is preservation and access of manuscripts. The digitization confronts many problems and requires utmost caution and research and exploration.

The project chain normally consists of:

- Instigate the project
- To assess and select the material
- Prepare for digitization

- To digitize
- Edit
- Delivery
- Support

Most archival programme begin as an idea which may stem from a new funding opportunity or it may be a part of institutions overall strategy in managing its rare collections. Thus the initiative can be either reactive digitization in response to external request or proactive digitization when authorities target an archive of manuscripts. In reality, many institutions in India operate in reactive manner when catching a new call or opportunity for sponsorship. This immediately follows to perform an initial assessment of the manuscripts under consideration and select material from it which could be digitized.

The medieval manuscripts are normally copyright free but need adequate information about the manuscript for its retrieval which involves expertise of orientalis, scholars, codocoligists, linguists etc at one or the other stage of the project. However, 'cherry-picking' is acceptable proposition (*i.e.* focusing a sized item within chosen archive when funds are limited and extended when funds are available) by using a matrix covering all varying categories by which an item can be assessed. This matrix needs to devise to meet diverse situation when many such examples can be located.

Digitization is the core of an archival project which need source item, capture device, computer with required storage to house the digital image and necessary software interface. The picture is clear when one focuses on three components *i.e.* anatomy of image, image formats and digitization hard-ware and software.

The anatomy of dots, pixels, resolution, bit depth, shade etc effect the quality of image. For example one major problem arise when resolution concerning the size of the image scanned compared with the original dimension of the manuscript but the resolution at which one chooses to scan is not always the "effective" resolution. This creates more problems especially in surrogate like microfilm but technology seems to remedy such problem in future.Bit depth and dpi are probably important factors which influence quality and dynamic range (Dmax-Dmin) all depending upon the hardware used. However it will be everyone's interest to opt for high quality though affected by many constraints and pressures. The most frequently cited reason for not choosing maximum resolution is resulting file size.

Simple formula for calculating the file size is:

- Resulting file size= dpi x dpi x bit depth x dimension/8

Let us assume one page of 10 inch square item scanned at 24-bit colour at a resolution of 600 dpi Applying formula it comes to:

- $600 \times 600 \times 24\ (10 \times 10)/8$

- = 864,000, 00/8
- =108, 00,000 bytes
- 108,000 Kb or 108 Mb

It clearly shows the file size extremely large—equivalent to 75 floppy disks and nine such images would fill 1 GB hard drive. There could be other reasons as well for sacrificing higher quality for better speed. However, one solution to the balancing of quality versus size is to employ some form of compression using encoding/decoding algorithm to make it much smaller. Ideally this would mean no loss of information but many file formats provide 'lossy' compressions although not necessarily obvious to human eye, do involve degradation in quality. Therefore TIFF is generally used for master images of bi-tonal documents for being 'lossless'.

Interpolation is also used in connection with compression but it is best to avoid it in capturing or resizing to maintain quality true to its original. Good number of file formats (.TIFF;.JPG;.GIF;.PCD;.PNG;.PIC;. BMP;.PDF;.DJVU; AND PYRAMID File) have their relative qualities and limitations but still TIFF is widely used as cross–platform and archiving format for high quality images to be saved without any loss in original capture but alone not tied to any particular scanner or displayed and conversion from TIFF to other formats is relatively straight forward.

However JPG and GIF prove ideal for displaying via web in all browsers. The others may have advantage for compression, printing etc but remains to be seen how far these may go. The digitization process has complexity in deciding about many problems of utmost importance which influences are curatorial concerns on how source material is to be digitized.

For example, handling of a rare and delicate item like manuscript or painting may be restricted regardless of digitization, one could not be able to run ones' fingers across an original copy and therefore certain types of scanning will be prohibited and this contact digitization (using flatbed scanner with bright light from CCD) is often prohibited for handling fragile manuscripts, as against non–contact digitization (like camera) at a distance with employing facilities (ultraviolet or infrared) illumination for controlling light to reduce heat.

So a survey of digitizing hardware (flatbed scanner; sheet feeders; drum scanners, slide scanners; microfilm scanners; different variety of digital cameras; oversized document scanners and scan backs) need to be undertaken so to arrive at right type of software for different types of manuscripts. Outsourcing to the reputed and well established firms can be another alternative for bigger archives, of course, with extreme care and vigilance. The digital software (covering capturing, processing and delivery of images) is required though much hardware comes bundled with a range of imaging software but as referred to earlier, many decisions are to be undertaken regarding file formats etc. Processing may involve many things like cropping, fine tuning, colour schemes, applying filters etc and creating of derivatives. After understanding hardware and software requirements, the archival body responsible for digitization should be able to perform digitization assessment as under:

- Suggest digitization procedure to meet objectives of the archive/library and satisfy needs and recommen-dations of curators/conservation experts
- Establish digitization from original material/or surrogate
- Place of digitization: In-house or out sourcing
- Establish cost of conversion (*i.e.* unit cost for digitizing each unit)

The next step is in the practical issue of actual digitization and steps involved therein before capturing image are:

- Material is to be checked and prepared
- Sample shots taken to allow for accurate bench-marking (process at the beginning of digitization project to set levels in the capturing process to ensure that the most significant is captured. It is a dual process involving not only the study of the source document itself but also sample shots and the bench marker should have full knowledge of present/future needs of the user)
- Cameras calibrated accordingly when digitalization is under way.
- Quality Assurance (Different from Benchmarking being post process check to verify decisions made earlier were right ones) checks to be undertaken to assure digital files match all applications.

ORGANISATION

Without a brows-able or searchable catalogue, end users will struggle through to find manuscripts in the collection they may seek. This descriptive information attached to digital archiving may be commonly referred to as metadata. This needs to be a thorough understanding and debate as one third of overall cost of a project of digitization is involved in it. Text based cataloguing provides most straightforward approach to recording of information about digital manuscripts and the director/manager has to decide the structure of its catalogues and its resultant format–an appropriate metadata system which should meet the current and future requirements of the library and its users.

Metadata as term crept into standard Vocabulary of IT related projects has invited much discussion, confusion and problems that a single accepted standard have not evolved and yet user requirements are eluded out of sight. However a successful metadata system should satisfy needs of cataloguers, users, technical experts and administrators. Thus it should be flexible, extensible and forward looking which allow easy searching and browsing by the user at different points of access to collection preferably as a part of online catalogue. Many large digital projects looked elsewhere leaving MARC or Dublin Core and RDF systems out strapped to cope up with the complexities. The solution that has been adopted is that of SGML/XML. However RDF is also used in combina-tion and has proven more logical and practical policy. The findings of the CEDARS (The CURL Exemplars for Digital archives) are extremely influential on future digital initiatives. Like many other projects, CEDFARS has recognized the need for a comprehensive metadata system and currently looking at open archival system.

JIDI (JISC image Digitization initiative) project has set out a lengthy set of definitions for metadata categories and has segmented cataloguing into five levels via Collection, Work, Visual document, Person and Organization. But RLGs working group on preservation issues on metadata has taken 16 categories under which digital image should be recorded. The CEDARS/JIDI/RLG is extensive, complex and overlapping and XML approach seems to offer best possible solution for the present.

Assuming that one accepts XML as the metadata system of choice, the next step is to decide the Flavour of XML i. e. which DTD is used. One may write ones own DTD, though most digital imaging project select an off the shelf DTD and at present two DTD that are greatly used are TEI and EAD. The Text Encoding Initiativer (TEI) was established in 1987 and reviewed in 1998 as TEI-lite. Besides its complexity, people have looked to other DTDs for their projects on account of the literary and linguistic background of TEI. The notable example being of EAD (Encoded Archival Description) seems to be attractive to both curator and librarians as it emanated from background of archival description.

Most digital archival projects chose TEI flavour (DTD) of XML; EAD occasionally or a combination of both. Some are started to embed Dublin Core metadata or others with XML and write their own DTD. The other aspect is describing content, file naming and creation of metadata. The knowledge about a manuscript, its relation with traditional knowledge, history and scholarship, lack of standard terms in vocabulary tools are problems which crop up very significantly and may affect the retrieval system especially at delivery stage.

The uniformity, consistency and expertise of the catalo-guers under the supervision of orientalists well versed in different languages will be of utmost importance. However, secondary tools (descriptive catalogues/Directories etc) will be of immense help at this stage especially in varied cultural and linguistic diversity of Asian subcontinent. One may have to follow different extremes—simply dealing with broad description of the manuscript and other to decipher the depth matter about the nature, significance and importance of the document.

The file naming of manuscripts is very useful especially if Meta get lost and thus should be meaningful and/or mnemonic conveying information about file and its relation to other files besides persistent and consistent. The first one need to convey is some form of meaning to a file name. The most obvious example would be using a file naming system that reflects the shelf mark/

accession numbers of the volume under digitization e.g. The filename "ms25fir.jpg" would suggest that it is an image of folio one, recto from manuscript number 25.

Similarly.jpg suffix may indicate that this is derivative of master image (.TIF). Some users are frequently frustrated by the fluid state of WebPages and their sudden disappearance, rendering URL obsolete. It is therefore important that the identifiers one uses for digital file are persistent-hence the notion of persistent URLs (PURLS).

DELIVERY AND DISSEMINATION SYSTEMS

Flat–file Browsing (series of Linked files) can be a quick and easy solution to many programmes but it is also extremely unsophisticated from both cataloguers and users perspectivc. Complicated searches are not available besides updating the site is always cumbersome. The structured approach is seen as desirable and database programme can be used to store the metadata and link it to image files. The simplest way is to use a standard desktop database system such as Microsoft access link aging images and can interface relatively easily with the web (using Microsoft ASP).

The second option is to choose a system designed specifically for image database—an option that has been chosen for many projects. These have limitations due to high cost, lack of interoperability and focused on museums and galleries. A third option is SGML/XML route to treat the catalogue as a text base. It will allow one to catalogue all the material in XML, place XML file or files on a server and allow user search the texts.

The user would probably do this in web form. Then, through CGI scripts the system could convert the users input (i. e search or browse) to syntax usable by XML search engine on the server. This search engine in turn would analyse the catalogue files and return the hits; with further set of scripts converting material back to HTML for web display (although with XML this intermediate conversion process will eventually will not be necessary). Experience shows that the solution works well and is customizable to such an extent as to satisfy the most demands of users.

This, however, needs knowledgeable and experienced staff. The first digital image the user sees is the thumbnails image-*i.e.* a small derivative of around 100 pixels high created from a larger image. The thumbnail is usually small enough (PFG file of up to 40:1 compression) to allow to download quickly and convey at the same time meaningful graphical information about full image. From Thumbnail, the user could be allowed to download an image of sufficient resolution (say 72 dpi–a screen resolution) to fit a low end monitor of 640x480 resolutions.

Some difficulty arises when one considers the next level of image for advanced analysis or study (e. g. 150-200 dpi). The files would be larger in terms of file size (and slower to network) and one may not be keen perhaps to allow such images to be freely available. Besides creating, delivery of the full text has invited decisions to choose between transcriptions or by OCR. Having done so, it is surrounded with some form of structural make–up using a recognized SGML/XML DTD, with level of encoding to be chosen by the project management.

Future copyright decisions, if any and image protection decisions are to be made at an institutional level. It will vary from collection to collection and importance and policy of the parent institution. However employing banners and water-marks may cut right across the image and always be visible and defeat the entire purpose of the programme of digitations. The dissemination programme can be offline using CD_ROM technology and need to save as a backup for future use and transfer to other media keeping the life span of the medium in consideration.

However to make the cultural and historical assets more visible on-line access will be the viable solution but proper organization and management is to be taken into account in keeping large size of the collection in view in each country of Asia. It is reported by National Commission of Manuscripts in India that there are 50 million manuscripts about India available in many media, languages and scripts. Thus such diversity in a particular country can't be managed by a single organization but needs to be organized according to the region, language, script and available expertise in the institution etc.

However coordinating bodies in particular country can coordinate and monitor in order to achieve possible unifor-mity, consistency and maintaining of accepted standards so that overlapping is avoided and interoperability is achieved in a cost effective manner. This will also solve the web-hosting problems to a greater extent and a Portal can be maintained by the coordinating agency so to serve a Gateway for important resources of Asia with links to global digital archives in the coming future.

DIGITIZATION INITIATIVES

Western Countries

Western countries have taken a lead in undertaking digital library projects for medieval manuscripts resulting in development of various lists, union catalogues of manuscripts in various libraries in the region or country. These have evolved into OPAC's of the manuscripts with many fields for their retrieval and displaying images of manuscripts with different resolutions.

The prominent among them is the prestigious programme of Laurentius digital library of the Lund university, MASTER (Manuscript Access Standards for electronic Records), "Medieval manuscripts of Bodleian Library", The Digital scriptorium, Oxford university manuscripts, Medieval Manuscripts Of Syracuse University Library, The Bibliotheque National De France, "Medical Manuscripts in NLM", "European Manuscript server Initiative" (EMSI), "Unesco Memory of World", "The Humanities Text Initiative (HTI)" and "Manuscript digitization Demonstration Project of LC".

These projects have used photographic and digital methods to develop a full or partial archival copy of the manuscripts available on-line using different software with JPEG format for image processing in association with different metadata initiatives. These attempts could be very useful in evolving a common strategy for digitization of vast manuscripts resources.

Indian Initiative

Khuda Baksh Oriental Public Library

It is one of oriental libraries having rich collection of Persian, Arabic, Urdu and other language manuscripts. The descriptive catalogue is in 30 vols which appeared in 1923 and reprinted in seventies, besides other catalogues and publications compiled by different authorities. Now the institution has launched a website and a link is given to the whole catalogue of the library in a tabular form.

The table has hyperlinks to different volumes of the catalogue which can be browsed as JPEG files and browsed from as a file from top to bottom. The whole project has been undertaken by National Informatics Centre. It has not introduced any retrieval mechanism as the document is treated as collection of image files in JPEG format. The catalogue, ironically, can't be accessed under metadata or any useful descriptor.

Raza Library, Rampur, Uttar Pradesh

The library developed under the patronage of "nawabs" contains a collection of about 10,5000 vols. has appeared recently on the web with an interface for the manuscripts. It displays information of two manuscripts on a single screen, giving brief bibliographic information in Romanized form along with a folio of the manuscript scanned. However the collection is limited to few manuscripts only and further work is in progress. The retrieval engine for the data is missing as they have not structured the data nor made use of any digital library software.

Kashmir University Project

The Department of Library and Information Science, University of Kashmir, Srinagar, JandK has undertaken a project sponsored by the UGC for designing a database of medieval manuscripts available in Kashmir. The work is in progress and is made accessible on web after proper test and assessment.

ISSUES

- High band communication with computer networks which support efficient image document transfer

- Data storage
- Data compression and interpolation
- Scanning and conversion technologies
- Planning and execution (in house, outsourcing, financial implications, funding etc)
- Data image file format(.TIF..JPG.GIF..PCD.PNG,and others like.PIC..PDF.BM)
- Text encoding initiative (TEI)
- Single interchange standard for both First level (abbreviated)and full description of the manuscript
- Development of the software for simple descriptive records and provide means for fully detailed records
- Link manuscript images and full text transcript
- Adaptation of Unicode for different scripts and languages and research thereof for developing multilingual databases.

NEED FOR DIGITIZATION: PROBLEMS AND PROSPECTS IN COLLEGE LIBRARIES

Information technology and networks are the major tools to shape our society in future. The application of information technology has the largest impact on library and librarianship. It has changed the way we perceive and disseminate information and has even threatened the traditional approaches to library and library professionals.

The impact of such technologies (Computer network, Internet, Hypermedia, Multimedia, CD-ROM etc.) has led to a paperless society. The convergent of computational storage and networking technologies now have a wider impact on society. The computers can record any information/document at high speed and disseminate information wherever required to the users. It is possible now to digitize and store information in the form of high quality graphics, network texts, colour images, voice signals and video clips at a relatively affordable cost.

DIGITAL LIBRARY

The term "Digital Library" in a broad sense is a compu-terized system that allows obtaining a coherent means of access to an organized, electronically stored repository of information and data. It is a relatively new concept. The term digital library explains the nature of its collection. This term became familiar towards the end of the 20th century. Resources in digital library are electronic store and access of information. Access to digital library is therefore, not based on space or time.

The Berkeley Digital Library Project, University of Cali-fornia "the digital library will be a collection of distributed information sources, producers of information will make it available and consumers will find it perhaps through the help of automated agents". The Stadford Digital Library project states "the integrated digital library will create a shared environment linking everything personnel information collection to collection of conventional libraries to large data collection shared by Scientists". Digital Libraries do not mean libraries in the classical sense but a network of multimedia systems.

NEED FOR DIGITIZATION

With the rise of information explosion libraries facing manpower and monetary constraints are able to acquire every document published under one roof and thus evolve the concept of resource sharing and network. Automation has helped libraries in improving library activities and accelerates their working. It saves the effort, time and manpower of libraries. In an automated system the information can be altered and updated without the repetitive work involved in the manual system.

With the development of computer, any information can be turned into sequences. So, any user can access into the sequence without any trouble and delay. It saves the time for the users, staffs and increases productivity and reliability. As a series of development the concept of digitization evolved in the field of libraries. The process of library culture is and shall be as follows– the traditional libraries shifted towards automated libraries; the automated ones towards electronic ones; the electronic ones towards digitization ones and ultimately to virtual libraries (libraries without walls).

CHARACTERISTICS OF DIGITAL LIBRARY

The important characteristics of digital libraries are as follows:

- Digital library is a digital object.
- Digital library provides faster access to information
- Digital library enables easy management of large amounts of data
- Digital library collections are fixed and permanent.
- Digital library support formal and informal learning procedures
- Digital library can be accessed by any user from any workplace.

FUNCTIONS OF DIGIRAL LIBRARY

The most important functions of digital libraries are:

- To provide friendly interface to users.
- To avail network facilities.
- To support library functions.
- To improve the cost effectiveness of library operations.
- To enhance advanced search, access and retrieval of information.
- To support in editing and publishing annotations and integration of information.
- To digitize documents for preservation and for space saving.

SCOPE OF THE STUDY

The scope of the study entitled "Need for Digitization: Problems and prospects in college libraries of Manipur" is limited only to some leading colleges of Manipur. In this paper an attempt has been made to study the problems and prospects of Digitization.

METHODOLOGY

The study was conducted through questionnaire and interview method.

Major Findings Colleges in Manipur

The development of college libraries in Manipur was very late and started only from the 1940s, when the first college of the state, the D.M. College, Imphal was instituted with a well furnished library. At present there are 32 affiliated government colleges and 8 government aided colleges, 22 affiliated private colleges and 8 permitted private colleges in Manipur.

Libraries have been set up in all the colleges of Manipur. Majority of them are, however, facing financial problems for the development of resources manpower, money and collection etc. Application of modern technology in the work of college libraries still remains bizarre in Manipur.

Library Collection

The most important factor of any library is its collection. It grows in value with the passage of time. If the book collection of library is efficient, ideal and satisfactory to the needs of the readers, the image of the library shall automatically enhance. The efficiency of the library service is governed largely by the quality and quantity of its collection. Table 8.1 shows the collection of 20 college libraries of Manipur.

Table. Library Collection

Sl. No.	College	Books	Journals	News-papers	Audio	CD ROM Video
1	C.I. College	10200	4	4	NIL	NIL
2	Churachandpur College	7955	11	2	NIL	NIL
3	D.M. College of Arts	27500	NR	7	5	NIL
4	D.M. College of Science	53500	24	6	NIL	50
5	G.P. Women College	33315	NR	NR	NIL	NIL
6	HTT College	3309	3	1	NIL	NIL
7	Ideal College	12000	7	5	NIL	NIL
8	Imphal College	20844	NR	5	NIL	NIL
9	Lilong Haoreibi College	6750	50	5	NIL	NIL
10	LMS Law College	12012	509	NR	NIL	NIL
11	Manipur College	19799	3	NR	NIL	NIL
12	M.B. College	14035	3	6	NIL	NIL
13	Modern College	11250	4	4	NIL	NIL
14	Oriental College	7157	5	3	NIL	NIL

15	Regional College	5000	2	2	NIL	NIL
16	Royal Academy of Law	3469	848	6	NIL	NIL
17	S.K. Womens College	5455	NIL	5	NIL	NIL
18	Thoubal College	14269	4	3	NIL	NIL
19	T.S. Paul Womens College	11000	5	4	NIL	NIL
20	Waikhom Mani Girls College	10288	8	5	NIL	NIL

Notes: (NR = Not Received)

Table 8.1 indicates the great difference in the collection of materials and the non-uniformity in standard and status amongst the college libraries of Manipur.

Manpower Structure

The greatest and richest resource of any library is its staff. The staff provides services. The staff builds or destroys the image of the library. A trained and motivated staff is an invaluable asset of any library. Table 8.2 shows the manpower structure of 20 college libraries in Manipur.

Table. Manpower Structure

Sl. No.	Name of the College	Professionals	Non Professionals	Professional Qualifications
1	C.I. College	2	1	BLISc
2	Churachandpur College	1	3	MLISc
3	D.M. College of Arts	3	2	MA/BLISc
4	D.M. College of Science	4	4	MLISc/Ph.D
5	G.P. Women College	1	3	BLISc
6	HTT College	1	2	MA/BLISc
7	Ideal College	1	2	BLISc
8	Imphal College	1	2	BLISc
9	Lilong Haoreibi College	1	4	BLISc
10	LMS Law College	1	3	MLISc
11	Manipur College	2	3	BLISc
12	M.B. College	2	3	BA
13	Modern College	2	2	MLISc
14	Oriental College	1	3	BLISc
15	Regional College	1	2	BLISc
16	Royal Academy of Law	1	2	BLISc
17	S.K. Womens College	1	3	MLISc
18	Thoubal College	3	2	BLISc
19	T.S. Paul Womens College	1	3	BLISc
20	Waikhom Mani Girls College	2	3	BLISc

It is clear from Table 8.2 that staff pattern is not propor-tionate to the national standard and libraries of Manipur are suffering from lack of well trained staffs.

Financial Resources

Since the Library is NFP (Not for Profit) organization it does not have its financial resources. A library is on the other hand supposed to be a growing organism. It cannot grow without adequate amount of fund.

Most libraries are run with government grants (Central and State) or public donations or contributions from the students. Table 8.3 shows the financial position of college libraries of Manipur.

Table. Source of Income

Sl. No.	Name of the College	Budgetary Technique Adopted	Sources of Income During the 9th Plan State/Central	Fees/Fines Donation	(UGC)
1	C.I. College	Lump sum	87,000/	1,25,000/	28,000/
2	Churachandpur College	Lump sum	35,000/	15,000/	Collected
3	D.M. College of Arts	Lump sum		40,000/	Collected
4	D.M. College of Science	Lump sum		7,02,000/	Collected
5	G.P. Women College	Lump sum		1,00,000/	Collected
6	HTT College	Lump sum	28,000/	NR	Collected
7	Ideal College	Lump sum	NR	NR	Collected
8	Imphal College	Lump sum	NR	NR	Collected
9	Lilong Haoreibi College	Lump sum	20,000/	1,80,000/	Collected
10	LMS Law College	Lump sum	1,22,950/	2,50,000/	Collected
11	Manipur College	Lump sum	45,000/	1,80,000/	Collected
12	M.B. College	Lump sum	5,000/	2,00,000/	Collected
13	Modern College	Lump sum	50,000/	2,00,000/	Collected
14	Oriental College	Lump sum	NR	1,00,000/	Collected
15	Regional College	Lump sum	NR	NR	2,78,000/
16	Royal Academy of Law	Lump sum	NR	NR	4,40,000/
17	S.K. Womens College	Lump sum	NR	2,00,000/	NR
18	Thoubal College	Lump sum	NR	NR	Collected
19	T.S. Paul Womens College	Lump sum	NR	NR	2,71,000/
20	Waikhom Mani Girls College	Lump sum	NR	1,00,000/	32,700

Notes: (NR = Not Received)

Table 8.3 vividly shows the lapses in financial resources of the college libraries in Manipur which would ultimately check their normal growth and development.

PROBLEMS

The manpower, money and collection in college libraries of Manipur are in a pitiable position. Without proper infrastructure and well-trained staffs, digitization of college libraries is not possible. The most important aspect in this regard is financial resources from the concerned authorities. Some burning problems in college libraries of Manipur may be noted as follows:

- Library facilities in the college libraries of Manipur are inadequate and disorganized.

- Training for manpower-development (library staff) is not yet seen in Manipur.
- The earmarked plan and non-plan fund allotted to the libraries are insufficient.
- Lapses in the management of the fund allotted to the libraries can be seen from time to time.
- Information technology is lacking far behind in the colleges of Manipur.
- Creation of posts and consequent appointment of trained staffs are not done.
- Lack of cooperation among the libraries in colleges of Manipur.
- Lack of reading habit in the libraries by the students.
- Non-application of modern advanced technology in college libraries of Manipur.

PROSPECTS

The changing information and communication tech-nologies have brought the creation, handling, delivering and storage of information in digital forms. In this changing environment using digital technology in the college libraries is of utmost importance. The college authorities (Principal, Libraries and Staffs) of Manipur are also aware of the same in the state.

The following points may be recommended/suggested in this connection for the College Libraries particularly in Manipur and in India as a whole:

- The government should take steps for providing library facilities with well-equipped modern tech-nology at par to the colleges.
- The concerned authorities should not grant affiliations and permissions to the private colleges until and unless they can keep the requisite library norms.
- Information technology may be facilitated for making network among the libraries.
- A committee consisting of library authority, staffs and user community may be constituted to initiate joint efforts introducing computerized service in the library.
- Availability of information technology facilities (like internet) should be considered and encouraged.
- E-resources training/awareness programme may be organized from time to time by the concerned authority.
- College management committee should take steps to take help/ assistance from the UGC (INFLIBNET) for the successful implementation of modern technology.
- Earmarked grants for the college libraries should be given.
- Libraries must be encouraged to renovate themselves in the modern trends.

- Adequate funds may be provided and utilized properly.

DIGITAL ARCHIVING: INDIAN SCENARIO

Before the advent of digital video storage analog recordings on films and video tapes were placed on the shelves with a card catalogue. Whenever the library has to make room for the inclusion of new material, some of the old materials were removed and stored off-site, which is properly viewed as an archive. These analog and physical archives had limited shelf life depending on the medium on which the content is stored. In the digital age archiving is in the digital form-that is migrating the content electronically to new media for the purpose of preservation.

The classic meaning of archiving is:

- To place the documents in a secure place for presentation.
- To remove the data or documents from common use and conserve for future use.

The word *'Archive'* derives from the Greek word *Arkheia* meaning "Public records". The word denotes local, regional and national government collections of documents and other records kept for consultation and research purposes. One of the earliest digital-archives was a use-net news group called Talkorigins, which was devoted to mainstream theories in geology, biology, cosmology, theology etc. Contributions arguing the Darwinian evolutionary line were posed and often sent to bear all the hallmarks of serious research arguments and bibliographic referencing.

DIGITAL ARCHIVING

Digitization is sometimes recommended as a preservation strategy for materials that are in fragile formats and which are not in frequent use. Images and audio-visual materials are being stored in digital formats more than ever before, for example, digitizing pages of delicate manuscripts, preserving images of texts which are important for scholars. The primary goal of digital archiving is the storage, retrieval and access of rare documents with the aid of electronic technology for image capturing and reproducing.

The aim is to create conditions, whereby the researcher can consult the manuscripts without physically handling the individual items and at the same time the artistic quality of the calligraphy and decoration of the manuscripts could be preserved for future generation. In each and every country of the world the *National Archives department* is responsible for the preservation of important documents of that particular nation. Digital Archives can be defined as Repositories of digital information, that are collectively responsible for ensuring through the exercise of various migration strategies, that the integrity and long term accessibility of the nation's social, economic, cultural and intellectual heritage is preserved in digital form.

ADVANTAGES OF DIGITIZATION

The most promising strategy for saving the intellectual and artistic content of endangered volumes is to transform or convert it to a different medium by copying it to a film or digital form. Digital archiving is a recent work of digital libraries and ensures long term storage and access. By digitizing the documents, lots of space can be saved-a stack of CD's will take much lesser space compared to the space occupied if the same information was to be stored as hard copies. In addition, Electronic-files can be accessed from any where, at any time and at a cheaper price.

MIGRATION OF DIGITAL INFORMATION

Refreshing digital information by copying it from medium to medium and the possibility of maintaining a complex set of emulators describe two distinct points on a continuum of approaches to preserving digital information. It is a periodic transfer of digital material from one hardware and software configuration to another or from one generation of computer technology to a subsequent generation.

CREATION OF INFORMATION IN DIGITAL FORM

Information objects in digital form have to be created, edited described and indexed, annotated, revised, re-created, modified, disseminated and retained for future use, by a complex interwoven community of creators and other owners, value-added services and institutional and individual users. The process of preserving digital information will vary with different kinds of objects like textual, numeric, image, video, sound, multimedia simulation etc.

ORGANIZATION OF DATA

Before scanning the documents for digitization, one has to organize the data, that is to be archived, so that the process will go on in a smooth way and the scanned data can be retrieved properly.

The most important steps which are to be followed are given below:

- Organize the data that is to be archived in to files.
- Decide how to organize the scanned file, for example-by subject, by code number, by chrono-logical order, by keyword, by author, by title etc.
- File names should be clearly identified, so that one can easily recognize the contents of the file.
- All the files or documents which are to be scanned should be kept in order.
- All the staples and paper pins, if present, should be removed.
- The paper folds and creases in the paper should be smoothened out.

Scanners

Different scanners are available for scanning the docu-ments but one has to select the scanner on the basis of materials, like

- Vacuum-fed belt scanners–can be used for fragile and odd shaped material.
- Plane-protected wide-angle scanners–can be used for book scanning.
- High-volume scanners can be used for–architectural drawings and other oversize materials.
- Flat-bed scanners can be used for–delicate and fragile materials.

METHOD OF SCANNING

After deciding the type of scanner and type of material to be used, one has to decide whether to scan the documents as images or with OCR (Optical Character Recognition).If the document is scanned with OCR, the files need to be saved in the form of application for easy editing. The benefit of OCR is that the documents are converted to an editable format. If the document is to be archived to maintain the integrity of the records for preserving, they should be scanned as images. The documents should be scanned at a minimum resolution of 150 ppi, through 300 ppi, for future use or print.

The choices available for saving the documents as images are:-

- *BMP:* Bit Map is the native image format for the windows operating system and will provide high quality images.
- *TIFF:* Tagged Image File Format is very detailed and it is supported by many operating systems.
- *JPEG:* Joint Photographic Experts Group format comprises the data, but it is enough for normal use.

STORAGE METHOD

When all the documents are scanned, they should be saved on CD zip disks or floppy disks or tape drives. For storing the files on the disks, labeled folders should be created, the disks as well as the disk cases should be labeled. In digital archives there may be many levels of storage on the basis of expected use for the retrieval. Seldom-used material may be stored offline, usually in tape media, which is less expensive. The data which is in high demand and where retrieval time is at a premium, online storage in magnetic media may serve best.

An intermediate solution is near-line storage, where the data can be stored on optical or tape media and loaded in jute box, which is more responsive to users demand than offline storage. The most promising strategy for saving the intellectual and artistic content of endangered volumes is to transform or convert it to a different medium by copying it to a film or digital form. Paper documents can be transferred to microfilms, DVD's (Digital Video

Data) and CD-ROM's (Compact Disk Read Only Memory).This process is known as Archiving. Digital archives can use any of the three methods.

RETRIEVING DIGITAL ARCHIVES

Digital archives must maintain the information in a form, so that the users can access the information over the net through search engines, print, audio etc. If the archives are saved on CD's, floppies or tape mediums they should be checked periodically for content redundancy. If the digital archives need to be accessed in a distributed network environment, the digitized data should be connected to networks using proper protocols and bandwidth suitable for retrieving the information.

ARCHIVING IN INDIA

Preservation of Indian culture and literature is one of the oldest traditions of India. Thousands of years ago, Indian philosophers, scholars and poets have expounded their knowledge through treatises, sacred songs, commentaries on scriptures etc. which were recorded on specially treated palm leaves and birch barks, in the form of engravings on brass and copper plates etc. for future use. Before the invention of the printing press, the texts were handwritten by the craftsmen so that the universal knowledge can be preserved for future use. This proves our theory that Archiving has existed since long in India.

Indian National Archives

Indian National Archives department, which is located in Delhi is making efforts through various conservation methods and photo duplication processes to preserve the important documents of Indian cultural art, political and economical and literature. Department of Indian National Archives is using a unique method of rejuvenating and repairing the old documents with the help of "Cellulose acetate foil and tissue paper", which is known as "Solvent of Hand lamination". The Conservation Research Laboratory is a department of Indian National Archives has been successful in retrieving palm leaves that have gone dry since the last three decades. The National Archives is trying to ensure the longevity of documents by microfilming and reprographing.

Preservation of Indian Art

C-DAC–Center For Development of Advanced Compu-ting is trying to digitally preserve and disseminate Indian Art in the form of paintings. By using HP (Hewlett Packard) equipment to capture, store and make available via internet to the researchers and art lovers.

In this project, using comprehensive suite of H.P. Technologies, the scientists capture images in extraordinary details using digital cameras to store and process the images on workstations and to develop new colour pallets and drivers to make the individual works and print realistic reproductions on large prints. By digitizing Indian art in this way not only the art is preserved but is also made available to a larger audience.

Muktabodha Institute-Archiving of Indian Manuscripts

Muktabodha institute is working in collaboration with libraries and institutions around India to make digital images of specific, rare manuscripts and texts. The institute recognizes the importance of saving the spiritual knowledge and preserved around 871 works in microfilm format. Around 262 of these works were converted to digital image format. The institute is launching the "On-line digital library" website with 74 volumes of the Kashmir series of texts and studies. These volumes were originally published in Sanskrit language.

The main contribution of this institute is in the preser-vation and accessibility of photographic images of rare manuscripts and religious scriptures, so that the valuable information is more easily available to scholars around the world. At present Muktabodha discontinued the practice of microfilming the manuscripts and started producing digital images directly from the manuscripts. Since the main objective of the institute is in the dissemination of old religious literature by digitizing and preserving them, the institute decided not to face the hassels of microfilming and adopted the process of digital imagery.

COMMERCIAL ARCHIVING ORGANIZATIONS

Many commercial organizations have come up and made it easy to have any time anywhere, to access to information. These organizations provide electronic publicizing, content management, digital archiving etc. for the E-Publishers, individual purposes and institutions like libraries etc. Some of the organizations of India are the following.

DPS (Digital Publishing Solutions)

The Digital Publishing Solutions (DPS) is a Pune based organization, which has digitized so far 3.5 million pages and made digital archiving a reality. It scans the data from paper, photographs, negatives, microfilm, microfiche, transparencies and then the data digitized using the OCR and stored the digitized data in E-book format. Now the data is sold online using DX Reader, online XML reader. This organization is a approaching the libraries interested in preserving the rare books, manuscripts etc. In India DPS is working for 15 libraries, National research Institute, Indian national science academy etc.

JALVA

Mumbai based Jalva Media provides solutions for media management, indexing, content archiving data distribution, with partnership of other companies like mediasite, Ibeam Broadcasting, Madge.web, microsoft, Real and Apple. Jalva and SGI are offering better technologies like MPEG2 (moving picture experts group 2) which allows archiving data in DVD (digital versatile disk) by providing longer storage like and cross-platform compatibility.

Sampradaya

SAMPRADAYA Which means *handling down of tradition*. It serves as a resource centre by documenting the various aspects of the South Indian (Karnatic) music. It was founded in 1980, by two students of South Indian music Michael, Nixon of Veena and Ludwig, Pesch of Flute, under the guidence of late Savitri Rajan with the purpose of documenting Sampradaya Sangeetam. The main contribution of this organization is to bring to light and preserve this music tradition by documen-tation, archiving of recordings, music books, journals, manuscripts etc. This organization is conducting in-depth taped interviews of eminent Carnatic musicians, and organizing seminars and workshops on important topics of South Indian Music. Sampradaya Audio listening library is only one of its kind in South India, where the public has free access to music recordings and archival collections. It has 8 separate music listening stations.

PROBLEM AND PROSPECTS OF DIGITAL LIBRARY

The world has become a global village due to the development of information technology especially computer technology. Computer technology plays a vital role for gene-rating and disseminating information in the network environ-ment. The rise of digital libraries has also brought phenomenal changes in the progress of collection, storage, preservation of rare documents, retrieval and dissemination of information. Computer technologies not only create and develop some modern libraries but also transform many existing libraries on the modern lines. A digital library is a global virtual library. And it can be defined as library with all the information available in the digital form. Data accessible through digital library system in addition to full text information includes non text information. With the advent of digital technology the possibility of horizontal and vertical integration of knowledge and information has increased significantly. As such there is every reason that the role and the status of traditional library will change.

DIGITAL LIBRARY AND DIGITIZATION

Perception of the term "digital library" is a bit like perception of the elephant in the poem 'The Six Blind Men and the Elephant" where each of six blind men gives different descriptions of the elephant according the elephant's body part they touch. The library communities have also used different terms over the years to denote this concept. The idea of easy and fingertip access of information conceptualized as digital library begins with Vannenar Bush's MEMEX MACHINE and has continued to evolve with each advances in information technology.

Today people give different definitions of digital library in arrays of terms such as electronic library, virtual library, hybrid library, library without walls, cybrary, spatial library, digitize collection, library of the future etc. While these are not necessarily synonyms of digital library, they do have some aspects in common and the term digital library is one most widely accepted. Digital library may be treated as repositories of massive amount of information content in digital form in different servers on diverse format permitting access over different electronic networks.

According to Edward Fox (Editor of ASIS and commu-nication of ACM) a digital library is an assemblage of digital computers, storage and cummunication machinery together with the context and software needed to produce emulate and extend those services provided by conventional libraries based on paper and other material means of collecting, cataloguing, finding and disseminating information. . . A full service digital library must accomplish all essential services of traditional libraries and also exploit the well advantages of digital storage, searching and communication.

Digital Library Federation in USA define digital library as "organizations that provide the resources, including the specialized staff, to select, structure, offer intellectual access to, interpret, distribute, preserve the integrity of ensure the persistence over time of collections of digital works so that they are readily and economically available for use by a defined community or set of communities".

A digital library "is that set of global internet worked libraries" that includes the following criteria:

- A collection of text, images, or data in digitized form
- A set of systems for indexing and navigating or retrieving in that collection.
- One or more defined community of users.

Christine Borgman opines that the term digital library has various meanings.

However, for her, it clusters around two themes:

- From research perspective, digital libraries are content collected and organized on behalf of users' communities,
- From library-practice perspective; digital libraries are institutions or organizations that provide information services in digital forms for the enhancement of information storage and retrieval system.

Similarly, Levy points out that "notably for librarians, digital library refers most directly to institutions that oversee digital collections. For the other professionals like computers and information scientist digital library refers to digital collections without regard to institutional settings in which they might be managed. More comprehensively, in digital libraries the information arrives as needed at the users' screen like the attending waiter ever filling the water glass before the glass is empty. However, these defined perceptions are likely to evolve as activities move research development endeavours to full scale practice.

Digitization, now a day, has become one of the key activities in libraries. These two terms Digital library and Digitization goes hand in hand, like the two sides of a coin, the elements that form both concepts can not be separated. Digitization can be defined as the digital conversion of library and other archival materials. Digitization is also a technique for data transmission at a very high speed.

It is the conversion of any fixed analog media – books, journals, and photos, paintings into electronic form through scanning, sampling, or even re-keying. Digitization provide solution to traditional library problems such as conservation, preservation, storage space, remote access to information collection, acquisition of original digital works created by other publishers, agencies, access to external digital materials and resources.

WHY DIGITAL LIBRARIES

Libraries have changed with time to time from mere static storehouse to dynamic service centers, serving all professionals and non-professionals utilizing useful need base collection. The emphasis of the users has also shifted from micro document to micro piece of information with the changed of the medium from clay tablets to paper and now to electronic and optical media. The worlds of both communication and production of information are changing at a very fast pace and the conver-gence of these had huge impact on libraries.

All this changes in libraries is due to the impact of information technology and this impact is seen in the form of digital library. Due to information explosion during the last few decades many techniques and technologies have emerged for handling the information more readily, speedily and effectively. Many computer specialists also succeeded in integrating text, graphics, audio, animations, and video converted into a digital media. People feel enthused to read from computer screens.

Varieties of software are now available which are capable of manipulating and rendering information. At the same time price of personal computers are getting cheaper and cheaper to a very affordable cost. Besides allowing remote açcess, bringing the diverse material together from scattered locations, solving space problems, raising the profile of institution, enhancing preservation, increasing in retrieval and dissemi-nation of information in digital libraries system, people in the library professionals shows increased concern in building digital library. Dwindling budgets of library and high information demand are also another factor.

NEED AND IMPORTANCE OF DIGITAL LIBRARY

We are in the midst of information explosion and information technology revolution leading to the emergence of electronics information era. Rapid advances in information processing, storage and communication technologies have revolutionized the role of libraries worldwide in disseminating information services to their users. Libraries therefore, are reconsolidating their services and information products, incorporating new technologies of upgrading information resources, changing information objects, models of communication and information delivery in order to add value to their services and to satisfy the changing information needs of user community.

In fact, impact of information technology on libraries and its users is an important factor for transformation of traditional organizational structure into new institutional entities. Infor-mation seekers are also no longer statisfied with the printed materials alone.

As a result the users demand for information delivery in digital form, considered more dynamic in electronics multimedia documents, at their desktop are increasing day by day.

Thus, there is a need to develop digital library and to adopt electronic media for its collection development so that it can fulfill the requirement of users. Libraries and other library professionals should make efforts for setting digital libraries and conversion of resources into a digitized format.

Some important features of Digital library can be summarized as:

- To introduce new service and material
- To provide remote access to information resources that are expensive and rare and easy searching that are impractical manually;
- To facilitate in the management of digital content
- To minimize in handling of rare and unique collection of traditional library
- To improve access to the latest information at a very high speed
- To support search and retrieval
- To provide users friendly interface
- To support formal and informal learning
- To reduce errors that would have occurred in the manual systems scientifically because of bar code
- Cost effectiveness and affordable and
- To raise library profile
- Digital libraries as global multilingual expository of data must attract people from all walks of life regardless of geographical locations.

Technical Architecture

Technical architecture is another factor that need enhance-ment for digital information service system. Therefore, libraries need to upgrade current technical architecture to accommodate digital materials.

The architecture includes the following components:

- Local Network with high speed and fast connection to internet
- Full text search engines to index and provide access to resources

- Variety of servers (FTP and Web server)
- Electronic documents management functions that will support digital resources
- A variety system functions to coordinate mange the entry and retrieve data
- Local Library system with adequate PCs having LAN
- Well trained and manpower
- Relational databases that support a variety of digital formats

Present Status of Library in Manipur in the present technological environment

In library information system, information technology has had a clear and persuasive impact in almost every area of the library. The most significant development in information technology over the last few years or so is digital technology. Digital technology is revolutionizing the traditional concepts of preservation and access in library and archive communities. The applications of digital system and computing system in the libraries have been a subject of interest to present day professional librarians.

More recently the libraries have sought to implement increasingly complex solution that involved distributed networking and access to remote information resources. During the eighties, the whole focus of the librarians shifted towards library automation but in the nineties it has shifted towards digitization. The phrase library automation has been generally accepted within the profession to encompass early automation activities, yet it does not do justice to the current state of affaires as libraries have move well beyond the automation of internal procedures. In Manipur, however, applications of technologies in libraries are lagging far behind.

There are two university libraries, 74 affiliated colleges, nine public libraries, one state central library at Imphal and others at different districts of Manipur and many high and higher secondary schools libraries. But most of the libraries function in the traditional way with conventional printed shelf collection except some libraries like Manipur University library, Central Agricultural Library, RIMS Library, DOEACC Library etc. These libraries have initiated automation. Manipur University Library started automation since 1989 in the areas such as cataloguing, serial control, information retrieval and circulation recently.

This library provides internet facility, OPAC and has become one of the important nodes in the academic libraries system. As far as college libraries are concerned collections of information resources which support the faculty and students are not up to the mark because of lack planned systematic approach to the development of resources. Many of college libraries built up their collection of printed materials as activities and services are yet to be automated.

Only one college library *i.e.* Modern College library has started Data entry using CDS/ISIS.

Books are still the only important channel for dissemi-nation of information. The librarian and other supporting professional staff are not well qualified and trained with the new modern technology. As far as infrastructures are concern a large majority of libraries have not yet automated their activities as they are handicapped to switch over to computeri-zation and modernization because of lack of infrastructural facilities like computer hardware, software, and human-ware. And most of the libraries are not provided internet facility.

Regarding school and higher secondary school libraries, majority of school libraries are not able to provide even the facilities of a traditional library. From the discussion it is evident that the libraries in Manipur, except some, automation of the operations and services progressing very slowly. Automation as well as conversion of digital library will not be possible within five year though plan for automation exist. In Manipur it is not an easy task to develop digital library system as automation in the library is totally absent. Keeping in views of the reasons, authority should take initiative for promoting library automation by implementing new IT in the libraries of Manipur so that users from different communities can get the universe of knowledge available in the digital format.

PROBLEMS

Problems faced while entering into a digital libraries systems in Manipur can be summarized as:

- Libraries exist only in the traditional form and there is no electronic library/digital resource;
- Most of the libraries function with inadequate number professional staff required for smooth functioning and there is a general unwillingness to develop digital library system;
- Even if the librarian and some professionals are qualified they certainly lag behind because of lack of awareness about value of information, cooperation and coordination in the resource building and sharing of information and poor communication skill;
- Libraries lack standardization of methods due to unwillingness to adapt to new requirements;
- Presently large majority of library have no computer and no internet facility and other infrastructural facilities required to exploit the opportunities provided by electronic media. Therefore, the best use of electronic publication on-line and network access are not possible;
- Total absence of hardware, software and trained human power is another reason;
- A highly irregular and unpredictable power supply; and
- Lack of financial support due to the acute financial problem the state is facing.

In fact, the main problems faced seem to be lack of financial resources and lack of computer education without which automation in the libraries are not possible.

PROSPECT

The dawn of information revolution is considered to be one of the marvelous achievements of the 20th century. The rapid growth and development of IT has resulted in the development of digital library, tools and skill relating to encoding information objects in digital format. The application of digital technologies within the library comes along with the development of computer technology. Keeping the points in view it is necessary to consider some perspective of digital library.

Digital library not only creates and develops modern libraries but also transforms many existing libraries. Digital Library introduced the concept of hypertext, facilitates networking in order to communicate and exchange digital information from source location to destination. It also facilitates preservation, storage, and communication of diverse multimedia objects but also provides intensive access from multiple locations and enrich teaching and learning environment which is not possible with the traditional library. Due to information explosion and existence of information society, everybody is aware of the newly developed technologies. This new developments are reflected in LIS education and in those libraries with existing infrastructure, services and network.

In fact, there is a complete change in activities, role of library, librarians and other professionals (staff). Most of the librarians in Manipur have now entered in the technological era of communication dominated by film and electronic media. The libraries are expected to be an automated information system having pervasive impact in almost every areas of library-be it the online catalogue, online database, online searching, document delivery, inter library loan, circulation etc. Clearly, the impact of automated system in libraries has been pervasive and significant.

DIGITAL PRESERVATION OF MANUSCRIPTS: A CASE STUDY

During the history extending over 5000 years, India has produced a large wealth of literature. This vast knowledge treasure was written on different kinds of material like birch bark, palm leaf, cloth, wood, stone and paper etc. India perhaps has one of the oldest and largest collections of manuscripts in the world. They are in the custody of different institutions like libraries, museums, monasteries, mosque and individuals. Many of them have disappeared and a large number are in a state of damage/decay. We already have lost huge manuscript collection in Buddhist monasteries like Nalanda, Taxila and Vikramshila.

Taxila at the North West front of India was destroyed by foreign aggression. Nalanda library known as Dharmganj had three sections Ratnadodhi, Ratnasagar and Ratna Rajak. Ratnadodhi was a nine storied library. First Hun king Michirkul damage the library in AD 450-470. In AD 1205 Bakhtiyar Khilji destroyed it completely and his soldiers use the manuscripts for boiling water. Let us hope no more Khilji is born in modern time and let us take step to save these manuscripts for further decay and damage that will destroy them. The public access of older manuscripts also leads to substantially quicker disintegration of the originals.

An appropriate alternative that could be the solution to the existing problem is preservation by way of microform or use of modern computer technology which is digitization of the manuscripts. The manuscripts, besides having information (the image data) also have visual information (secondary image data). The information regarding physical form, binding, paper, history of manuscript, source of acquisition, its present market value which is often high, is called physical data. All these are very important in manuscripts.

There are many libraries in the world where rare manuscripts of Indian origin are preserved and some of them are:

- Copenhagen Royal Library (Denmark);
- Bibliotheque Nationale (France);
- Preussiche States Bibliothek,
- Universitats Bibliothek,
- Staats Bibliothek,
- Bayershe Staats Bibliothek(Germany);
- British Library,
- Royal Asiatic Society,
- Bodleian Library,
- India Institute,
- Cambridge University Library (United Kingdom);
- Darbar Library (Nepal);
- Punjab University Library (Pakistan);
- Museum Library (Sri Lanka).

In India Manuscripts are maintained usually by univer-sities and research institutes.

They are as follows:

SL.	Name of the Institutions	Manuscripts
1	Sampurnanand Sankskrit University, Varanasi	1,40,000
2	Rajasthan Oriental Research Institute, Jodhpur	1, 16,123
3	Govt. Oriental Manuscript Library Chennai	72,620
4	TSSM Library, Thanjovour	47,625
5	Adyar Library and Research Centre, Chennai	40,000
6	Orissa State Museum, Bhubaneswar	37,000
7	Asiatic Society, Kolkata	32,000
8	Andhra Pradesh Orinetal Main Library	23, 115
9	Khuda Baksh Oriental Public Library, Patna	20,060

10	Scindia Oriental Research Institute, Ujjain	18,695
11	Punjab University, Chandigarh	18,395
12	State Central Library, Hyderabad	17,000
13	Vishwabharati University, Shantiniketan	15,354
14	Rampur Raza Library, Rampur	15,000
15	Rajasthan State Archives, Bikaner	14,000
16	Kameshwar Singh Darbhanga Sanksrit University, Darbhanga	13,000
17	University of Calcutta, Kolkata	13,000
18	Aligarh Muslim University,Aligarh	12,000
19	Govt. Manuscript Library, Allahabad	11,000
20	Banaras Hindu University,Varanasi	10,500
21	Safdarjang Museum, Hyderabad	10,00
22	Central Institute of Buddhist Studies, Leh	10,000
23	Osmania University Library, Hyderabad	6,428
24	Shivaji University Library, Kolhapur	5,673
25	Kurukshetra University, Kurukshetra	5,500
26	Poona University, Poona	4,416
27	Patna University, Patna	3,700
28	Tamil University, Thanjavur	3,365
29	National Library, Kolkata	3,258
30	Guwahati University, Guwahati	3,248
31	Utkal University, Utkal	3,053
32	Andhra University Library, Hyderabad	3,000
33	Sanskrit Academy, Osmania University, Hyderabad	3,000

A Survey made by Indian National Trust for Art and Cultural Heritage (INTACH) under National Manuscript Mission in the year 1988-90 found that there were various types of manuscripts:

SL.	Types of Manuscripts	No. of Manuscripts
1	Manuscripts in India (estimated)	5,000,000
2	Indian manuscripts available in European countries	60,000
3	Indian manuscripts in South Asia and Asian Countries	150,000
4	Number of manuscripts recorded in catalogues	1,000,000 (approx.)

Percentage of Manuscripts Language Wise:

- Sanskrit 67%
- Other Indian Languages 25%
- Arabic/Persian/Tibetan 8%

HISTORICAL BACKGROUND OF UJJAIN CITY

Ujjain is an ancient, historical pilgrimage city of India. It is known as cultural capital of India. Ujjain was called by ancient people Vishala, Kanak Shiringa, Amaravati, Pratikalpa Awantika, Ujjaini, etc. It is situated on the fertile land of Malwa. Ujjain which has always been known for its sanctity stands on the right bank of river Shipra. This city is one of the seven sacred cities of the Hindus. Where one of the Jyotir-lingMahakal rests and during 'Simhstha Mela' or 'Kumbh Mela', a festival held in every twelfth years, people went there to have a dip in the holy water of 'Shipra' on the auspicious days.

Also known as city of Mahakavi Kalidasa is also famous for Guru Sandipani Ashram where lord Krishna completed his education. Historically, this city was the capital of the famous king Vikramaditya who was famous for his judgment and Navratna of scholars. Sawai Jaising of Jaipur had erected here an observatory which is still standing.

Scindia Oriental Research Institute (SORI)

Scindia Oriental Research Institute, Ujjain a pioneer manuscript library of India, was ranked 11th in India as per the Indian National Trust for Art and Cultural Heritage (INTACH) survey.

Establishment

The history of Oriental Institutes begins with establish-ment of Asiatic Society of Bengal in 1789. Royal Asiatic Society of London was established much later to it in 1823. Its Bombay branch was established in 1829. These institutes were established with an aim to collect manuscript. After that many institutions started colleting rare manuscripts in India and abroad. In India Baroda, Mysore, Kashmir, Kochin and Travancore etc., started collecting manuscripts. Bhandarkar Oriental Research Centre, Poona was established. In Madhya Pradesh, Bhelsa (Vidisha), Maheswar, Mandesaur, Ujjain, Dhar and Chanderi had rare manuscript collections but in neglected state.

The manuscript from Ujjain were being sent out of Ujjain, a few of them to Oritental Institute, Baroda. In 1931, king of Baroda, Maharaja Siyaji Rao Gaekwad wrote to Regency Council of Gwalior State about scattered manuscripts in Ujjain and recommended its colletion and preservation. On this, a manuscript library named Oriental Book Collection was established on 20th October, 1931. It was started with only 11 manuscripts in a rental house in Pan Dariba. This was increased to 2000 by July 1933. On 1st July, 1933, it was transferred to Madhav College, Ujjain.

A galery was constructed for their display which is still in very good condition. Dr. Divakar started caring these manu-scripts. In 1936 and 1941 the manuscript catalogues were published.

Maharaja Jiwaji Rao Scindia set up a committee in 1938 under the Chairmanship of Sir Manu Bhai Desai with Dr. Radhankrishnan, Dr. Amarnath Jha and Professor Paranjbe as its members to establish permanent memory of Maharaja Vikram celebrating Vikram era festival. The committee recomm-ended establishment of Vikram University, Vikram Kirti Mandir including Archeologoical Museum, Scindia Oriental Research Institute and a Conference hall.

During independence movement, it was delayed. In 1941, Vikram Bi-Centinary festival was organised in Ujjain when the earlier oriental book collection was renamed as Scindia Oriental Institute and was included in normal budget of education department of Gwalior State for financial help. President of India Dr. Rajendra Prasad lay fouindations of Vikram Kirti Mandir on 8th May, 1951. But due to delay in its progress, the Scindia Oriential Research Institute was transferred in a rental house-Nawab Saheb Bangla near Madhav Club.

After state reorganisation in 1956 and establishment of newly carved Madhya Pradesh, the SORI was transferred to the control of Deputy Director of School Education in M.P. Government. Finally Vikram University was established in 1957 and on 06/11/1960 an Memorandum of Understanding (MoU)was signed between M.P Govt. and Vikram University. On 26/06/1961 the institute was transferred to the Vikram University. In 1966, it was shifted to newly constructed Jiwaji Rao Library building. In August 1968, after construction of some parts of Vikram Kirti Mandir, the institute was shifted to its own place.

Staff

In the beginning (till 1956) the institute has the post of one Curator, one Shastri, one Librarian, one assistant cataloguer and one clerk.

The following posts are sanctioned posts and their designations with grades are given Table 8.4:

Table 8.4. Staff and Designation

Sl. No	Class	Designation	No. of Posts	Grade
1.	I	Director (Vacant) *	One	16000-19500
2.	I	Joint Director (Vacant)	One	12000-15990
3.	II	Lecturer (Vacant)	One	8000-13500
4.	III	Curator (Vacant)	One	Not available
5.	III	Sastri	One	4500-7000
6.	III	Research Assistant	One	8000-13500
7.	III	Upper Division Clerk	One	4500-7000
8.	III	Archivist	One	4000-6000
9.	III	Cataloguer (Vacant)	One	950-1530
10.	III	Assistant Cataloguer	One	3050-4590
11.	III	Microfilm Operator	One	5000-8000
12.	IV	Khallasi/Daftari	One	2550-3200
13.	IV	Sweeper	One	2550-3200
14.	IV	Servant/Peon	One	daily wage
15	IV	Chowkidar	One	daily wage

Notes: *Acting Director working from Sanskrit Department.

Budget

The expenditure/budget of the institute in 2002-2003 and 2003-2004 are as follows (Table 8.5):

Table 8.5. Expenditure and Budget

Sl. No.	Items	Actual Exp. 2001-02	Original Budget 2002-03	Revised Estimate 2002-03	Original Budget 2003-04
1.	Contigency	7000	10,000	10,000	10,000
2.	Books and Megazines	–	30,000	30,000	20,000
3.	Furniture and Equipments	2000	25,000	20,000	20,000
4.	Water and Electricity	2000	20,000	20,000	25,000
5.	Microfilm Unit	–	10,000	10,000	10,000
6.	Maint. and repair of old and rare manuscripts	–	10,000	10,000	40,000
	Total Rs.	11,000	1,45,000	1,40,000	1,75,000

Salaries are not included in this which is high as compared to other heads.

Collection

Collections of this institute are very rare and important. Only a small portion of the present collection of manuscripts was made available from Ujjain. Remaining collection was brought from different places mainly from Lashkar, Gwalior, Mandsaur, Poona, Jalgaon, Sagar, Ratnagiri, Banaras, Jalone, Indore and Srinagar (Kashmir). After the establishment of SORI in 1931 the growth of manuscripts is shown in the table.

The progress made by the institute is as under Table 8.6:

Table 8.6. Growth of Manuscripts

Sl.No.	Year	No. of Manuscripts	Sl.No	Year	No. of Manuscripts
1.	1931	11	12	1942	6160
2.	1932	58	13	1943	7033
3.	1933	483	14	1944	7369
4.	1934	1891	15	1954	9794
5.	1935	2700	16	1969	14146
6.	1936	4459	17	1986	18122
7.	1937	4853	18	1989	18122
8.	1938	5392	19	1990	18562
9.	1939	6057	20	1991	18695
10.	1940	6090	21	1993	18695
11.	1941	6125	22	2003	18695

Here we can see that only 473 manuscripts have been added since 1986.There are various kinds of manuscripts in the institutes. More than enough manuscripts are collected in Sanskrit language but the other manuscripts are written in many languages like Marathi, Hindi, Gujrati, Aarabic, Persian, Bengali, Maithali and Telegu etc.

Many kinds of writing materials cab be seen here like:

- Papers,
- Palm leaves,
- Brich barks,
- Metal plates etc.

There are also manuscripts which are written in different kind of scripts. The scripts are:

- Devanagari,
- Brahmi,
- Gupta,
- Jain,
- Maithili,
- Modi,
- Sharada,
- Muriya,
- Farasi,
- Bangla,
- Telegu,
- Tamil, etc.

Acquiring Manuscripts

Whether it becomes known that a particular manuscript is being sold the 'Sastri' and other staff members of the institute goes to the place to purchase and study the manuscripts. The 'Sastri' knows about the collection of manuscripts in the institute and after seeing the catalogues it is decided whether or not the manuscript is useful for the institute. The pages are checked if found useful. It is checked whether the pages are in agreeable state and written by a single person or two or more persons. Thereafter, meeting is convened and the draft for purchase is proposed before the committee. If the proposal is assed then the cost of the manuscript is assessed and after due assent of the seller and the manuscript.

Types of Manuscript Available in SORI

- *Palm Leaf Manuscript:* In India maximum manuscripts of ancient period are written on palm leaves. Palm leaves are usually 37 inch in length and three inch in width. The palm leaves were boiled and then were rubbed by couch shell for smoothness. Then with the help of iron pen, letters were scratched and ink was pasted on them-simultaneously. This method was popular in South India. Hot atmosphere is harmful for palm leaves. The palm leaf manuscripts if kept in paper or cloth, is mutilated. In SORI only three palm leaf manuscripts are available.
- *Birch Barks Manuscripts:* Birch tree is found in Himachal Pradesh. Its inner bark is just like papers which were used for writing. Some times its length is found to be 60'. These were cut into pieces as per requirement and then were written with different inks. The manuscripts written on birch barks are generally found in Kashmir

and north India. In SORI only 3 manuscripts of this type are available.

- *Paper Manuscripts:* It is said, that first of all, the paper was made by Chinese peoples. In ancient India also the paper was made. In our country, many types of papers are famous for writing, like Kashmiri, Moghulai, Ahmadabedi, Daulatabadi, etc. The paper used, was prepared by hand using different raw material like bamboo, cotton, etc. In SORI most of the manuscripts available are on paper. Leather, Cloth and Wooden manuscripts are not available at SORI.

Publications of Scindia Oriental Research Institute

The institute has published the following titles under the 'Scindia Oriental Series'

- *Tattvasara* (Marathi), 1936, 414p.
- *Alankara Manjusha* (Scindia Oriental Series no.1), 1940, 384p.
- *Ancient Jaina Hymns* (Scindia Oriental Series no.2), 1951, 178p.
- *Sastrattva Vinirnaya* (Scindia Oriental Series no.3), 1952, 136p.
- *Chikitsa Manjari* (Scindia Oriental Series no.4), 1959, 206p.
- *Journal of Scindia* Oriental Institute, Vol. I (1955) and Vol. II (1956).
- A descriptive catalogue of manuscripts in the Scindia Oriental Institute, Vol. II, (literature),
- Part-I, 1983, 282p. 8. A descriptive catalogue of manuscripts in the Scindia Oriental Institute, Vol. II, (literature), Part-II, 1985, 414p.

It may be noted that for some reasons Volume I (Vedic Sahitya) is not published and Volume III to XII ready but yet to publish.

In addition the following three Vikram volumes have been published in commemoration on the completion of 2000 years of Vikram era:

- Vikram Volume (English), 768p.
- Vikram Smriti Grantha (Hindi), 927p.
- Vikram Smriti Grantha (Marathi), 568p.

Micro-filming of Manuscript

Some 4190 manuscripts of importance have been microfilmed by Indira Gandhi National Centre for Arts (IGNCA) at SORI. One copy of the microfilm is available with SORI. The IGNCA has microfilmed 2,50,000 manuscripts in 66 libraries running to 11 million folio. Other manuscripts at SORI are yet to be microfilmed due to lack of staff though a microfilm processing unit is available. Department of culture, Govt. of India has started National Mission for Manuscripts which will convert manuscripts into electronic record as one of the activities.

Besides preparation of catalogue, search of manuscript in society through surveys and building up of a National Manuscript Library. The institutions have been provided fund to start the mission. ₹10 millions has been allocated to launch the mission. A total of ₹265 million is estimated for building, cataloguing, conservation, microfilming, and digitization starting from the year 2002-2007.

Besides ₹25 million will be spent on purchase of manuscript from the customers. SORI is recognized as Manuscript Resource Centre (MRC) for all Madhya Pradesh for the preparation of accession catalogue, launch awareness programme in society. In total 23 such MRCs have been recognized in India. Under the project SORI is getting grants and the preliminary work has started.

MANUSCRIPTS DIGITAZATION PROCESS

The digitization process at SORI is yet to start. In this section we have studied technologies available at present so that options can be selected at final stage. There are various options available for digitization of reading material. The re-typing is not possible in case of manuscripts. Scanning is the only possibility in case of manuscripts. It is nothing more than a picture of printed page in digital form. Digital imaging technology convert manuscripts into digital images and can be made available over electronic networks-a digital image is composed of set of pixels.

The text can be retrieved, printed and modified using appropriate software. The scanning of manuscripts using computer image scanner is done carefully due to variations in text and colour and images. Aperture of can also be made by digital camera or other feasible imaging devices. The digital images can be captured at varied of density or bits pixel. Simple binary scanning in black and white is not always complete in digitizing manuscripts as coloured illustrations are also valuable with texts. Light and darkness of document is to be considered before digitization.

Colour images are more complex because they need encoding of shades. Resolution of image is measured in dot per inch (dpi). Higher dpi leads to better resolution and quality of image but larger image file. 300 to600 dpi are recommended for better resolutions. File compression is another important aspect because image capturing takes more space. Various types of scanners such as Flatbed, sheet feed, drum scanners and digital cameras are available to scan manuscripts. Mircofilm scanners are used to convert roll film, fiche into digitized form. Video Digitizer are also available now a days which may be also used for scanning.

DIGITIZATION EXPERIENCES

There have been few manuscripts digitization projects in the world to point problems and solutions of digitization of manuscripts. The experiences may be helpful in deciding technological options. A few experiences are given here. UNESCO project entitled "The Memory of the World" aim to initiate to support the safeguarding of existing document for future. Under the programme in 1993 first memory disk was published on two CD ROMs having digital form of two entire manuscripts that National Library of Czech Republic to test the possibility of digitization of manuscripts.

Latter more CDs were made. These two projects studied the problems of manuscripts digitization. Each image 2.40 MB and display of original image was very time consuming. More such experience was made to get high resolution. The present technology has enabled approximately 100 on a CD-ROM with full preservation of colour and passed resolutions. Manuscript digitization demonstration Project sponsored by Library of Congress is carried out in cooperation with National Library Digitization act. Digitization of Manuscript of the National Library of India undertook a pilot project entitled "Down Memory Lane" to digitize its rare and brittle books in 90's.

A local private agency was given the responsibility to scan and clean the documents. Between the year 1999 and 2001 approximately 6601 books/ manuscripts containing 2.5 million pages were scanned and archived in 548 CD-ROMs. National Library has 3000 volume of paper manuscripts and 334 palm leaf manuscripts in Arabic, Persian, Urdu, Bengali, English, Hindi, Tamil and Sanskrit language. Many of them with beautiful illustrations fine epigraphy and elegant bindings. The sample project was undertaken for the digitization of these manuscripts. The project was undertaken in collaboration with Trinetrix Technologies, Calcutta.

A Persian Manuscript – Tutinamah was sample project. The image was captured by a digital camera (Nikon D100 with bayonet mount 28-70mm f/2.8 ED–IF AF-S Zoom-Nikon lens) mounted vertically on the photographic copy stand (Bojen System 800 Repro Copy Stand W/bb 1740), with side illumination through 40 watts incandescent lamp. The background was chosen to be slightly lighter than the document colour in order to minimize shadow and optimize digital transfer. The digital camera had special colour metric filter that enabled the camera to capture a broader spectrum of colour than most digital scanners.

The lighting was also provided selectively from by two 1000-watt Elinchrome Strobe lights (daylight balance) at 45% angle to copy surface, with multiple diffusion filters between copy surface and light to soften shadows and reduce glare for specific pages with illustrations. The image processing station was a HP Brio, PC with Pentium IV processor, 128 MB DDRAM. The workstation had the image processing software like Kodak Imaging, Abode Photoshop 6. There was an image transfer device connected to the USB port, which gathered images from the memory card of the digital camera. The lighting environment was adjusted as per the specific requirement document using light meter.

The manuscript was set on the Photography copy stand bed opening it at angle of 120 degree to avoid the stress to the binding of the manuscript. The image was captured from the manuscript at the different aperture, focal length and shutter speed and the captured images were transferred to the image processing Station. Final images were at suitable Aperture Focal length shutter speed. First for all right hand side pose and then for all left hand side pages in colour as uncompressed 8 bit per channel (24 bit RGB) TIFF files at 300 dpi. The images were then transferred to the Image Processing Station. The files were converted to three basic formats as per the requirements namely, PDF, TIFF and JEPG.

The individual image PDF files were tagged and a composite PDF file was prepared as per the original document pagination and sequence. The images were stored in CD-ROMs and were made resident in hard disk of the central server. The images produced have minute tonal variations due to shade of colour and illustration. A white light is more helpful to minimize tonal variations. Software Adobe Photoshop version 6 is very resource consuming. From the experiment it is clear that digitization of manuscript is not as simple as one can understand as photocopying and scanning.

It is much more complicated need expertise, costly and time consuming. It requires costly digital cameras, work stations and high quality hardware and software. The images need to be as close to the original as possible, with removal of worm marks, stain marks. The images need to be clear and the details of the illustrations of pages have to be captured to the best possible extent. Cost-benefit analysis on the project with the long-term view on the scope of project in large scale is to be considered. The project estimations and determination of the time frame of completion of digitization of the entire collections of manuscripts is to be decided.

INSTITUTIONAL REPOSITORY OF INFLIBNET CENTRE USING DSPACE

INFLIBNET Information and Library Network is an Autonomous IUC of the University Grants Commission (UGC) started in 1991 with its Headquarters located at Gujarat University campus, Ahmedabad.

The Programme is directed towards modernization of libraries and Information centres, and establishment of a mechanism for information transfer and access, to support scholarship, learning and academic pursuits. It also aimed at establishing a National Network of Libraries and Information Centres in Universities, institutions of higher learning and R & D Institution in India. It is basically a co-operative endeavour in resource development, sharing and its utilization at national level.

The main objective being to evolve a National Network, interconnecting various Libraries and Information Centers in Universities, deemed universities, colleges, UGC information centers, Institutions of National importance and R&D institu-tions, the centre has taken the initiative of building Dspace INFLIBNET an Institutional Repository using the open source software Dspace to support the long term preservation of the digital material for the Academic community.

So far the centre has already hosted the CALIBER proceedings, Course materials, Newspaper clipping etc. The Academic community can also submit their resourceful articles in this repository centre and preserved it for future use.

The building of an Institutional Repository is needed in the present scenario of digital world because of the following certain changes:

- Technological changes.
- Significant increase in the overall volume of research.
- Increasing dissatisfaction especially on the part of Librarians with traditional print and electronic journals price and market model that have become less relevant and more difficult to sustain in a period of rapidly escalating prices and relatively flat library budgets.
- Increase uncertainty over who will handle the preservation archiving of digital scholarly research materials.

All these factors have evolved and combined to create new expectations in the Academic community for the production, distribution and interchange of scholarly communication and to force a rethinking of the relative roles of authors, librarians and publishers as well as the possibility of entirely new actors who will emerge as the publishing model. In such an environment Institutional repository might act well to preserve an Institutional intellectual work product.

INSTITUTIONAL REPOSITORY

An Institutional repository is a digital archive of the intellectual output of an Academic Institution. It makes the quality and breath of scholarship produced at that Institution accessible to others world wide over the internet. It is a set of services that a University/Organization offers to the members of its community for the management and dissemination of digital material created by the institution and its community members. It is most essentially an organizational commitment to the stewardship of the digital materials including long term preservation.

An effective Institutional repository of necessity represents collaboration among librarians, Information technologies, archives and record managers, faculty and University administrators and policy makers. At any given point in time, an Institutional repository will be supported by a set of Information technologies but a key part of the services that comprises an Institutional repository is the management of technological changes and the migration of digital content from one set of the technology to the next as a part of the organizational commitment providing repository services.

The basic and fundamental level of an Institutional repository is that it is a recognition that the intellectual life and scholarship of an University will increasingly be represented documented and shared in digital form and that a primary responsibility of our University is to exercise stewardship over these riches both to make available and to preserve them. It is the mean by which a University/Organization will address the responsibility both to the members of their communities and to the public. It is a new channel for structuring the University contribution to the border world and as such invites policy and cultural reassessment of this relationship.

IMPORTANCE OF INSTITUTIONAL REPOSITORIES

Institutional repositories centralize, preserve and make accessible the knowledge generated by Academic Institution. It also form part of a larger global system of repositories which indexed in standardizes way and searchable using one interface, providing the foundation for a new model of scholarly publishing. Institutional repositories often employ a method of article submission known as author self-archiving and rely on user communities to control the input of content.

These can include academic departments; research centers administrative groups and other sub-group who will determine what content merits inclusion and act as arbiters for their own research communities. Author self-archiving is the broad term often applied to the electronic posting of author-supplied research without publisher mediation. It involves a simple web interface where the depositors types or copy/pastes in the metadata and then attaches the full text documents. Institutional repositories also have roles beyond dissemi-nating and managing the works of individuals scholars that are part of the dialog of scholarly communication and it is also a place where we can put much of the material that research libraries identify as worth collecting and they offer a frame-work for organized stewardship and accessibility of these materials. It can encourage the exploration and adoption of new forms of scholarly communication that exploit the digital medium in fundamental way.

They can support new practices of scholarship that emphasizes data as an Integral part of the record and discourse of scholarship. They can structure and make effective otherwise diffuse efforts to capture and disseminate learning and teaching materials symposia and performances and related documentation of the intellectual life of Universities. Institutional repositories benefit both the Institution and its scholars by raising the Institutional profile while also bringing broader.

Dissemination, increased use and enhanced professional visibility of scholarly research others benefits are:

- Improved visibility and impact-Institutional, National;
- Contribute to institutional knowledge management;
- Improve Research collaboration-interdependent, inter-Institutional, International;
- Enhanced status and reputation;
- Enhanced research capacity.

Realizing the needs of the scholars and the benefits of building an Institutional Repository Centre the INFLIBNET (Information and Library Network Centre) being the nodal point of all the Indian University has started this Institutional Repository Centre called Dspace INFLIBNET using the open source software package dspace developed by MIT and Hewlett-Packard (H P).

DSPACE

Dspace is an open source software platform that enables institution to:

- Capture and describe digital works using a sub-mission workflow module;
- Distribute an institutions digital works over the web through a search and retrieval system;
- Preserve digital works over the long term.
- The mission is to create and establish an electronic system that captures, preserve and communicates the intellectual output.

The vision is a federation of system that makes available the collective intellectual resources of the world leading research Institution. It supports all manner of digital format (*e.g.* Articles, preprint, working paper, technical reports, and conference papers).

- Books
- Thesis
- Datasets
- Computer programmes
- Visualization, simulation and other models
- Multimedia publication
- Learning objects.
- The other facilities which are available in this open source software package are:
- Browse
- Search
- Advance search
- Communities
- Collection
- Sign on to Dspace
- Submit
- File format
- My Dspace
- Edit profile
- Subscribe to e-mail alerts

INSTITUTIONAL REPOSITORIES, OPEN ACCESS MOVEMENT AND OAI-PMH COMPLAINT SOFTWARE

Institutional repositories of scholarly content have been receiving increasing attention recently. The main purposes of institutional repositories are to bring together and preserve the intellectual output of a university. The number of signifi-cant developments, such as the launch of MIT's Dspace, University of California's eScholarship and the growth of repositories based on the University of Southampton's EPrint software, have brought the issue of institutional repositories increasingly to the fore.

Further the open access and open archives movement and the changes in scholarly communication to remove barriers to access have begun driving the establishment of institutional repositories. Keeping in view the recent changes in scholarly communication, emergence and various standards and protocols, and trend towards open access INFLIBNET being a national Centre for library and information Centre too is exploring the possibility of institutional repository and archiving faculty publication of universities in India.

During the course of development of experts database and research projects database of academic and scientific community in India, it was observed that faculty generates enormous amount of information, which is untapped and not available for access. These content needs to be managed, preserved, and maintained for larger access to the users. Faculty members want additional visibility for their resources. INFLIBNET in future aims to provide a comprehensive system for managing these resources and play a pivotal role of repositories of these valuable resources. In this direction, Centre has opted Dspace open source software for achieving institutional publications including CALIBER and PLANNER proceeding.

WHAT IS INSTITUTIONAL REPOSITORIES

An institutional repository (IR) is a digital collection of a university's intellectual output. Institutional repositories centralize, preserve, and make accessible the knowledge generated by academic institutions. IRs also form part of a larger global system of repositories, which are indexed in a standardized way, and searchable using one interface, providing the foundation for a new model of scholarly publishing.

An institutional repository (IR) is defined to be a web-based database (repository) of scholarly material, which is institutionally defined as opposed to a subject-based repo-sitory; cumulative and perpetual (a collection of record); open and interoperable (*e.g.* using OAI-compliant software); and thus collects, stores and disseminates. In addition, most would include long-term preservation of digital materials as a key function of IRs.

Definition

Despite of the amount of press that the topic of institu-tional repositories has received in the past few years, providing a concrete, precise definition of an institutional repository (IR) is difficult to do. Clifford Lynch (2003), executive director of the Coalition for Networked Information, describes an IR as "a set of services that a university offers to the members of its community for the management and dissemination of digital materials created by the institution and its community members." Other than replacing "a university" with "an organization," this definition reflects how IRs are discussed in this report.

Lynch's definition is particularly appropriate because services, and not technologies, are the emphasis. Nevertheless, even with this definition in hand, the question remains: what exactly comprises this "set of services" to which Lynch refers? Unfortunately, this question has no single, correct answer because an institutional repository must be *institutionally defined.*

To be successful an IR must provide the set of services needed by its unique community of users, and these services will and should differ from institution to institution. The SPARC position paper on IRs has been influential in setting the agenda for the IR debate.

Crow argues that there are two key rationales for IRs:

- Reform of scholarly communication, and in particular scholarly publishing;
- To enable the institution to enhance its prestige by making visible the fruits of its faculty's academic and research labours.

CORE FEATURES OF INSTITUTIONAL REPOSITORIES

Despite this ambiguity, all IRs share some common features and functions, and it is this combination of features and functions that distinguishes IRs from other types of services. The first of five common features, and perhaps most obvious, is that an IR contains digital content. The range of different types of digital content can be vast, including text, audio, video, images, learning objects, and datasets. The material may be born digital or of a physical medium that has been digitized, such as scanned images. A second core feature of an IR is that it is community driven and community-focused.

The community of users not only determines what should be deposited into the IR, but they are individually responsible for making the deposits. The members of the community also are the authors and copyright owners of the content. As a result, the IR reflects or showcases the scholarship, research, and interests of an organization. A third core feature is that the IR has institutional support. An institutional repository is not a simple or cheap undertaking.

A successful IR requires collaboration among divisions across an institution, which is accomplished most easily with top-down institutional support. Moreover, an IR necessitates ongoing, long-term financial support to ensure, for instance, the integrity of the content through digital preservation. Without an institutional commitment to the project, the costs and obligation of an IR likely are too great for any one department or unit to bear on its own. An assumption of durability and permanence is the fourth common feature of an

IR. When a digital file is deposited into an institutional repository, the author expects that the document will remain there for the perceivable future. Finally, an IR is not a black archive; the content in an IR is not hidden from the entire world. With some exceptions, the content of an IR can be accessed by more than just the content's owner because the material within an IR is meant to be shared. Access can vary greatly from just a few people within a department to the entire world, but the cost and scale of an IR discourages its use as a person's private, digital dumping ground.

ISSUES FOR INSTITUTIONAL REPOSITORIES

There are various issues which needs to be properly addressed before establishing any Institutional Repositories.

The main issues for establishing arc:

- *Cultural Issues Affecting Faculty Take-up:* The biggest problem facing those setting up IRs is persuading faculty to use and contribute the content from them. Outside a few disciplines (*e.g.* physics, computer science and economics) there is little tradition of preprints or working papers and apparently still little interest in self-archiving. There is a great deal of inertia in the current publishing systems. The organisers of IRs need money for advocacy (marketing campaigns, meetings, flyers, websites, e-mails, etc.), for training users and producing guidelines, and for ensuring the interface design does not put off potential users.
- *Intellectual Property Rights/Copyright:* Institutional repositories raise issues of rights-not just copyright but other intellectual property rights such as patent rights. The copyright issues have been extensively reviewed by the RoMEO project, in UK. As RoMEO notes, there are rights associated with metadata as well as with the content itself.
- *Existing Digital Collections:* New IRs at most organisations will have to take account of existing collections. Some of these *viz.* personal self-archiving websites may be best source for the IR
- *Organisation and Administration:* Who will manage the IR? Where will it be located? What will be the rela-tionship between the centre and the departments?
- F*unding/business Model:* How will the IR be funded, and what business model will it adopt?
- *Preservation:* This is very important issue. The long-term preservation of digital objects are very far from solved.
- *Accession Policies:* The IR has to decide:
  - Who is allowed to deposit materials;
  - What types of materials can be deposited (*e.g.* pre-prints, post-prints, working papers, theses, chapters, datasets, etc.);
  - What digital formats will be accepted (and which formats will be migrated);

  - Quality assurance procedures (*e.g.* none, or approval by departmental head, or even peer review);
  - Storage limits etc.
- *Open Access:* Although IRs can be seen as part of the open access movement, this is not necessarily the case. IRs may well want to restrict access to part of their content to their own network only.
- *Central vs. Institutional Repositories:* This argument is somewhat theological. Central, subject-based repositories have been very successful in a few fields (physics, computer science, economics, cognitive science) but have failed so far to migrate to other disciplines. Institutional repositories may offer a new route to reduce the inertia among the non-archiving communities. From the perspective of a web-based searcher (*i.e.* reader), however, there is (in theory) no difference between the two repositories, as articles are discovered on the basis of metadata independent of location (author, title or whatever), collected via the same OAI protocol. The searcher would be using an interface on a third party site, *i.e.* an OAI service provider. In practice, of course, there are significant benefits in centralised systems, for instance in terms of standardisation, single metadata schemes, etc.
- *Metadata:* Without at least some metadata, nothing can be found. But too comprehensive a metadata requirement will inhibit users. Decisions also have to be taken on which metadata schemes to use. Metadata requirements may vary from field to field. Most of existing repositories are using Dublin core Metadata scheme.

WHAT IS THE BENEFIT OF INSTITUTIONAL REPOSITORIES

Institutional repositories benefit both the institution and its scholars by raising the institutional profile while also bringing broader dissemination, increased use, and enhanced professional visibility of scholarly research. The main reason for universities to have institutional repositories is to impact of the research output of the university, its publishing faculty, and the institution itself.

Few broader aspects of benefits of IRs are listed below:

- Researchers benefit through wider (and more rapid) dissemination of their work, resulting in more "research impact".
- PG and UG students benefit, as university publica-tions are readily accessible via the institution's virtual learning environment, library system and institutional portal.
- The university benefits from a higher profile by making all output publicly (and freely) available.
- The university benefits by having a comprehensive managed and preserved record of its research output.

WHY INSTITUTIONAL REPOSITORIES

There has been a convergence of technology develop-ments and other initiatives that have made IRs possible. Technology costs, especially storage costs, have dropped significantly so that repositories are now affordable. Standards such as the open archives metadata harvesting protocol are in place and work is being done on the metadata itself. Awareness of the needs for, and challenges of, digital preservation has accelerated. Developments in web publishing such as open archives initiatives, open access journals and disciplinary archives are pointing the way to opportunities to enhance scholarly publishing.

The launch of the DSpace IR at MIT in November 2002 and the subsequent release of the DSpace software under an open source license have been seen as a seminal event and a trigger for the development of IRs. However the release of the EPrint software from Southampton University in January 2001 predated this by nearly two years and at present there are more functioning IRs running on EPrints than on the DSpace platform.

THE OPEN-ACCESS MOVEMENT

For some years now there has been a movement towards "open access" to academic publications. This argues that sources of scholarly information, usually in the form of articles, should be freely available to all on the internet. The establish-ment of repositories contributes towards easy open-access publishing online. By ensuring that access to the results of academic research is not confined solely to subscribers to expensive journals, it allows them to reach a much wider audience. There are over 20,000 peer-reviewed scholarly journals in existence; no academic library can come anywhere near stocking even a tiny proportion of titles appropriate to the needs of the research staff in an institution.

This being the case, individual scholars cannot get access to some – perhaps much – of the literature that is pertinent to their work with the result that the efficient exchange of scholarly information is impaired. To exacerbate this problem, over the last two decades the so-called 'serials crisis' has become a more and more acute issue. Journal prices have risen faster than both the rate of inflation and the increases in library budgets, resulting in the cancellation of subscriptions to journals in large numbers.

This has happened all over the world and India universities have been no exception: indeed, it is there that the problem has been seen to be most extreme. Data collected by the Association of Research Libraries show that in the 16 years between 1986 and 2002, inflation rose by 64% (in the US), library materials budgets rose by 184% and serials unit costs rose by 227%.

One way in which publishers have reacted to the seriousness of the serials crisis has been by developing the 'Big Deal' whereby parts or all of a publisher's journal list were offered to a library (or a group of libraries within a consortium) at a price that equated to less per journal than the library had originally been paying but which included journals that had not been required. These practices seem to conflict with the aims of scientists and scholars who, it is argued, primarily publish research papers for research impact, *i.e.* in having their work read, cited and built on in the research of others. This lead to the open access initiative and movement.

Open Access Initiatives

In the last three years there have been several key events that serve as milestones for the movement. In December 2001, the Open Society Institute organised a meeting in Budapest to assess the state of play on open access and to see how the various initiatives up to that point could be progressed. The outcome of this meeting was the Budapest Open Access Initiative (BOAI). This took the form of a public statement in support of open access for scholarly journal articles. In addition, a website was launched in February 2002 where supporters could add their signatures.

The Budapest Initiative formally announced its endorse-ment of two strategies for open access–the establishment of open access journals and self-archiving by scholars of their work. The Budapest Open Access Initiative defines open access as: "free availability on the internet, permitting users to read, download, copy, distribute, print, search, or link to the full texts of these articles, crawl them for indexing, pass them as data to software, or use them for any other lawful purpose, without financial, legal, or technical barriers other than those inseparable from gaining access to the internet itself.

The only constraint on reproduction and distribution, and the only role for copyright in this domain, should be to give authors control over the integrity of their work and the right to be properly acknowledged and cited. Even mainland Europe is getting in on the act. In October 2003, the leading research associations of Germany, France and Switzerland signed what has become known as the "Berlin Declaration"—another call for free access to research findings. One of the groups behind the declaration, Germany's Max Planck Society, is now changing its employment contracts to require staff to return the copyright of their work to the society.

At the moment it gets assigned to the publishers. Although the society's researchers will still be able to publish in journals, their work must eventually be put into an online repository. The Open Society Institute continues to donate resources to the open access movement The Budapest Open Access Initiative and later Berlin Declaration promote the development of open access electronic journals and digital repositories, free to anyone with internet access.

It may be possible in some fields to support open access journals by authors or research funding bodies covering the costs with article fees, following the economic model of BioMed central and the Public Library of Science. For example, BioMed Central currently charge $500 per paper as an 'article processing charge,' while the PLoS initiative has estimated that authors will be asked to pay around $1,500 per paper when their journals become available sometime in 2003.

A US House of Representatives committee has recomm-ended that the National Institutes of Health (NIH) provide free access to all research it funds and asked the NIH to submit a plan by December 1, 2004 for how to implement the new policy in fiscal year 2005. UK parliament Science and Technology Committee recommended Open Access self archiving of funded research. The Australian Government has recently done the same for Australian universities along with numerous other institutions around the world.

SPARC (The Scholarly Publishing and Academic Resources Coalition) has recently proposed a hybrid model, whereby each article in a journal would be made electronically available only to subscribers, unless its author chooses to pay, in which case it would be freely available to all. There are other subject specific model *viz.*, covering physics, mathematics and computer science repository operated by Cornell University.

This was set up at the Los Alamos National Laboratory (LANL) in the early 1990s to facilitate the communication requirements of high-energy physicists. Now based at Cornell University, it remains one of the largest e-print repositories with almost 230,000 papers, growing by more than 30,000 per year. Other subject-based e-print repositories exist, *e.g.* for cognitive sciences (CogPrints) or chemistry (the Elsevier-run Chemistry Preprint Server), but there is now a growing interest in the creation of interoperable repositories based on research or educational institutions.

Today, about 5% of academic publishing follows the open-access model. But the model is quickly gaining ground, including among both for-profit (BioMedCentral-BMC) and not-for-profit (Public Library of Science PloS) publishers. In fact, more than 80% of conventional journals already allow their authors to deposit their postprints in OA repositories. Most OA repositories are interoperable in the sense that users can search them without knowing which repositories exist, where they are located, or what they contain.

TECHNICAL DEVELOPMENTS

The existence of institutional repositories has been made possible by the development of standards and tools that facilitate interoperability between multiple repositories. The most important of these is the Open Archives Initiative Protocol for Metadata Harvesting (OAI-PMH). The OAI-PMH was developed from the 'Santa Fe Convention' agreed at the initial meeting of the Open Archives Initiative (OAI) in 1999. Version 1.0 of the protocol was issued in January 2001; the latest version (Version 2.0) being released in June 2002. The protocol provides an interoperability framework based on the harvesting of metadata. To that end, it defines a simple set of metadata that can facilitate federated resource discovery. The protocol divides users of the OAI-PMH into two main categories: Version 1.0 of the OAI-PMH was released in January 2001 for experimental use, the latest in June 2002. A growing number of open-source software tools that help support the implementation of the protocol are now becoming available. For data providers, the most important of these are the University of Southampton's EPrints software and MIT Libraries's DSpace system.

WHAT IS OAI-PMH

The OAI-Protocol for Metadata Harvesting (OAI-PMH) defines a mechanism for harvesting records containing metadata from repositories. The OAI-PMH gives a simple technical option for data providers to make their metadata available to services, based on the open standards HTTP (Hypertext Transport Protocol) and XML (Extensible Markup Language). The metadata that is harvested may be in any format that is agreed by a community (or by any discrete set of data and service providers), although unqualified Dublin Core is specified to provide a basic level of interoperability.

Thus, metadata from many sources can be gathered together in one database, and services can be provided based on this centrally harvested, or "aggregated" data. The link between this metadata and the related content is not defined by the OAI protocol. It is important to realise that OAI-PMH does not provide a search across this data, it simply makes it possible to bring the data together in one place.

In order to provide services, the harvesting approach must be combined with other mechanisms. Open Archives Initiative Protocol for Metadata Harvesting is a protocol which facilitates access to heterogenous web-accessible material from various repositories. The Open Archives Initiative develops and promotes interoperability standards that aim to facilitate the efficient dissemination of content. The OAI protocol provides access to metadata from OAI-compliant repositories.

There are two classes of participants in the OAI-PMH framework:

- Data Providers administer systems that support the AI-PMH as a means of exposing metadata; and
- Service Providers use metadata harvested via the OAI-PMH as a basis for building value added services.

"OAI-compliant" means that the archive complies with the metadata harvesting protocol of the Open Archives Initiative (OAI). This makes the archive interoperable with other compliant archives so that the many separate archives behave like one grand, virtual archive for purposes such as searching. This means that users can search across OAI-compliant archives without visiting the separate archives and running separate searches. Hence, it makes your content more visible, even if users don't know that your archive exists or what it contains.

SOFTWARE

There are a handful of open-source packages for creating and maintaining such archives. The four most important are eprints (from Southampton University), DSpace (from MIT), CDSWare (from CERN), and FEDORA (from Cornell and U. of Virginia). In addition to this there are few more software, which is being used for archiving. I have listed them with brief description, these are:

Arno

The ARNO project—Academic Research in the Netherlands Online—has developed software to support the implementation of institutional repositories and link them to distributed repositories worldwide (as well as to the Dutch national information infrastructure). The project is funded by IWI (Dutch acronym for: Innovation in Scientific Information Supply). Project participants are the University of Amsterdam, Tilburg University and the University of Twente. The ARNO system was released for public use in December 2003. It has been in use at the universities of Tilburg, Amsterdam, Rotterdam, Twente and Maastricht.

CERN Document Server Software (CDSware)

The CERN Document Server Software (CDSware) was developed to support the CERN Document Server. The software is maintained and made publicly available by CERN and supports electronic preprint servers, online library catalogues, and other web-based document depository systems. CERN uses CDSware to manage over 450 collections of data, comprising over 620,000 bibliographic records and 250,000 full-text documents, including preprints, journal articles, books, and photographs. CDSware was built to handle very large repositories holding disparate types of materials, including multimedia content catalogues, museum object descriptions, confidential and public sets of documents, etc. Each release is tested live under the rigors of the CERN environment before being publicly released.

DSpace

The DSpace software has been purpose built in collaboration between Hewlett Packard and MIT to offer IR services. It is specifically designed to manage diverse heterogeneous types of digital content. It offers interoperability via OAI-MHP (Open Archive Initiative–Metadata Harvesting Protocol–a software standard that allows specialised search engines to gather article metadata from compliant websites) and built-in support for Dublin Core metadata (Dublin Core is an agreed metadata standard used in library cataloguing and elsewhere, though other metadata schemes are possible). It uses persistent identifiers (which are like URLs but have the benefit that unlike ordinary URLs they do not change when the linked document's physical location is changed) via the CNRI Handle system.

Eprints

The Eprints software has the largest and most broadly distributed installed base of any of the repository software systems described here. Developed at the University of South-ampton, the first version of the system was publicly released in late 2000. The project was originally sponsored by CogPrints, but is now supported by JISC as part of the Open Citation Project and by NSF. Eprints worldwide installed base affords an extensive support network for new implementations. The size of the installed base for Eprints suggests that an institution can get it up and running relatively quickly and with a minimum of technical expertise. The number of Eprints installations that have augmented the system's baseline capabilities—for example, by integrating advanced search, extended metadata, and other features—indicates that the system can be readily modified to meet local requirements.

Fedora

The Fedora digital object repository management system is based on the Flexible Extensible Digital Object and Repository Architecture (Fedora). The system is designed to be a foundation upon which fullfeatured institutional repositories and other interoperable web-based digital libraries can be built. Jointly developed by the University of Virginia and Cornell University, the system implements the Fedora architecture, adding utilities that facilitate repository manage-ment. The current version of the software provides a repository that can handle one million objects efficiently. Subsequent versions of the software will add functionality important for institutional repository implementations, such as policy enforcement, versioning of objects, and performance enhancement to support very large repositories.

i-TOR

i-Tor — Tools and technologies for Open Repositories—was developed by the Innovative Technology-*Applied* (IT-*A*) section of Netherlands Institute for Scientific Information Services (Dutch acronym: NIWI). NIWI calls i-TOR "a web technology by which various types of information can be presented through a web interface," irrespective of where the data is stored or the format in which it is stored. i-Tor aims to implement a "data independent" repository, where the content and the user-interface function as two independent parts of the system.

In essence, i-Tor acts as both an OAI service provider, able to harvest OAI compatible repositories and other databases, and an OAI data provider.

Because i-Tor is able to publish data from a variety of relational databases, file systems, and websites, the system allows an institution considerable latitude in the way it organizes its repository. It can create new databases for the repository, but it can also use already existing relational databases. Further, i-Tor supports harvesting of data directly from a researcher's personal home page Because of this design, i-Tor does not enforce a specific workflow on a group or subgroup. Rather, i-Tor gives an institution tools (for example, fine grained security, notification, etc.) to set up any required workflow required by the organization, without integrating this workflow into the i-Tor system itself. i-Tor's design might make it an appropriate choice for an institution that wishes to impose a repository on top of an existing set of disparate digital repositories.

MyCoRe

MyCoRe grew out of the MILESS Project of the University of Essen. The MyCoRe system is now being developed by a consortium of universities to provide a core bundle of software tools to support digital libraries and archiving solutions (or Content Repositories, thus "CoRe"). The bundle is designed to be configurable and adaptable to local requirements (hence, the "My"), without the need for local programming efforts.

In contrast to MILESS, which provides a hard-coded Qualified Dublin Core data model, the MyCoRe data model is completely configurable. Further, MyCoRe provides a sample application, based upon a "core" of functionality, that shows users how to build their own applications using metadata configuration files. The core contains all the functionality that would be required in a repository implementation, including distributed search over geographically dispersed repositories, OAI functionality, audio/video streaming support, file management, online metadata editors etc.

INSTITUTIONAL REPOSITORY AND ROLE OF INFLIBNET

In India most of the research is being funded and supported by the Government. The software for implemen-tation of IR is available free of cost and has been used to establish an e-print archive at very few institutions. The prominent among are the Indian Institute of Science and DRTC. The US and UK openaccess proposals are inspiring and encouraging steps for other countries. In UK, JISC has funded number of e-print repositories.

A US House of Representatives committee has recomm-ended that the National Institutes of Health (NIH) provide free access to all research it funds and asked the NIH to submit a plan by December 1, 2004 for how to implement the new policy in fiscal year 2005. In our country, we too need such initiative and we should move towards open access. In last one decade INFLIBNET has published reasonable amount of content in the form of database on it's central server. The foundation of repositories has already been established at the Centre, it further aims to provide many more potential services to support academics.

On experimental basis, INFLIBNET has configured DSpace software and content is being archived. Establishing IR though seems very simple but while implementing it has been observed that collection of content and faculty participation and pursuing them to submit the content are major issues.

Thus success and failure of IR is reply upon these two factors. In order to implement IR successfully, we need to study the existing model of IR and adopt best model for universities in India. It is need of ours to develop a series of national, discipline-focused services through which the higher education community can access the collective output of e-print papers available from compliant Open Archive reposi-tories, particularly those provided by universities.

A policy and strategy in collaboration with UGC and universities has to be framed and faculties need to take the lead in ensuring that their papers are suitably archived. INFLIBNET can play major role by establishing central/ discipline based repositories and fecilitate to create and maintain these archieve. UGC and other funding agencies should put a condition on research grants to submit the finding of research in to central repositories. When a grant recipient publishes the results of funded research in a journal, pre-print of the article should be submitted to INFLIBNET central repository.

Similarly, faculty courseware and submission of full text of Phd Theses in digital form from universities at central repository should also be made available from INFLIBNET. Long-term preservation of these content has to be addressed by framing a policy with proper guidelines, involving UGC, INFLIBNET and universities so that repository can offer digital hosting, preservation and more effective web dissemination to the users.

3

Managing Information Technology in the Networked Libraries: Issues and Strategies

OPERATION AND DEVELOPMENT: SORTING SEARCH RESULTS OF LITERATURE DIGITAL LIBRARIES

An OLDL (Online Literature Digital Library) is a library in which collections, *i.e.*, publications from one or more domains of study, are stored in digital formats and accessible by users through the Internet.

Examples of well-known OLDLs are:

- IEEE Xplore
- CiteSeer
- Google Scholar
- PubMed

Digital libraries are rapidly growing in popularity. For instance, ScienceDirect, the world's leading scientific, technical and medical information resource celebrated its billionth article download in November'06 since, launched in 1999. Besides usage, digital libraries are also rapidly growing in terms of size and diversity of topics.

For instance:

- In Computer Science, ACM Digital Library has close to one million full-text publications collected over 50 years, to search and download.
- In Electrical Engineering and Computer Science, IEEE Xplore, another OLDL, provides users with on-line access to more than 1,700 selected conferences proceedings.

These high growth rates introduced several challenges facing the information access capability of OLDLs. Next we list few challenges that probably guides future research related to LDLs.

CHALLENGE 1: LARGE SIZES AND TOPIC DIVERSITY OF SEARCH OUTPUT RESULTS

Search outputs of OLDLs tend to suffer from the 'topic diffusion' problem, where commonly, keyword-based searches produce a large number of publications over a large number of topics, where not all topics are of interest to the user. One way to solve this problem is to assign scores to search results. Assigning scores to publications helps OLDLs to present the most important relevant publications to the user first, Citation-based publication score measures are commonly used for ranking publications. At the present time, OLDLs lack effective and accurate publication ranking.

CHALLENGE 2: LACK OF EFFECTIVE SCORING FUNCTIONS FOR PUBLICATIONS

At the present time, OLDLs lack effective and accurate publication rankings. Providing accurate publication scores can help users in reducing the time spent in searching OLDLs, and thus enhances the scalability of OLDL usage as users can quickly identify important relevant publications to their topic of interest.

CHALLENGE 3: LACK OF EFFECTIVE SCORING FUNCTIONS FOR SEARCH OUTPUTS

In the field of literature digital libraries, citation analysis is employed to order digital library search outputs. Examples of citation-based measures are citation-count and PageRank. However, as noticed by, citation-based measures compute popularity of publications based on the 'current' state of a citation graph that continuously changes and evolves.

Thus PageRank is effective in capturing the popularity of publications based on the current citation-graph inhand. We show that PageRank may assign inaccurate popularity scores for both old and recent publications. And thus PageRank cannot be used to rank OLDL search outputs. We therefore need effective techniques to order search results based on their importance and relevance to users' interests.

EVALUATING PUBLICATION SCORING FUNCTIONS IN DIGITAL LIBRARIES

This section deals with the issues of defining score functions for publications in digital libraries, and evaluating how good they are.

Presently, digital libraries do not assign scores to publications, even though they are potentially useful for:

- Providing comparative assessment, or 'importance', of papers; and
- Anking papers returned in search outputs.

Using social networks or bibliometrics, one can define a number of publication score functions. Existing citation-based publication score functions are all based on the notion of prestige in social networks and bibliometry. The well-known PageRank algorithm determines the importance of a publication by the number and importances of publications with links to it. The Hyperlink Induced Topic Search (HITS) algorithm is similar to the PageRank algorithm in that HITS involves computing two scores for each publication; hub and authority scores. Authorities represent high-prestige publications, whereas hubs are publications that have links to authorities.

Other citation-based score functions can be derived as follows:

- Use normalised citation count as the basis for a score function.
- Revise the score of a paper using the score of its publication venue.
- Add weights to citations, *e.g.*, citations by an 'important' author's work are more significant.
- Revise the score of a paper using temporal distributions of citations; *e.g.*, citations in the last 10 years are more significant than earlier citations.
- Revise a paper score using the score of its citation venue; that is, capture the notion of a hub or an authority, *e.g.*, survey journal represents a hub, whereas a research paper represents an authority.
- Revise a paper score by the score of its author.

Citation-based Publication Score Functions

PageRank

Importance of papers that cite a particular paper determines its importance. PageRank and HITS were designed based on this assumption. PageRank scores is computed recursively using the formula

$$P_{i+1} = (1-d)M^T P_i + E$$

Where *Pi* and *Pi+1* are the current and next iteration PageRank vectors respectively. *M* is a matrix derived from the citation matrix *C* by normalising all row-sums in *C* to *1*. *C*, in turn, is the adjacency matrix of the graph *G* formed as follows; the papers represent the graph nodes, and the citation relationships between these papers represent the edges. *C* is of size *NxN*, where *N* is the total number of papers in the system.

Finally, *d* and *(1-d)* are the future citation probability. Given that an author *A* who is writing a new paper and already cited paper *u* which in turn cites paper *v*, and let *w* be a paper in AnthP selected randomly.

The parameter *d* represents the probability that A will cite *w*, and *(1-d)* is the probability that *A* will cite *v*. To guarantee the algorithm convergence, it is assumed to have a hidden link between each pair of the graph nodes. This link is represented by the user-defined parameter *E*. A variation of *E* is simply *E1=d*. Another variation of E that is used in is,

$$E_2 = d / N[1_N]P_i.$$

Hubs and Authorities

Authority score of paper *P* is computed by summing up the hub scores of the papers citing *P*. Hub score of *P* is computed by summing up the authority scores of the papers that *P* cites. Computation is recursive until results converge after a number of iterations. One difference between HITS and PageRank is that the first one works on papers in the result set of a query, while the latter considers all the papers independent of the query.

Citation Count

A paper, normally, does not cite another paper unless the cited paper is relevant. And, large number of citations to a paper gives an indication that the paper is important. Based on this fact, one can use citation count as a measure for paper importance. For a given paper *P*, let CitationCount (*P*) be the number of times paper *P* is cited by other papers. Using the number of citations, paper *P* is as important as those papers that have the same number of citations and more important than those papers that have fewer citations. As suggested, refer to this paper ranking measure as PCitation_Count.

Evaluating Publication Score Functions

Figure shows the three score functions, namely, PageRank (PPgRank), Authorities scores of HITS (PAuth) and, the Citation-count (PCitCnt). As it is clear from the figure the three functions are highly skewed, and do not separate scores well over the interval. This figure is based on the AnthP digital collection from the field of data management. In the author observed the skewness and inseparability of these functions independently in computer science and life sciences publications as well. And, it is shown that distributions of citation-based score functions are also highly skewed and decay very fast. Studies show that the cause is topic diffusion since, scores are computed with respect to the full publication set.

In the authors compared and evaluated several publication score functions, including PageRank and Authorities scores, both adopted from the www search domain, and citation-count scores from the bibliometrics domain. The authors observed the separability problem with all of these functions which is that none of these scoring functions assigns scores that distribute well over a given scale, *e.g.* Instead, distributions of existing publication score functions are highly skewed, and decay very fast resulting in a much less useful comparative publication assessment capability for users.

This lack of separability is caused by the 'rich gets richer' phenomena, *i.e.*, a very small number of publications with relatively high numbers of in-citations have even higher chances of receiving new citations. Yet, these scoring functions are still not very accurate, probably caused by topic diffusion in search outputs. In the following section, and by using the research-pyramid model proposed in, the authors in normalise scores of publications within their own research pyramids, which allows for a fair comparative assessment of publications as publications are compared to their peers in their own research pyramids.

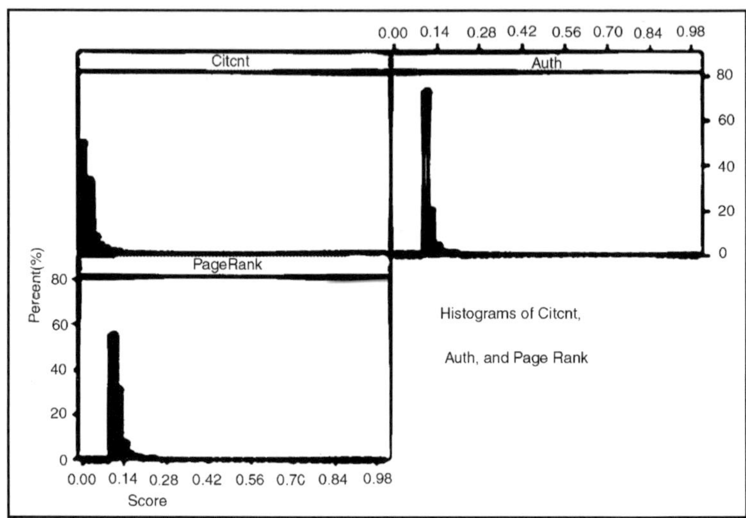

Fig. Skewness of Score Distribution of the Three Main Citation-based Publication Score Functions

IMPROVED PUBLICATION SCORES VIA RESEARCH PYRAMIDS

Providing accurate publication scores for search results and ranking publications returned as search results accurately can help users in reducing the time spent in searching OLDLs. And, better publication rankings are also useful for comparative assessments of publication venues and scientists as well. At the present time, OLDLs lack effective and accurate publication rankings. For instance, ACM Digital Library returns rankings of publication search results that are unexplained and not useful to users.

Moreover, search outputs of OLDLs tend to suffer from the 'topic diffusion' problem, where commonly, keyword-based searches produce a large number of publications over a large number of topics, thereby producing scores that are non-specific to topics. The research evolution model proposed in suggests that citation relationships between research publications produce multiple, small pyramid-like structures, where each pyramid represents publications related to a highly specific research topic. A research pyramid is defined as a set of publications that represent a highly specific research topic, and usually has a pyramid-like structure in terms of its citation graph.

Publications within an individual research pyramid are:

- Motivated by earlier publications in the topic area is motivated in part by citations; and

- Use techniques proposed in publications from other research pyramids in part uses some of the techniques presented in citations.

Other 'reasons' for citations may also be observed. In this section, our goals are to:

- Provide a solution to the OLDL search output ranking problem due to the topic diffusion problem, by grouping search outputs at the most-specific topic level and without identifying the topics themselves;
- Eliminate the low separability problem of score functions; and
- Improve the accuracy of three score functions, namely, PageRank, Authorities and Citation Count score functions.

The research pyramid (RP) model is used to improve the separability and accuracy of publication scores, and is based on normalising publication scores within a limited scope, namely, within individual research pyramids. These improvements come from the fact that publications are now compared to their peers within their peer groups, namely, their own research pyramid publications that are on the same topic. In two approaches to identify research pyramids are presented and evaualted.

The first, called LB-IdentifyRP, uses Link-Based Research Pyramid identification, which captures research pyramids by identifying pyramid-like structures from the citation graph of the publication set. The second approach, called PB-IdentifyRP, uses Proximity-Based Research Pyramid identification, utilises a graph-based proximity measure, namely SimRank to compute similarities between publications, and then restructures the k-most-similar publications into a research pyramid.

Properties of Research Pyramid Model

In the authors have observed three properties of research publications in three separate data sets, namely, ACM Anthology which is a collection of 15,000 publications and computer sciences and life sciences publication sets, each with 70,000 publications. These properties are utilised in the identification of research pyramids.

Property 1 (Maximum Citation Age)

In OLDLs, most publications receive most of their incitations within a fixed number of years after their publication dates. We refer to this value as the Maximum Citation Age, and denote it by CAgeMax. It has been observed in that, in the AnthP, CSSet and the LSSet datasets, most publications receive 90 per cent of their in-citations in 10 years, *i.e.*, CAgeMax=10.

Figure presents the citation age distributions in AnthP. We give a tighter bound for citation age within which topical similarity within an RP is maintained between citing and cited publications. In rare cases, publications may cite works older than CAgeMax.

It is found that a great proportion of these citations are for historical reasons, which we interpret as: old cited works:

- Have coarse similarity to citing papers; and
- Do not belong in the RP of the citing publication.

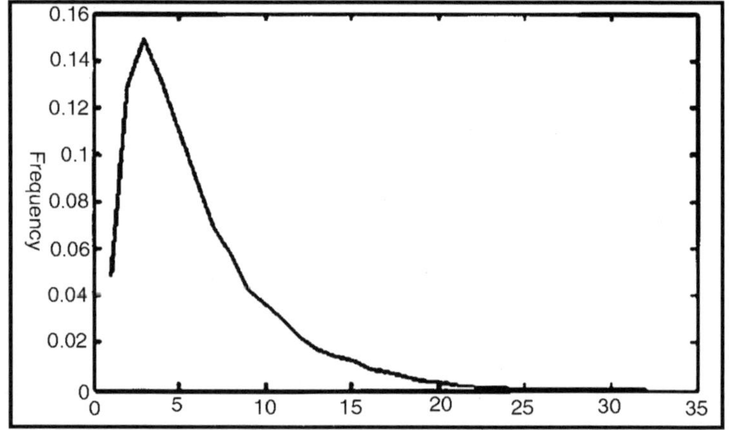

Fig. Citation Age Distribution Curve of AnthP

Property 2 (Topic Specificity Over Time)

Scientific research publications quickly become very topic-specific over time, usually referable via a highly specific topic.

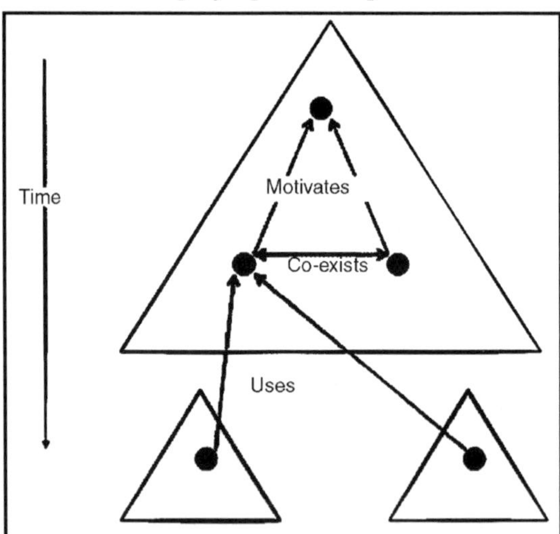

Fig. The RP-based Model

As illustrated in figure, an old research pyramid that covers a certain research topic leads to instantiations of new research topics, and thus to creations of new RPs, that use techniques proposed in the publications of parent RP(s). Again, such old citations carry topical similarity between the citing and cited publication at a coarse granularity level. Possible citation exchanges between different RPs also occur and are of type 'uses', *i.e.*, the citing paper uses techniques proposed by the cited paper.

Example

Codd's paper E. F. Codd, 'A Relational Model of Data for Large Shared Data Banks', Commun. ACM 13(6): 377-387 is about the topic relational model, and cited around 580 times. A new and more specific topic of 2000's say, rank-aware join algorithms, is coarsely related to the more general topic relational model in that, a publication P in the RP of rank-aware join algorithms and citing Codd's paper 'uses' the techniques proposed in the RP of the relational model.

Property 3 (Topic Similarity Decay Over Citation Path)

After very small citation path distances, topical similarity between papers decays significantly. From figure, after a citation path of length 3, the topical similarity, as measured by SimRank, significantly decays. We refer to this value by LMax-TopicDecay. This observation led the authors in to build RPs of height at most 3 in the experimental results section.

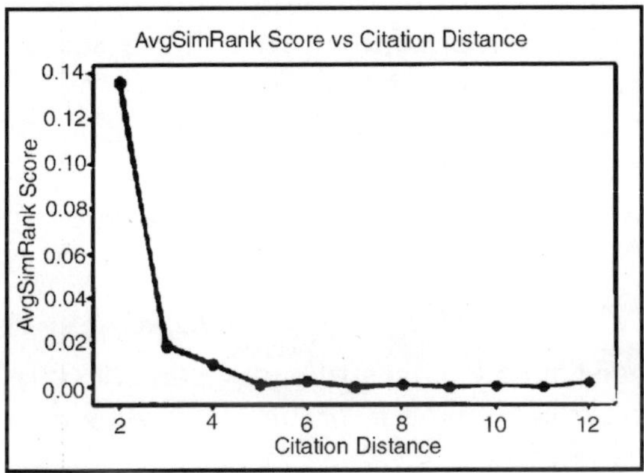

Fig. SimRank Scoer Change with Citation Distance

Property 4 (Topic Similarity Decay Over Citation Age)

After a certain citation age, topical similarity between the citing and the cited papers significantly decays. From figure, in the AnthP set, after a citation age of about 5 years, the topic similarity between the citing and cited papers decays significantly. We refer to this value by CAgeMax-TopicDecay. This observation led the authors in to build RPs in the experimental results section such that the maximum citation age within an RP is 5 years. The two characteristics that identify a research pyramid RP are.

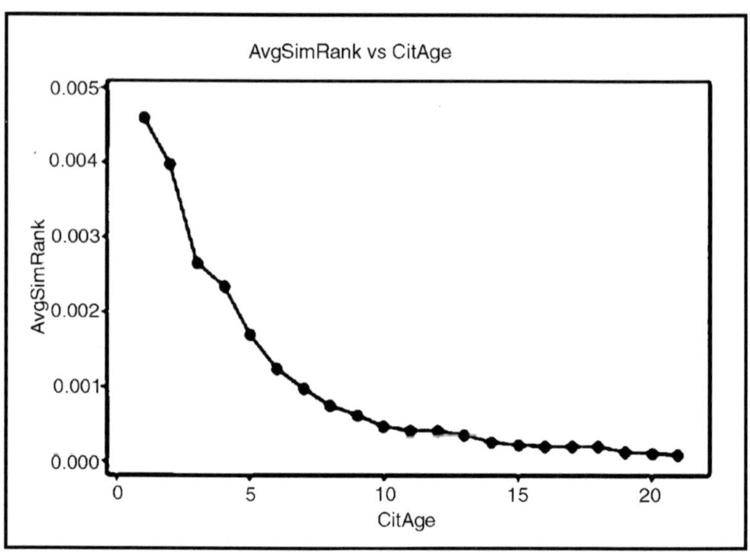

Fig. SimRank Score Change with Citation Age

RP-Property 1 (High Topic Specificity)

An RP, usually organisable into a pyramid, is a set of publications that represent a highly specific research topic. We maintain high topic specificity of RPs by applying properties 3 and 4, and keeping the height of research pyramids low. Note that we make no attempts to identify the topic associated with an RP, as our approach does not need the topics explicitly. But, in interactive environments, providing topics to users is useful.

RP-Property 2 (Research Pyramid Construction)

RPs are arranged into pyramid structures either directly by using citation graphs (*i.e.*, the link-based approach) or indirectly using the publication times and close proximity of papers.

Research Pyramid Identification Procedures

Based on the properties of publications and characteristics of RPs, next we propose two offline research pyramid identification procedures, namely, the link-based (LB) and the proximity-based (PB) RP identification procedures. Both procedures start by choosing a candidate root node for an RP, called the cornerstone paper. The paper that is located at the root of a research pyramid receives more citations than others as other publications within the research pyramid are 'motivated' by it, and directly or indirectly cite it. Thus, our approach is to identify papers with high in-citations as cornerstone papers (*i.e.*, the roots) of RPs to be constructed. The link-based procedure locates research pyramids by identifying pyramid-like structures in the citation graph of the publication set. In summary, within an individual RP, publications are topically related and motivated by each other and we use the four properties to identify citations within RPs—as summarised next. In AnthP, the average number of citations to a paper, denoted by ÇI, is 2.066. Note that, in our experiments, we consider only the AnthP citations that are completely within AnthP; any citation from a paper within AnthP to a paper that is not in AnthP is removed. Using Property 3 and RP-Property 1, we limit RP heights to 3. Thus, the expected number of papers within a research pyramid RPP with paper P as the root and with height 3 is |RPP| = 1 + CI + CI2 + CI3 H' 15. Of course, the actual identified RP sizes vary.

Some RPs may deal with active research topics, and, in such cases, the number of in-citations of publications are noticeably higher than CI, leading to noticeably higher RP sizes as well. Figure presents the link-based LB-IdentifyRP procedure. The proximity-based PBIdentifyRP is similar, except that the function call to LB-FormRP is replaced by the function call PB-FormRP.

The procedure LB-IdentifyRP:

a. Selects a cornerstone paper P from the existing publication set as an RP root, by simply picking the current most-cited publication;
b. Calls LB-FormRP to locate the RP set RPP of P; and
c. Eliminates RPP from the current publication set CurrAnthP, and repeats (a)-(c) again, until no more publications are left in CurrAnthP.

Note that our approach in this chapter is to create distinct and non-overlapping research pyramids. An alternative approach, not reported here due to space limitations, is to allow overlapping research pyramids as follows: Do not to eliminate any papers from the original publication set; instead, simply colour each selected publication, and continue until all publications are coloured, meaning that, when the algorithm ends, each paper belongs to at least one RP set, and possibly more.

The two main functions of the link-based LB-IdentifyRP procedure are ChooseRoot and LB-FormRP. ChooseRoot chooses publications that are cornerstone papers, or roots of research pyramids. The function LB-FormRP forms the RPP of a root publication P by adding direct citers of P into RPP, and indirect citers of P at a level up to the LMax; in experiments, we choose LMax as 3, by following the property 3. The function Citers(P, 1, CAgeMax-Topic-Decay) returns the set of publications that cite P at a level 1 (which is at most LMax) where the citation age of the citing paper with respect to P is less than the maximum citation age CAgeMax-Topic-Decay. In more detail,

- Paper-id pidP of root P along with its level 0 is inserted into RPP and the queue Q, which holds paper-ids for future expansions and their distances to the root paper P.
- Two-tuple <Pi, A > in Q is dequeued, and expanded by locating direct or indirect citers of Pi so long as their levels with respect to P

is at most LMax-TopicDecay and their citation age with respect to P is less than the maximum citation age CAgeMax-TopicDecay. All expanded publications and their level info with respect to P are inserted into the queue Q.

- The above two steps are repeated until Q is empty; then RPP is returned.

```
proc LB-IdentifyRP(AnthP, RP-Sets)
{
RP-Sets:= Ø;
CurrAnthP:= AnthP;
while (CurrentAnthP = Ø)
{Root:=ChooseRoot(CurrAnthP);
RPRoot:=LB-FormRP(Root,LMax-TopicDecay);
RP-Sets:=RP-Sets U RPRoot;
CurrAnthP:=CurrAnthP-RPRoot;
}
}
(a) Procedure LB-IdentifyRP
funct ChooseRoot(CurrAnthP)
return TopCitedTopicDecay(CurrAnthP);
(b) Function ChooseRoot
funct LB-FormRP(P, LMax)
{Set RPP:={P}; Queue Q;
Q.Enqueue({P},0);
while(Q is not empty)
{<Pi, A>:=Q.Dequeue;
if(A<LMax)then
{CiterSet=Citers(Pi, A, CAgeMax-TopicDecay);
Q.Enqueue(CiterSet,(A+1));
RPP = RPP +CiterSet;
}}}
Return RPP}
(c) Function LB-FormRP()
Funct PB-FormRP(P, LMax)
{Set RPP={P}; Queue Q;
Q.Enqueue(P,0);
while(Q is not empty)
{<Pi, A>:=Q.Dequeue;
if(A<LMax) then
{CiterSet(Pi):=Citers(Pi, A, CAgeMax-TopicDecay)
TopSimSet:=TopSim(Pi,|CiterSet(Pi)|, CAgeMax-TopicDecay);
Q.Enqueue(TopSimSet, A +1);
RPP= RPP+TopSimSet;
}}
Return RPP}
(d) Function PB-FormRP()
```

Fig. Functions of LB-and PB-IdentifyRP Algorithms

The function PB-FormRP of the proximity-based approach utilises a graphbased proximity measure, namely SimRank to compute similarities between publications.

It captures RPP of the root publication by locating publications that are most similar to P and yet:

- Are linked to P with a citation path length of at most LMax-TopicDecay; and
- Have a citation time distance less than CAgeMax-TopicDecay. SimRank iteratively computes similarity scores between nodes in a graph G following the rule that "two nodes are similar if they are linked with similar nodes".

In other words, the SimRank similarity between two nodes a and b, S is iteratively computed using the formula:

$$S(a,b) = \left[C/|I(a)|\ |I(b)\ |\right] * \sum_{i=1}^{|I(a)|} \ \sum_{j=1}^{|I(b)|} S\left(I_i(a), I_j(b)\right)$$

where I(a) and I(b) are sources of in-links of a and b, respectively. C is the decay factor between 0 and 1. We choose C=0.8. If |I(a)|or|I(b)| = 0 then S(a, b)=0 by definition, in the case where a=b, S(a, b)=1. The space complexity of the naive SimRank algorithm is O(N2) where N is the graph size. We prune as in by considering node pairs that are near each other in the range of radius r. We choose r=6, which is twice the value of the expected research pyramid height.

PB-FormRP receives as input the root P, the maximum level LMax from root, and utilises the maximum citation age CAgeMax-TopicDecay and returns the RP set RPP of publication P following the same main steps of LB-FormRP with one main difference: the way the twotuple <Pi, t > dequeued from Q is expanded, as follows:

- Top |Citers Pi, A,CAgeMax-TopicDecay| similar papers, based on SimRank, to Pi are identified. The number of citers of Pi is used to capture the density of the RP being identified, and thus to expand RP at Pi accordingly;
- The identified similar papers are added to RPP and also enqueued to Q for further expansion, this time with the level increased by 1. Similar to LB-FormRP a maximum level of LMax-TopicDecay is employed.

Advantage of PB-FormRP over LB-FormRP is that it successfully captures co-existing members of RP as well as those that are not reachable through any citation path from RP's root. We give an example.

Example

Figure shows two RPs; RP1 and RP2. RP1 contains two co-existing roots Λ and B. Such a case occurs when two researchers work on the same problem simultaneously. At some point of our RP identification process, A will probably be recognised as a root of a new RP, say RP3, as it has more in-citations than B. And, since, B is not reachable through any path from A, LB-FormRP will fail to identify B as a member of RP3. PB-FormRP will succeed to place both A and B into RP3 in this case as B is very similar to A.

A similar problem will be observed with paper C that is not reachable through any path from the root. Furthermore, LB-FormRP may incorrectly identify F, that probably 'uses' a technique proposed in A, as a member of RP3 when F is really a member of RP2 which co-exists with RP3. PB-FormRP successfully repels F from RP3 as F is not similar to A or any of RP3's members, based on SimRank. We observe here that PB-FormRP may capture pyramid-like structures, but not exactly pyramid structures.

SimRank computes similarity between two papers P1 and P2 by averaging the similarity of the citers of both. However, note that similar papers to a member of an RP will be the other members of the same RP since, members of an RP are usually cited by each other.

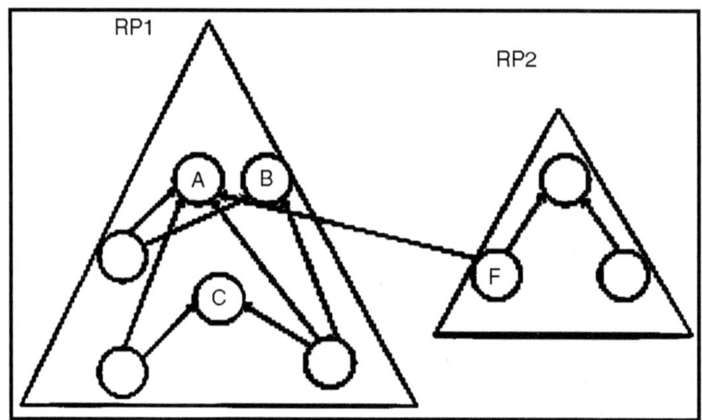

Fig. Examples where PB-FormRP is more Successful than LB-FormRP

Improved Publication Scores Via the RP-Model

In the authors have applied the two RP-identification algorithms on the AnthP set. After that, they normalized publication scores within the research pyramids identified. The authors observed that, for RP-based scores, the observed skew values range in the RP-based scores. In comparison, the original scores showed highly skewed values that range between 8.12 and 13.04, which mean that they are sharply left-skewed. They also observed that, for RP-based scores.

In comparison, in the case of globally normalised scores, Kurtosis values range between (113.28) and (291.10). The enhancement of score distribution comes from the fact that publications are being compared to their peer groups, *i.e.*, publications that belong to the same scope, and thus have the same chances of receiving new citations.

The observations on PageRank (PPgRank, PPgRank-LB, PPgRank-PB) also apply to Authorities scores (PAuth, PAuth-LB, PAuth-PB).

Table. 6.1 The Means, InterQuartile Ranges (IQR), Skewness, and Kurtosis Values of the Publication Score Functions Applied on the AnthP set

	Mean	IQR	Skewness	Kurtosis
CitCnt	0.02527	0.01845	8.12	113.28
Auth	0.11352	0.01134	13.04	291.10
PageRank	0.12091	0.01733	8.84	134.65
LBCitCnt	0.55698	0.88462	-0.05	-1.81
LBAuth	0.81266	0.37723	-1.02	-0.26
LBPageRank	0.77649	0.46181	-0.80	-0.84
PBCitCnt	0.20802	0.21910	1.88	2.65
PBAuth	0.62386	0.32036	-0.07	-0.58
PBPageRank	0.55653	0.31615	0.30	-0.60

Here we report only PageRank-related results as we have observed that PAuth and PPgRank scores are highly correlated with a correlation coefficient of 0.98, and the correlation between PPgRank and PCitCnt is 0.74. The authors in have also performed multiple searches and manually evaluated the accuracy ranking publication via the RP-Model.

They observed that research-pyramid-based scores resulted in 16 per cent-25 per cent more accurate search outputs than the PageRank-based quality scores. Accuracy was measured for the top-k publications in the result sets, where k is 10.

Section Summary and Conclusions

The Research-Pyramid model proposed in used to solve the separability and accuracy problems of publication score functions.

We showed that:

- Normalising publication scores within their research pyramids provides more accurate and less skewed scores, moreover;
- Ranking search results by these scores promises to give higher accuracy compared to ranking by globally normalised publication scores due to reduction of topic diffusion effect.

However, as noticed by citation-based measures compute popularity of publications based on the 'current' state of a citation graph that continuously changes and evolves. Thus PageRank is effective in capturing the popularity of publications based on the current citation-graph in-hand. We show that PageRank may assign inaccurate popularity scores for both old and recent publications.

And thus PageRank cannot be used to rank OLDL search outputs. We therefore need effective techniques to order search results based on their importance and relevance to users' interests.

ON POPULARITY QUALITY: *GROWTH AND DECAY PHASES OF PUBLICATION POPULARITIES*

In the field of literature digital libraries, citation analysis is employed to evaluate the impact of publications and scientific collections. It is also employed to order digital library search outputs. Examples of citation-based measures are citation-count and PageRank.

However, as noticed by citation-based measures compute popularity of publications based on the 'current' state of a citation graph that continuously changes and evolves. Next we present two scenarios where usage of such popularity scores becomes problematic.

Example

Table shows a sample search output from Google Scholar, a digital library search tool by Google, for keywords 'top-k query processing for semistructured data'. On the left-side of table, relevant documents are ordered based on text-based relevancy to query terms and the citation-based popularity of the document. On the right-side, documents are ordered based on their publication date.

The most relevant document to our query, the one entitled by 'TopX: efficient and versatile top-k query processing for semistructured data', is published in 2008, and appears at the top of the right-side search output list. Given that users usually check only a few pages of a returned list of documents, this publication may not even have a chance to develop popularity unless, in time, awareness of readers increases, *i.e.*, it becomes known to users.

Table. Searching Google Scholar for 'Top-k Query Processing for Semi-structured Data.'

All Articles	Recent Articles
[PDF] Top-k query evaluation with probabilistic guarantees-all 6 versions »	TopX: efficient and versatile top-k query processing for semi-structured data
M Theobald, G Weikum, R Schenkel-... Conference on Very Toronto, Canada, 2004-cse.iitb.ac.in... error relative to 'exactly top-k' queries, translatable into guarantees about queryresult precision... on algorithmsthat process index lists by...	M Theobald, H Bast, D Majumdar, R Schenkel, G ...-... VLDB Journal Large Data Bases (VLDB), The International Journal on Very Large Data ..., 2008–Springer... As for our data model, we focus on a tree model for semi-structured data, thus following the W3C XML... TopX: top-k query processing for semi-structured data...
Cited by 85-Related Articles-View as Search IO-Top-k: query processing-all 5 versions »	Web Search- BL Direct IO-Top-k: index- HTML-Web index-access optimised top-k query access optimised top-k processing-all 5 versions »
H Bast, D Majumdar, R Schenkel, M Theobald, G ...-... of the 32nd	H Bast, D Majumdar, R Schenkel, M Theobald, G ...-... of the 32nd

international conference on Very large data ..., 2006-portal.acm.org... index-access steps in TA-style top-k query processing in the... In these cases, the query optimiser needs to find a... attributes that are relevant for top-k queries...	Very large international conference on data ..., 2006-portal.acm .org... index-access steps in TA-style top-k query processing in the... In these cases, the query optimiser needs to find a... attributes that are relevant for top-k queries...
Cited by 20-Related Articles-Web Search -BL Direct SPIDER: a multiuser information retrieval system for semi-structured and dynamic data-all 3 versions »	Cited by 20-Related Articles-Web Search-BL Direct [PDF] Top-k query evaluation with probabilistic guarantees-all 6 versions »
P Schäuble -Proceedings of the 16th annual international ACM SIGIR ..., 1993 -portal.acm.org.. The retrieval of information from semi-structured data collections is supported by an appropriate re... Let q be the user's query and let k be the... The top k exact...	M Theobald, G Weikum, R Schenkel-... Conference on Very Large Data Bases (VLDB), Toronto, Canada, 2004-cse.iitb.ac.in... error relative to 'exactly top-k' queries, translatable into guarantees about queryresult precision... on algorithms that process index lists by...
Cited by 40 -Related Articles-Web Search	Cited by 85-Related Articles-View as HTML-Web Search

Example

The two plots in figure show in-citation counts of two relatively highly cited publications from CiteSeer.

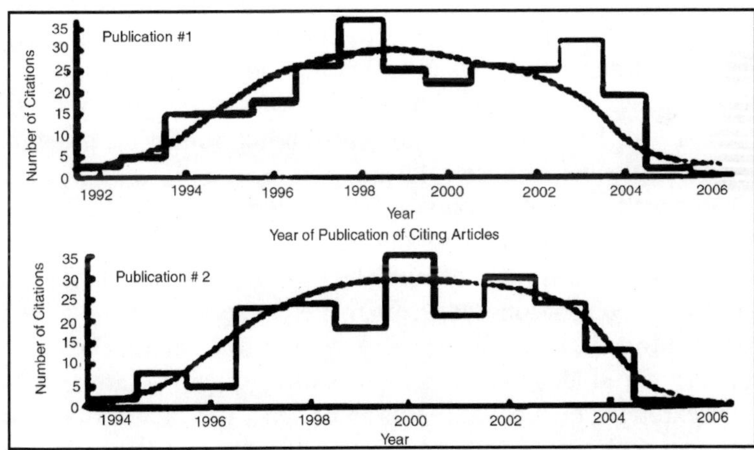

Fig. Citation Count per Year for Two Publications that Appeared in 1992 and 1994 and Cited Around 300 Times each

Notice that the popularities of the two publications have dropped significantly after 2004. We observe that the probability that a publication receives new citations drops as it gets older. And, we also observe that PageRank scores of old publications reach a certain value, and do not change after that, even when they are not cited anymore. The reason is that citations do not age or disappear, and as we shall shortly explain, citation graphs around old publications minimally change.

We thus conclude that PageRank scores of old publications represent their peak popularity but not their current popularity. This means that, even though old publications may in time be of lower interest to present users, their PageRank scores do not change. Based on the examples, we argue that, although PageRank is effective in capturing the peak popularity of publications, PageRank may assign inaccurate popularity scores for both old and recent publications.

In a web-user model is introduced and a new popularity growth model of webpages is presented. Using the growth model, Cho *et. al.* derived a quality estimator to compute webpage quality as opposed to its peak-time popularity. We experimentally validate the popularity growth phase model of publications proposed.

Moreover, we observe the following differences between publication citation and web-link graphs that the popularity growth model does not take in consideration:

- Publication citations do not ever disappear like web links;
- Unlike web links, once two papers are published, no new citations between them are added;
- Also unlike web links, new citations to old papers are very unlikely to occur; and
- Indirect citations to a publication are of lesser effect on its PageRank score.

We observe that these differences result in popularity decay for old publications overtime, which we refer to as the publication popularity decay phase. These differences guide us in extending the popularity growth model to accurately capture popularity decay of publications in technology-driven fields of study where authors tend not to cite publications that get older, and publication quality becomes less relevant.

We demonstrate that our proposal successfully assigns accurate publication scores that are in turn useful for two tasks:

- *Ranking Search Results of user Queries in Literature Digital Libraries:* Accurate publication scores may help users retrieve new and yet promising publications; and new publications may contain undiscovered ideas at the frontiers of the topic of interest for users. Our extended quality estimator identifies high quality papers, presents them to the user, and thus gives new papers a better chance to accumulate awareness more quickly.
- *Modelling Popularity Life Cycle of Publications:* Coupled with the probabilistic model of researchers' citation behaviour popularity life cycle of publications in different publication venues can be modeled. Cho *et. al.* analytically verified that the quality estimator they propose can successfully be used for pages with changing quality. However,

they did not investigate the popularity decay of pages probably because of the difficulties in capturing such web data and the complexity of web-link graph dynamics. Studies show that, for literature digital libraries, the popularity decay phase can be successfully modelled and integrated with the popularity growth phase.

Our two-phase publication popularity model, *i.e.*, the popularity growth and decay model, is in heavily different than the webpage popularity model. To illustrate the differences, figure shows two popularity growth and decay curves, one for a webpage and another for a publication.

Notice that the popularity of a webpage keeps increasing as the webpage becomes known and those who 'like' it place links to it in other pages. After the webpage reaches the peak, its popularity decays until it reaches a steady-state popularity value. In comparison, the decay of publication popularity has a much different curve. Studies show that researchers rarely cite old works, especially in fastmoving fields like computer and life sciences. Consequently, we show that, by properly modeling users' citation behaviour along with accurate publication quality estimators, we obtain realistic publication popularity growth and decay curves similar to the dashed curves of figure. Empirically, we observe that the majority of publication 'citation count per year' curves conform to this growth and decay model.

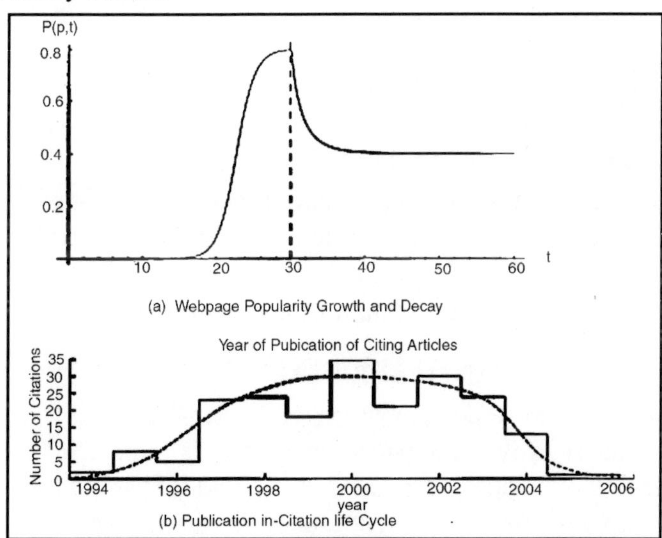

Popularity Drop of Webpages, as Opposed to Observed In-citation Life Cycle of Publications

Page Quality and Webpage Popularity Evolution Model

Cho via a simple user-web model, developed a formula for the popularity growth of webpages, and then used the formula to estimate page quality.

Publication quality, based on the web-user model, is defined as the popularity of the publication given that all possibly interested authors are aware of it and those who like it have cited it.

After getting published, a paper goes through two main phases:

- A popularity growth phase where its popularity increases as more authors become aware of it and cite it. After some time, the publication's popularity reaches to a certain value. During the growth phase of the publication;
  - — Researchers develop awareness of the publication, *i.e.*, more authors get to know it; and,
  - — Research problems inspired by the paper get studied by authors. This means that the longer the growth phase of a paper, the better the quality of the paper; and
  - — The authors who like the paper cite it in their works.
- A saturation phase: after the transient growth phase, the publication's PageRank score settles at a certain value, and minimally changes.

Definition:

- The growth region of a publication is the time interval during which the publication popularity grows.
- The saturation region of a publication is the time interval that starts at the saturation point; and, afterwards, the publication usually does not receive new citations.
- The popularity function p (p, t) of publication p, is a function that computes the popularity of p at time t.
- Publication quality Q (p) is the intrinsic and (saturation-time popularity) quality of a publication.

We empirically calculate an estimation $\tilde{Q}(p)$ for the publication quality Q(p) of publication p as the PageRank score at the saturation region. Or, $\tilde{Q}(p) = PR(p, t_{sat})$ where $PR(p,t_{sat})$ is PageRank score of p at the saturation time point t_{sat}. The popularity growth function P(p,t), proposed in is derived as:

$$P(p, t) = Q(p)/(1 + C_{1.e} - \beta t).$$

Note that the function P(p,t) is monotonically increasing with time t. The constant Q(p) is the intrinsic quality of the publication p (that is estimated as p's PageRank score in the saturation region), constant C_1 is the rate of PageRank score growth in Cho's PageRank score growth model. For new publications, $P(p, 0) \cong 0$. In time, the exponent component, $e^{-\beta t}$, approaches zero as t increases, and, consequently, P (p,t) converges to Q(p) the intrinsic quality score of the publication, over time.

Remark

The popularity of a publication p at time t is estimated as the p's PageRank score based on the citation graph at time t. Also, the quality of publication p is estimated as the PageRank score at saturation phase. The remark forms a bridge between the PageRank score change curve and Cho et. al.'s popularity growth model base their model on the fact that the quality of a page is time-invariant and does not change overtime.

Thus; Q (p) is assumed to be a constant estimated at any time as the sum of:

- The current popularity or PageRank score of p, and
- The relative popularity (PageRank) rate of change, *i.e.*,

$$\tilde{Q}(p) = PR(p,t) + \frac{1}{c}.\frac{dP(p,t)}{dt}.\frac{1}{PR(p,t)}$$

where $0 < c \leq 1$ is a constant which we choose to be 0.1. A high quality publication is one with a scientific value, and one can intuitively estimate the quality of a publication based on its impact on other authors. Quantitatively, the quality can be measured as the conditional probability that an author will like the publication (L_p) given that s/he has became aware of it (A_p). Mathematically, $Q(p) = P(L_p | A_p)$.

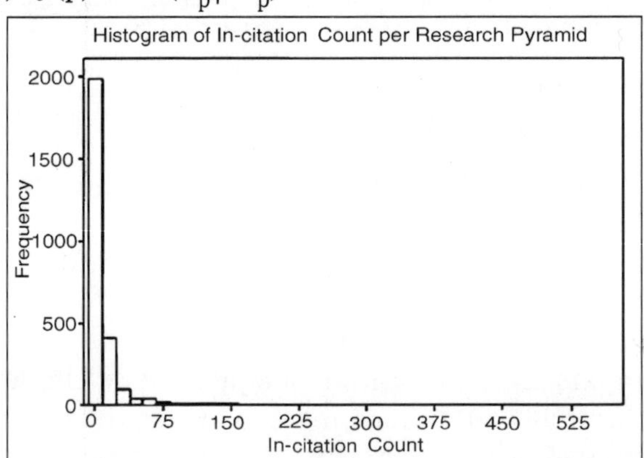

Fig. In-citation Per Research Pyramid (Inter-research Pyramid, *i,e.* Citations from Publications outside an RP to Ones inside it.)

We argue that we need to distinguish between two measures of quality for a publication:

- The first measure represents the scientific value of that publication. This value is time-invariant and is represented by Q (p).
- The second measure represents the value of the paper to the user at the time s/he is searching the digital library. This value, in contrast to Q (p), is time-dependent, especially in fast-moving fields of study. We refer to this quality measure as the Publication Quality with Aging Factor.

We show that publications go through the popularity growth phase during which publications gain awareness and thus popularity. We empirically show the popularity growth curves conform to the 'sigmoidal' evolution pattern derived.

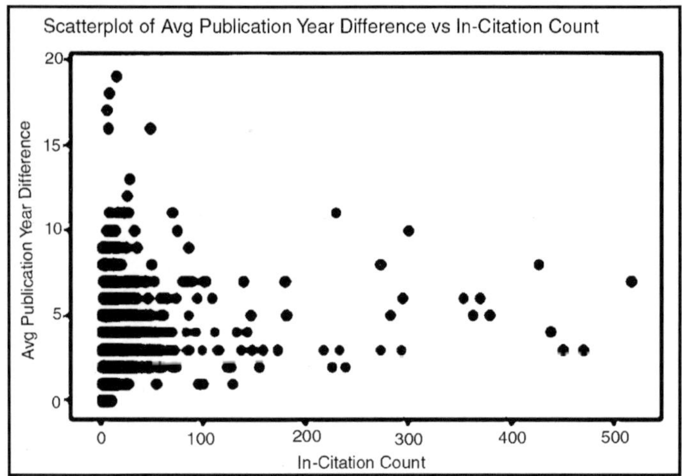

Fig. Inter-pyramid Citation count (x-axis) *vs.* the (average Difference in Publication Dates of Publications in a Research Pyramid).

Properties of Publication Citation Graphs and Research Pyramids

In this section we validate Cho et. al.'s popularity growth phase by:

- Using PageRank as a popularity indicator; and
- Utilising the research-pyramid model of research evolution to show that popularity scores of publications converge to a steady-state value that can be estimated by equation.

We first note one difference between a publication citation graph from a web citation graph: Publication citation graph evolution behaviour is to some extent more controlled than web graphs and can be anticipated.

A webpage that has been on the web for a relatively long time may still receive new links; old publications, however, are rarely cited. Consequently, publication citation graphs are highly unlikely to face structural changes around relatively old publications. This special characteristic of publication citation graphs allows for developing accurate mathematical models for changes to publication's PageRank scores, and thus better estimation of publication quality. In contrast, a web graph may face abrupt structural changes at any time in any part of the graph. Studies show that, every week, around 8 per cent web pages are replaced and that about 25 per cent new links are created.

Next we describe the research-pyramid (RP) model of publications that also suggests time-dependent growth patterns in publication citation graphs. The RP-Model is based on the observation that citations between research publications produce multiple, small pyramid-like structures, where each pyramid represents publications related to a highly specific research topic. A research pyramid is defined as a set of publications that represent a highly specific research topic, and usually has a pyramid-like structure in terms of its citation graph. The RP-Model suggests that publication citation graphs evolve in a time-controlled manner through the stimulation of most-specific research topics from one another as follows. A publication that deals with a new specific research problem appears, and proposes the first solution for it. More publications appear after that publication, addressing the same problem and proposing enhanced or refined solutions to that problem.

In time, the research problem:

- Is either solved.
- Settles down with 'good-enough' solutions, or; and
- Subdivided into more specific research problems.

Publications within an individual research pyramid are:

- Motivated by earlier publications in the topic area, or
- Use techniques proposed in publications from other research pyramids.

We have observed that citations between different research pyramids conform to a highly left-skewed distribution which indicates that as research pyramids of a particular research topic is formed and new research pyramids are instantiated, the RPs already formed receive few external citations from other research pyramids.

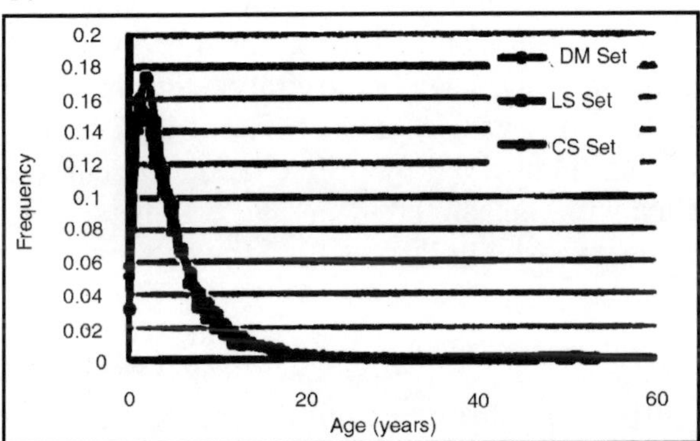

Fig. Empirical Citation-age Probability Distribution Curves (*i.e.,* Citation Age *vs.* Frequency of Citations with that age) of Publications in Three Datasets *(i)* Data Management *(ii)* Life Sciences and *(iii)* Computer Science.

Consequently, publication citation graphs are highly unlikely to face structural changes within an already constructed research pyramid because:

- Citations do not disappear like web links.
- Once two papers are published, no new links between them are added;
- New citations to old paper are less likely to occur, and
- Indirect citations to a publication are of lesser effect on its PageRank score.

Structural changes affect only the developing research pyramids. Thus, popularity of publications is expected to converge over time to a steady-state value, which is the essence of the popularity growth model.

The User Citation Behaviour Model

Figure shows that user interest in citing a particular paper significantly decays over time. The best probabilistic distribution that fits the citation-age PDFs of figure is the Weibull distribution.

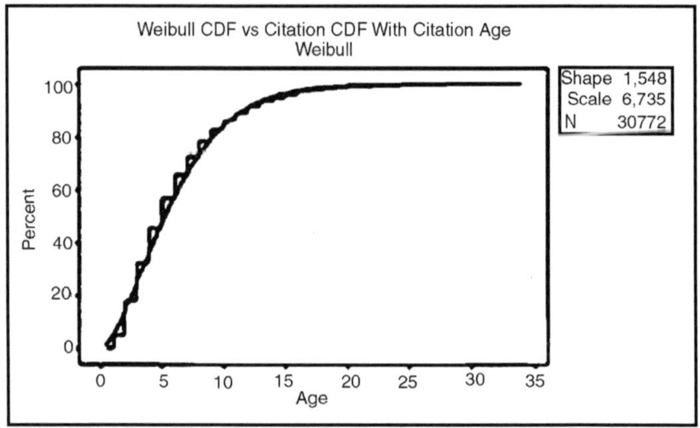

(a) Age vs Frequency of Citations of Publications.
(b) Weibull Distribution CDF.

Figure contains the cumulative distribution function (CDF) of the Weibull distribution, and the empirical CDF of the citation-age distribution for the data-management dataset. The two CDF curves show a high match. Using Minitab, 2008 software, we have observed that the citation age curve conforms to the Weibull distribution with the estimated parameters shape (g)=1.548 and Scale (a)=6.735. Thus, the probability P (u → v) of the citation from u to v to occur, is computed as,

$$P(u \rightarrow v) = f_{weibull}(|age(u, v|; \gamma, \alpha)$$

where |age (u, v)| is the absolute time difference (in years) between the publication years of u and v. The probability density function of Weibull distribution is given by,

$$f_{weibull}(x; \gamma, \alpha) = \frac{\gamma}{\alpha}.(x/\alpha)^{\gamma-1} e - \left(\frac{x}{\alpha}\right)^{\gamma}$$

assuming that $f_{weibull}(x; \gamma, \alpha) = 0$ for $x < 0$ (which is true in our case as a publication will not receive any citation if it is not published). We use this formula in estimating the publication quality considering the aging factor.

Publication Quality with Aging Factor

Assume that a user issues a search query at time t. Viewing the user as a potential author of an upcoming publication, the user will probably follow the Weibull distribution in his/her citations. *i.e.*, the user cites a relevant publication v with probability equal to $f_{weibull}(t - t_{Year}(V))$ where $t_{Year}(v)$ is the publication year of v.

Thus, we argue that considering both the publication quality and the aging factor together leads to a better search output ranking.

One possible way to order user search query results is to consider three factors:

- Text-based relevancy of v and the query terms;
- The publication quality; and
- The probability that the user will cite the publication given the ages of relevant publications.

Thus, for a given search query term w, and output (publication) v, one possible form of combining the three factors is as follows,

$$\text{final}_{score(v)} = \text{Sim}(w, v) * \hat{P}(p, t)$$

where Sim (w,v) is the text-based similarity between w and v, and $\hat{P}(p,t)$ is the temporal popularity of the publication at time t which is computed as,

$$\hat{P}(p, t) = f_{weibull}(t - t_{Year}(v); \gamma, \alpha) * P(p, t)$$

EXPLORING DIGITAL LIBRARIES THROUGH VISUAL INTERFACES

Libraries are long standing institutions, providing an important service of making information widely available. So it is with Digital Libraries (DL), but this evolution into a computerised format does not come without its own unique challenges. The variety and quantity of information available in the digital space is truly astounding. However, as this growth continues, traditional methods for searching are becoming less effective to support the needs of users to find information quickly and easily.

The conventional library book search system provides several attributes associated with books as a response to the users' enquiry. This includes title, author, publication year, ISBN, page total, and similar information. While considering the increasing volume of data, the current text-based approach to result presentation is not an ideal solution for the modern digital environment. Particularly in the case of comparing a lengthy list of search results, this approach is ill-suited, as it is inefficient and non-intuitive. Assistance, such as ranked results, can aid in such problems but the user will still be relied on to investigate the top results individually. Additionally, the current popular approach of presenting a summary of content may not accurately reflect what is of value to the user. The advancements and trends that allow for the rapid growth of DL also permit more elaborate interfaces with which to access them. Information Visualisation is one such avenue, which has proven to be an effective approach in acquiring information from a large compilation of data. By making use of users' perceptual cognition for navigating extensive digital workspaces, their ability to understand, and speed with which they review the information space is improved. Previous studies have proven the significance of visualisation in the users' information forage.

One common approach to assist users' search activities uses visualisation techniques combined with information filtering. The users' interaction defines the attributes of interest that easily filter out unrelated data. The following visualisation procedure transforms the remaining data into graphical illustrations. FilmFinder and HomeFinder are interactive visual interfaces which assist the user to narrow down the search scope and easily compare results using the visualisation. Another common approach focuses on presenting the underlying information through visualisation.

A novel text visualisation interface, TileBars, shows the distribution behaviour of a set of query terms. This presentation allows users to compare multiple documents compactly and concurrently. Other visualisation techniques in this category concentrate on showing a portion of the information at a great level of detail while maintaining the overall structure of the information. Information clustering is another method for supporting navigation of a large data collection. Related documents are clustered together, whose notable characteristics are visualised using a mixture of attributes. Visualisation methodologies have shown that the illustration of data has contributed to improving the user's ability to comprehend information quickly.

This, in turn, leads to increased speed and accuracy in finding desired information. We can apply these kinds of visual abstractions to enhance searches on different types of data domains. By presenting information in such a way, a large amount of content can be displayed in a format which is more intuitive. This has the benefit of allowing the user to analyse data more effectively, increasing the user's ability to comprehend results and make better content selections. Periscope, for example, is a visualisation system targeted at web search results.

It provides a series of different visualisations which users can utilise to analyse and explore the result set. A holistic interface can be used to organise documents into various categories, such as language and format, or web related attributes such as DNS domains. An analytical interface allows for up to seven attributes to be relayed at a time, through use of X, Y, Z axes, colour, size, shape, and animation. The search based on the underlying content will increase the accuracy in finding targeted information from the available resources. Think for a moment how one might search a physical book for a topic of interest.

The logical place to start would be the index. Indexes are valuable resources for referencing major terms which appear in a book. The categorical and hierarchical layout of terms in the index allows us to identify associated topics easily, along with their relationships without reading the underlying contents. The page numbers coupled with each entry makes it possible to estimate the amount information relating to a particular subject. The index will represent the overall layout of entire book contents. Due to a lack of readily available sources, this valuable information has been under utilised. The current trend of digitising books in recent years allows us to exploit content in searches, instead of just depending on superficial book attributes.

The visualisation techniques utilising this information will further enhances the user's search on the DL system. The main objective of this stage is on the utilisation of visualisation techniques for exploring the DL system. The following stage will survey and summarise various visualisation approaches which applied to DL. As suggested, introduce a visual interface which presents general book information through iconic representations. This stage also proposes a novel visualisation which utilises the book index for mimicking the content analysis.

It will allow for detailed comparison of index-based information between selected works. Two different visualisations for this detail view are implemented, each with different strengths. The procedure and analysis of results for a usability test follow, along with discussion and future possibilities, and final conclusions.

RELATED WORKS

The efficacy of visualisation in searching a large information space has been proven in many previous studies. DL are one promising area that should exploit visualisation techniques in searching on various forms of archived information, such as text, imagery, multimedia, citations, and even computer mediated communication. The 3D Vase Museum is one example applying visualisations for browsing photographs in a digital library collection. A Focus+Context type visualisation displays a set of Greek vases in the Perseus digital library in a simulated 3D virtual museum. By moving around the virtual space, users can appreciate vases with accompanying text data. Christel and Martin introduced visualisation techniques for browsing and navigating another type of multimedia, video documents. Meanwhile, Chen proposed a novel approach utilising a different side view of information in accessing the digital library.

It visualises semantic structures and co-citation networks extracted from a collection of documents. This method displayed the author co-citation networks in a 3D virtual space attempting to reveal the structure of a field of hyperlinks with co-citation patterns of authors. Borner and Chen explained that there are three common usage requirements for visual interfaces to the DL: *First*, to support the identification of the composition of retrieval result. *Second* is to understand the interrelation of retrieved documents to one another. *Lastly*, to refine a search, gain an overview of the coverage of a DL and to visualise user interaction data in relation to available documents.

The goal would be to evaluate and improve DL usage. Clarkson *et al.,* developed a visual interface emphasising on the hierarchy of the repository in presenting the DL search results. They used the hierarchical representation in digital repositories for developing an interface for enhancing query-based search engines. A treemap, a well-known technique, is used to organise results in a space-efficient hierarchical display.

The system, known as ResultMap, maps each document in the hierarchical tree structures to a treemap where items matched with given query are highlighted. ResultMap presents the full contents of a hierarchical dataset while providing a view of underlying levels. The experimental results from two controlled lab studies showed that participants expressed preferences to use ResultMap system and produced comparable performance to a text-only engine. When using physical books, people tend to view multiple at once.

This is to better compare and review information across multiple sources, and to have a better overall understanding of the domain. In their study, Good et al, identify this to be a major weakness in current DL displays. To address related issues, researchers have conducted studies applying visualisation techniques for book searches and presenting various forms of search results for easy comparison. Envision is a visual interface presenting book search results in a rigid matrix. The search results are presented as icons in a 2D grid where the visual attributes represent the characteristics of returned documents. Envision allows the user to organise the visualised output interactively based on their information needs.

The Graphical Interface for DL (GRIDL) and ActiveGraph adopted a similar approach in presenting search results. The GRIDL displays a hierarchical cluster of the relevant data to a query on two-dimensional display. This system provides an interactive grid layout, the axes of which are selectable from a variety of different attributes. Results were displayed within each cell as a collection of different size icons, colour coded by document type. ActiveGraph presented search results based on scatter plots. ActiveGraph also provides similar functionalities to specify shape, colour, and size of nodes representing various forms of digital resources. Because ActiveGraph system results in much more node clustering and overlap, a logarithmic transformation is provided, along with the ability to filter out unwanted items.

Many studies mainly focus on aiding the user in comparing the search results effectively by presenting book properties such as book title, author, publication, year, through various visual attributes, but they don't express in detail the amount of content related to user interest. Citiviz is a visual interface tool kit combining text mining and information visualisation. In order to present the insight of similarity among documents as well as traditional document attributes, this system used two visualisation techniques: an animated 2D scatter plot to represent document attributes and a dynamic hyperbolic tree to show hierarchical relationships among documents.

By allowing users to manipulate the manner in which data is displayed, these visualisations provided a better chance to find patterns within the data that may not typically be apparent. Lin proposed another approach through a graphical table of contents (GTOC) that tries to exploit a different perspective of underling information by utilising the table of contents of the book. GTOC showed the dimension of items in the table of contents based on Kohonen's self organising feature map algorithm. The paper introduces how documents can be organised and then visualised to allow the user easy access of underlying contents.

The GTOC prototype describes various interactive tools to assist the user exploring document contents and analysing relationships among terms in the table of contents. Both the attributes associated with documents and its underlying contents are valuable resources finding the relevant information of the users' interest. The increasing computing power and performance of graphics devices make it possible to exercise these information in presenting search results. The following section introduces a newly developed visualisation system that will assist the user's search while utilising the book index, which has been underutilised as a visualisation resource.

METHOD

The Visual Interface for Digital Library Search (VIDLS) system utilizes an Overview+Detail approach for presenting book search results. This is a visualisation technique that uses multiple images to display the entire data space, as well as show an up-close, detailed view of the data. Similar to traditional library searches, the overview will present outline of the book search results through graphical illustration. The user interactively selects a subset of visualised icons that will allow them to execute content level exploration. When a user provides search terms of interests, the Detail view presents a visualisation which relates, in depth, the information presented by the index. For our pilot study, we developed two possible visualisations for this view of the index, each with its own strengths. One emphasises space utilisation, whereas the other is designed to focus on clearly presenting term relationships.

Visualisation

The Overview allows the user to perform a general search on the data space, similar to traditional library tools. This visualisation utilises a tabular layout which offers a familiar spread-sheet style organisation of book search results. The attribute of each axis can be independently selected by the user, allowing for a more targeted display and increasing the users' comprehension of the data set. This functionality will assist the user in customising the search based on their own judgement of which attributes are more important. In the Overview, each book is represented as a circular node, located in the appropriate cell based on the axes.

To deliver the estimated amount of content, node size is determined by the normalised page count of the book compared to the rest. Books with a greater number of pages naturally map to the largest nodes. This will allow users to quickly identify the amount and distribution of content available.

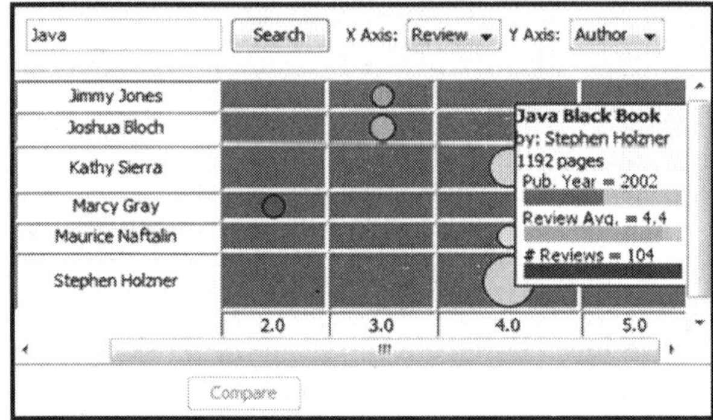

Fig. Overview Interface Displaying Search Results with Tool-tip

The system presents other book attributes through a colour coding scheme. The green component is derived through collaborative filtering. This is a content-filtering technique based upon the opinion of users whom have already evaluated the item in question. This will be a valuable piece of information to know regarding the quality of the book. In the case of VIDLS, collaborative filtering would be done by collecting user reviews, much like you found find at a merchant web site. Higher intensity of the green component would indicate a more positive response from reviews.

The accuracy of the content-filtering is highly correlated with the number of evaluators and their preferences. As an example: the mean score of a book which has a low number of reviews could potentially be misleading and unreliable.

To account for this, the Overview associates the blue component with the number of unique evaluations given to a book. The publication year is a valuable attribute to find the most up to date information.

This metric has been represented through the red component. With the utilisation of the RGB colour scheme, the larger more recent books with a solid review will be closer to white in intensity, while older, smaller, poorly reviewed works tend towards black. If the user needs to know more precise information for the components, or other detailed information of the work, the system provides this via a tooltip interface.

Detailed Visualisation

Once a user makes a set of selections from the Overview, the system will provide a detailed view of those items. This display is tasked with presenting visualised index data for each book, allowing the user to perform more refined queries, and compare and contrast each work in detail. Two visualisations were implemented on a data model to present the same information while emphasising different attributes: one a radial graph, and the other a sunburst-like display.

Data Model

The underlying model for the detailed visualisations relies on several important characteristics associated with a term in the index. These are: number of pages, number of occurrences, content density, and location relative to the parent term. Although this information is readily available in the index, it is unintuitive in a text format. Presenting these attributes via graphical illustration, the user should gain greater understanding of the content, and make more informed choices of which books to choose.

The number of pages associated with a term by the index is a potential indicator as to how much coverage a topic receives in a book. A work with a greater number of pages on a subject is intuitively going to have more potential value than one with less. Naturally, this attribute is represented by size in the visualisations. To assist the user in quickly making general comparison between each book, this attribute is further expanded to be a cumulative page total of the term along with its sub-terms. The number of occurrences and content density are related through a colour code.

This is intended to give the user a better understanding of the comparative value of each term being displayed. Term occurrence within the book is related by the green component. Although one work may have more information referenced in a single index entry for a topic, that does not necessarily make it the better choice. If another book contained references of a particular term in many different locations within the index, that may be an indication of a greater breadth or complexity of coverage on that topic.

The number of term occurrences are normalised across the display, with the instances of greatest coverage mapping to the highest green intensity, and the one with the fewest having no green intensity. Although two books may have the same total of pages for a particular topic, this should not be taken to mean they have equal value. Consider the situation in which one index allocates ten pages for a topic, but they are separate and not listed as a single range of pages.

Another index containing the same topic, but listed as a single range of ten pages, such as 152-161 may be more valuable to the user. The first may have fragmented references of the topic, but no detailed coverage, whereas the second may have a full section or stage dedicated to the subject. To relate this information to the user, the content density is mapped to the blue colour component. The value is given by calculating the ratio of page continuity to the total number of pages for a term. This is shown by *equation 1,* where *Cib* is the blue intensity for term $i, \sum_{j=o}^{n} P_j^c$ is the number of individual page ranges for *i*, *Ti* is the total number pages for the term *i,* and *Imax* is the brightest intensity of blue possible on the machine. This gives terms with more concentrated information a stronger representation in the visualisation.

$$C_{ib} = \left(1 - \left(\frac{\sum_{j=0}^{n} P_j^c}{T_i}\right)\right) * I_{max},$$

The last attribute represents the relationship between a sub-term and its parent. Similar to the previous attribute, a sub-term which is located close to its parent within the book could be an indication of cohesive coverage of the topic. A user may regard such a case with more value than one where the sub-term is more removed from the parent's location. The value of this attribute is calculated by *equation 2.*

$$D_j = ABS\left(\frac{NORM\left(\sum_{k=0}^{n} P_j^k - \overline{Root_i}\right)}{N}\right)$$

Dj is a normalised distance between the root node and associated sub-node j; P_j^k is the page number contains sub-term j; $\overline{Root_i}$ is the mean page number having the root word *i;* and *NORM* and *ABS* are a normalisation and absolute function respectively.

Visualisations

The two visualisations share several aspects, in addition to the attributes described previously. Each displays the matching term of the search prominently in the center, with the sub-terms radiating outward. Since, each term is sized based on the cumulative page count of itself and sub-terms, the root node will give users a quick guidance as to which book has more content. Additionally, each graph has a context side-bar that indicates which term is currently moused-over, along with a histogram displaying its colour components. The similarities end here for the two visualisations.

The first visualisation approach employs a radial graph layout; with each term presented as a circular node branching off the parent. Sub-terms are sized in the same way as the root, with node size directly correlated to the total number of pages. The largest sub-terms start from the top towards the bottom of the visualisation. This is done to prevent over-crowding of the display. Terms with the fewest pages are considered less important, and are collapsed into a single node, indicated by a red outline, if not enough space is available. Another way in which space is conserved is by displaying only the first level of sub-terms.

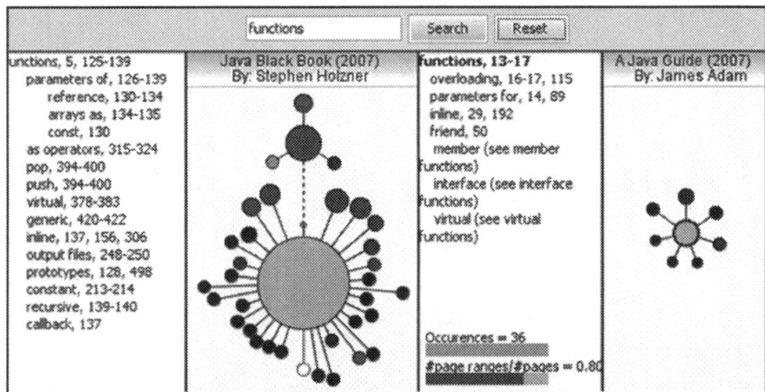

Fig. Diagram shows Two Books being Compared in the Detail View. The Left Shows Expanded Sub-terms and an Overflow Node. The Right has Context Highlighting of Text List and Bar Display from User Interaction.

A node with hidden sub-terms has a ridged outline. These along with the red 'overflow' node can be clicked show the hidden terms. In contrast, the second visualisation follows a sunburst-like design. Sub-terms are displayed in concentric sections around the center, extending from their parent term. Each sub-term 'slice' is sized as a percentage of its page allocation from the parent's. This has the benefit that all terms can be displayed compactly without hiding any. No additional user interaction would be required to explore the full term hierarchy. One potential downside of this design, compared to the previous one, is that terms are crowded together. This may cause difficulty in picking them out from their neighbours.

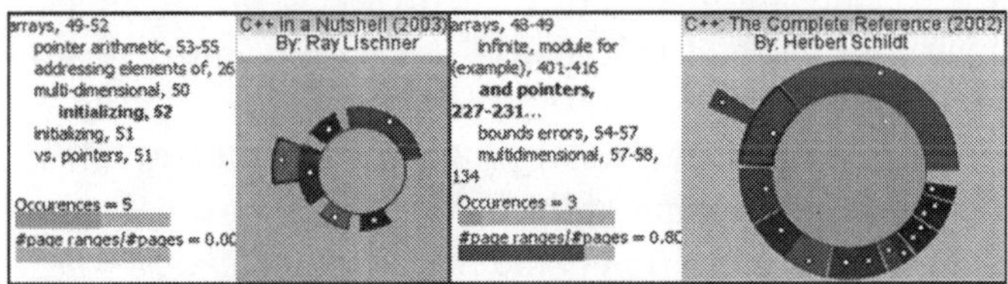

Fig. Alternate Sunburst Detailed View.

In the radial graph, the relation between a sub-term and its parent is indicated by the branch length. Terms which appear on pages near those of the parent naturally are drawn with shorter branches. Since, the sunburst approach has forgone branches to conserve space, a different analogue is required. Each slice instead contains a bubble, which will relate this information. As the closeness to parent is normalised, the term with the closest relationship has a bubble at the base of the slice, while the term with the most distant has a bubble on the outer edge of its slice. As was previously noted, the chief difference between the two visualisations is their concern for space conservation. With its emphasis on the term relation branch, and distinct nodes, the radial graph may have more clarity, but at the cost of poorer space utilisation. This results in the need to hide terms considered less important. The other visualisation puts more value in making better use of space, and is able to display all terms efficiently. However, when many terms are displayed at once, the resultant crowding could make smaller slices difficult to see. The addition of the bubble overlay to each slice can add to this difficulty.

EXPERIMENT

To measure the effectiveness of VIDLS, a series of usability tests were performed to compare it to more traditional text-based interfaces. In this set of experiments the VIDLS system, using the radial graph detailed layout, was used in conjunction with a text-only interface for the same information. Each usability test consisted of a small group of three to five students, comfortable in the use of computers, whom had no prior experience with VIDLS.

Each group was given a brief orientation presentation, and then allowed to acclimate to the functionality of both applications for a few minutes. The tests then began, with each user asked to search for books and information with the text-only application and then with the visualisation based approach. Once the test concluded, participants then filled out a survey to measure their quantitative and qualitative feedback of VIDLS in comparison to the text-based format. The questionnaire has 14 questions which utilise a 5 point Likert scale; 5 indicating the highest level of satisfaction, and 1 the lowest.

Table shows the survey results that summarises the user's feedback to VIDLS over a text-based library search system. Participants overall found the VIDLS system to be satisfactory, with some comments highlighting that unfamiliarity with the visualisations led to preference of the text-based design. The Overview visualisation was well received, with 82 per cent of testers responding that it improved their ability to quickly identify desirable books.

This was supported through the exploratory aspects of the system, which participants indicated positively as giving meaningful result displays, and facilitating better understanding of the information.

The radial graph visualisation of index level information was also seen in a positive light, as 65 per cent found it to be a useful representation, and only 11 per cent preferring the familiar text-only listing of results. As with the Overview, testers considered the Detail View to also be useful in expressing the concentration of information, and improving selection among the results. Table shows a summary of survey results.

Table. Post Experiment Survey Results

Question	Pos.	Neut.	Neg.
VIDLS overall was preferable to a text-based search	53%	35%	12%

The Overview improved identification of desirable books	82%	6%	12%
Use of the selectable axis facilitated a better understanding of a set of books.	71%	24%	5%
The Overview helped in selecting a subset of books.	65%	29%	6%
It was easy to discern book attributes based on node colour	53%	18%	29%
The Detailed view was preferable to a text approach	65%	24%	11%
It was easy to discern term attributes based on node colour	47%	24%	29%
The Detail view made relevant book selection easier	88%	12%	0%
The relation between a term and it's child was understandable	65%	35%	0%
The Detail view helped identify terms related to the search	94%	6%	0%

AUTOMATING THE MAINTENANCE OF GREENSTONE COLLECTIONS

Many applications generate multimedia documents, such as images and video, on a daily basis. For example, many municipalities have a photo-radar system to catch vehicles that violate traffic laws such as speeding or ignoring red lights. Many pictures of vehicle licence plates are created every day. If these images are organised into a digital library, the collection would need to be updated regularly to incorporate new images. Another example is a traveller who wants to update a digital library of trip photos with new pictures of her travels while travelling around the world. When documents and metadata are added to a digital library collection on a regular basis, such as hourly, daily or weekly, an automated and scheduled approach to collection maintenance is preferred over having to manually update the collection. In addition, an automated approach should be simple to use, therefore making time available for other important tasks. Digital library software such as Greenstone, DSpace and Fedora require that items be added manually to the collection.

In Fedora, data is retrieved at the time of viewing. However, a location needs to be manually configured. Further, although Fedora and DSpace do provide Application Programming Interfaces (APIs) to extend functionality, programming knowledge is required for using an API and for setting up tools based on it. We present a solution for automating and scheduling updates that occur on a regular basis. Our solution is implemented in the Greenstone digital library software system and comes in two parts. The first part of our approach is a command-line scheduling module. The Scheduler both automates the construction and modification of a collection, and schedules the construction to occur at specific intervals, such as hourly, daily or weekly.

In addition, the owner of a collection can update the collection manually, without affecting the scheduled collection builds. Further, the Scheduler interacts with the existing task scheduling mechanism on the host system, which keeps the Scheduler minimal, yet powerful. The second part of our approach involves incorporating the Scheduler into the Greenstone Librarian Interface (GLI). This will allow users who are more comfortable with managing collections through a graphical user interface to take advantage of the functionality of the Scheduler. In addition, this allows us to handle certain tasks associated with scheduling in a uniform and flexible manner.

GREENSTONE

Greenstone is a suite of software for creating digital library collections and making them available locally or via the Internet. A collection can contain documents of different formats, including images, PostScript and PDF files, audio, formatted and unformatted text, and many others. A collection built using Greenstone can be customised in many ways. For example, a collection owner can customise the types of documents that can appear in the collection, the appearance of the interface to the collection, and how the collection will be accessed by other users. In addition, Greenstone is extensible.

For example, functionality to support other data formats that are not provided with Greenstone can easily be added to a collection. There are two types of accessors in Greenstone. The first is an index that provides support for searching. The second is a classifier that provides support for browsing. A collection can be configured for browsing by any metadata that is specified by the collection owner or extracted by Greenstone. Furthermore, a collection can be configured for searching on the same metadata fields, as well as full text.

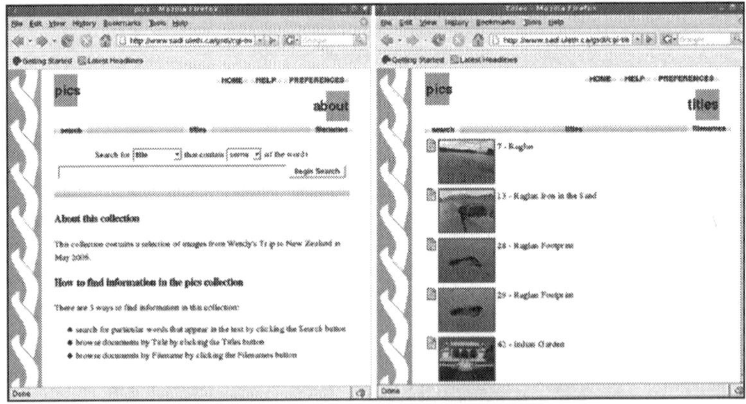

Fig. Pics Collection in Greenstone *(a)* Front Page of Pics Collection *(b)* Viewing Pics Collection.

Figures *(a)* and *(b)* depict a Greenstone collection called pics. The pics collection is configured to accept images only. Figure *(a)* shows the front page of the collection, which provides general information on the collection. In addition, the collection is configured for both browsing and searching by either Title or Filename. Figure *(b)* shows a display of some images from the pics collection. In this view, the collection is being browsed by Title. The user can click on any image to obtain a larger image for viewing.

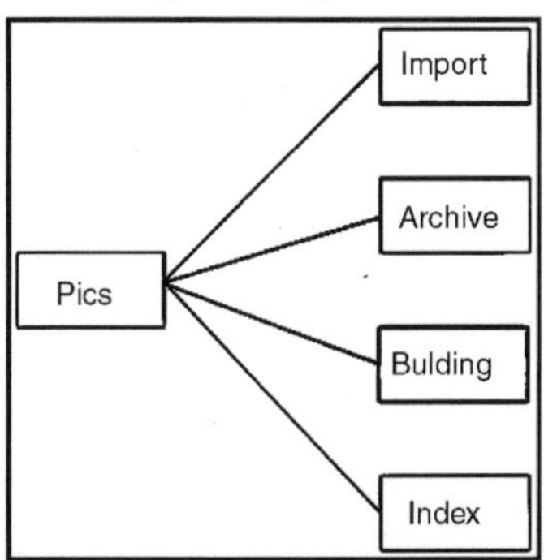

Fig. Internal Representation of a Greenstone Collection.

Figure depicts the internal representation of a Greenstone collection. Here, the four main directories of a collection—import, archives, building, and index—are displayed.

The purpose of each is described below:

- *Import:* The import directory contains all documents that are to be added to the collection. If desired, the documents can be organised in a hierarchical directory structure within the import directory.
- *Archives:* The archives directory stores all documents that have been processed from the import folder and added to the collection. All documents in the archives directory are represented in a canonical XML format.
- *Building:* The building directory is a working directory for creating all indices and classifiers that are specified for the collection.
- *Index:* The index directory contains the indices and classifiers after they are created.

A Greenstone collection is created or modified by the following four steps: document addition, document importation, accessor creation, and collection activation.

Each step is described in detail below:

- *Document Addition:* New documents that will be added to a collection are placed into the import directory for the collection.
- *Document Importation:* Each document in the import directory is processed for inclusion by creating a canonical XML representation for it. This is accomplished by specifying an import command. Different importing options can be specified by the user. For example, documents in the import directory can be added to an existing

collection by using a–keepold option. Alternatively, all documents in the import directory—new and existing—can be used to create a new instance of the collection by using a-removeold option. All imported documents are placed in the archives directory.

- *Accessor Creation:* After the documents in the import directory are added to the collection, indices and classifiers are set up by processing the canonical XML representations of all documents. This is accomplished by specifying a build command. New indices and classifiers can be built by specifying a–removeold option. Alternatively, existing indices and classifiers can be modified by specifying a-keepold or-incremental option. The resulting indices and classifiers are located in the building directory.
- *Collection Activation:* Finally, thc collcction is activated by moving the indices and classifiers from the building directory to the index directory. The collection is now viewable online.

The command for each step can be executed in a terminal or command window, or via the Greenstone Librarian Interface.

GREENSTONE LIBRARIAN INTERFACE

The Greenstone Librarian Interface (GLI) is a graphical user interface that provides a user-friendly method to build and configure Greenstone collections. It incorporates the steps above. The only steps that are required by the user are to place documents to the import directory via the Gather panel, and to add the documents to the collection via the Create panel. In addition, the Librarian Interface allows a user to create new collections, select metadata sets, configure which document types to allow, and select import and build command options. Figure shows the Librarian Interface.

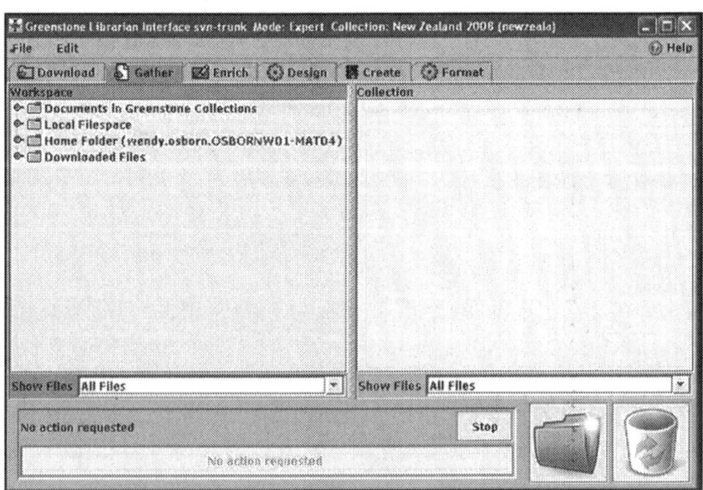

Fig. The Greenstone Librarian Interface.

CRON

Cron is a programme for users to schedule tasks that will run automatically at a specified time. A task can be one command, or a script containing several commands that are executed in sequence. Initially, Cron was implemented for Unix and Linux platforms, with most systems running Vixie Cron. Mac OS X also runs Vixie Cron. In addition, versions of Cron now exist for Windows platforms, such as Pycron. We summarise the general ideas behind all implementations of Cron that are applicable to our work. Cron runs continuously in the background of the operating system. Every minute, Cron reads several task configuration files. Each such file is called a crontab file.

A crontab file contains a record for every task that is scheduled for execution. Cron locates and runs all tasks that are scheduled at the current time. The format of a crontab record is, where min, hr, dom, moy, and dow are the minute, hour, day of month, month of year and day of week, respectively, user is the username that the command will run under, and task is the command or script that is executed at the specified time.

A task can be scheduled to run hourly, daily, weekly, monthly, or yearly:

- *Hourly:* An hourly scheduled task executes every hour at a specified minute.
- *Daily:* A task that is scheduled daily executes at a specific hour, which is required, and a specific minute. If no minute is specified, execution will occur every minute during the specified hour.
- *Weekly:* A weekly scheduled task runs on a specified day, which is required, and at a specified hour and minute. If no hour is specified, execution will occur every hour during the specified day.
- *Monthly:* A monthly scheduled task runs on a specified day.
- *Yearly:* A yearly scheduled task runs on a specified month.

Any unspecified values are replaced with an asterisk in the crontab record. Systems that use Vixie Cron support two types of crontab files-system crontab and user crontab. The system crontab files are primarily for system administration and maintenance tasks. Also, even if all tasks have a specified low-level username, root privileges are required for modifying a system crontab file. User crontab files, on the other hand, can be set up by any user on the system to execute tasks under their own username. Assuming the user has permission to execute the task, no root permissions are required. In addition, Pycron only supports user crontab files. Therefore, the Scheduler will employ a user crontab file.

```
30 * * * */ collect/pics/gsdl.pl
59 23 * * * /usr/bin/cleanup.bash
00 6 * * 7 /home/someuser/alarm
00 0 1 1 * echo 'Happy New Year!'
```

Sample Crontan File

Figure displays a sample user crontab file. It contains 4 tasks that are scheduled for specific times. The first task,/collect/pics/gsdl.pl, is scheduled to be run at 30 minutes past every hour.

The second task,/usr/bin/cleanup.bash, is scheduled for execution daily at 11:59pm. The third task, home/someuser/alarm, is scheduled every Sunday at 6:00am. Finally, the fourth task, which echoes 'Happy New Year!', is schedule for execution every January first at 12:00 AM.

THE SCHEDULER

We first present our design for the Scheduler command-line module in Greenstone. The Scheduler is written in Perl and runs on Linux, Windows and Mac OS X. It also utilises the Cron scheduling service for scheduling collection re-building. We chose Perl bccause a Perl script can be executed across different platforms without the need to recompile. Similarly, we chose Cron because it is available for Linux and Mac OS X. Therefore, we can maintain the the crossplatform requirement of Greenstone.

The Scheduler requires the following parameters from the user as input:

- The collection to be rebuilt;
- The full import command that is required to import documents into the collection;
- The full build command required to construct the indices and classifiers for the collection; and
- A specification of either an hourly, daily, or weekly build.

For example, if the user wants the collection pics to be scheduled for construction on a daily basis, the parameters would look something like this:

- Schedule.pl pics 'import.pl–removeold pics'.
- 'Buildcol.pl–removeold pics' daily.

Where pics is the name of the collection, 'import.pl–removeold pics' is the Greenstone command for importing documents into the collection pics, 'buildcol.pl–removeold pics' is the Greenstone command for creating the required indices and classifiers for pics, and daily indicates that the collection will be scheduled for construction on a daily basis.

Using the arguments provided by the user, the Scheduler performs two main tasks:

- Create a script that automates the building of the collection; and
- Create a crontab record that schedules the execution of the build script at specified intervals.

Automation Script Generation

The Scheduler generates a build script for any import and build command, and for the Linux, Windows or Mac OS X platforms. The build script contains all instructions that are required for building the specified collection. The commands include those for setting the Greenstone environment variables required for the collection building process, the import command and the build command.

```
#!/usr/bin/perl
SENV{'GSDLHOME'}=' /gsdl';
SENV {'GSDLOS'}=' linux';
SENV {'GSDLLANG'}='EN';
SENV {' PATH'}='/usr/local/gsdl/bin/script:/usr/local/gsdl/bin/
linux';
system('import.pl-removeold pics');
system('buildcol.pl-removeold pics');
system('\\rm-r/gsdl/collect/pics/index/*');
system('mv /gsdl/collect/pics/building/*
/gsdl/collect/pics/index/');
system('chmod-R 755 /gsdl/collect/pics/index/*');
```

Fig. Sample Automation Script for Linux.

Figure 6.15 shows a sample build script for Linux that contains the instructions for building the collection pics, as specified in the schedule.pl command above. The first four instructions set the environment variable that are required for the import.pl and buildcol.pl commands.

The next two instructions are the specified import and build commands. The remaining instructions handle cleanup in order to activate the collection.

```
#!/usr/bin/perl
SENV{'GSDLHOME'} ='C:\\gsdl';
SENV{'GSDLOS'}='windows';
SENV{'GSDLLANG'} ='en';
S E N V { ' P A T H ' } = C : / /
gsdl\\bin\\windows\\perl\\bin;C:\\gsdl\\bin\\windows;
C:\\gsdl\\bin\\script;C:\\Perl\\bin\\;
C:WINDOWS\\system32;C:\\WINDOWS;
system('import.pl pics');
system('buildcol. pl pics');
system('rd\/s\/Q \'C:\\gsdl\\collect\\pics\\index\'');
system('md \'C:\\gsdl\\collect\\pies\\index\'');
system('xcopy \/E \/Y \'C:\\gsdl\\collect\\pics\\building\\*\'
\'C:\\gsdl\\collect\\pics\\index\\\'');
```

Fig. Sample Automation Script of Windows.

Similarly, Figure shows a sample build script for Windows that is generated for the same schedule.

Crontab Generation

A crontab record is created to execute the automation script at a specified interval. The user has the option of specifying an hourly, daily or weekly build. An hourly build is scheduled for the beginning of the hour, a daily build is scheduled for midnight, and a weekly build is scheduled for Sunday morning at midnight. After creating the crontab record, it is added to the crontab file or replaces an existing crontab record.

```
0 0 0 * * * /gsd;/collect/pics/gsdl.pl
```

Fig. Crontab Record for Linux.

Figure 6.17 depicts the daily crontab record for the automation script in figure, while Figure 6.18 depicts the crontab record corresponding to the automation script in figure.

```
0 0 0 * * * C:\gsdl\collect\pisc\gsdl. pl
```

Fig. Crontab Record for Windows.

EVALUATION

The focus of our experiments is to evaluate the Scheduler for correct execution in specific situations.

For correct execution, we looked at the following:

- *Crontab:* Does the Scheduler generate a correct crontab record? A crontab record is correct if: 1) it is accepted by the crontab programme, and it causes Cron to execute the automation script at the proper time.
- *Automation Script:* In addition, does the scheduler generate the correct automation script to build a collection. An automation script is generated correctly if the collection it is created for is rebuilt correctly given the parameters that are specified when the script is created.

We conducted three experiments. The first is an hourly build of one collection. The second is an hourly build of two collections. The third is a daily build of one collection. All three experiments were performed on both Linux and Windows. These tests were not performed extensively on Mac OS X. However, the scheduler was executed many times on this platform to ensure that it does work.

Hourly Build of One Collection

The focus of this experiment is to ensure that the Scheduler produced a correct crontab record and automation script to re-build a collection of images every hour for 24 hours. To determine that each execution of the automation script was successful, we looked at the following. For Linux, Cron was configured to send an e-mail message containing the output of the automation script.

The e-mail message for each of the 24 builds contains an output for a successful Greenstone build. For Windows, Pycron maintains a log that contains two records for each automation script execution–one record indicating the start of execution, and one record indicating the end of execution and a return code. The terminating records for all 24 builds have a return code of zero, which indicates a successful execution of the automation script. In both cases, a visual inspection of the collection was also performed periodically to verify the success of the Scheduler.

Hourly Build of Two Collections

The focus of this experiment is to ensure that if multiple collections are scheduled to be rebuilt at the same time, they are successfully rebuilt. We scheduled the building of two collections on hourly intervals for 24 hours. A perusal of e-mail messages (for Linux) and the log (for Windows) verify that both collections were rebuilt successfully.

Daily Build of One Collection

The focus of this experiment is twofold. The first is to ensure correct daily execution of an automation script generated by the Scheduler. The second is to simulate a situation of a collection that has images added to it on a daily basis. We schedule one collection to be built daily for seven days. The collection starts with 10 images, and 10 images are added daily. In addition to the successful daily build, the collection did reflect the addition of the new images that arrived daily.

SCHEDULING IN THE LIBRARIAN INTERFACE

The Scheduler is a minimal, yet powerful tool for maintaining Greenstone collections. It hides the details concerning the collection building process, and also the details for scheduling a Cron task. However, the Scheduler has two main limitations.

The first is that the user is still required to know the syntax and command-line parameters for both the import and build commands in order to perform scheduling.

The second is that, currently, notification of collection building success—or failure—is still dependent on the version of Cron (and indirectly, the operating system it is running on) that is used. The Librarian Interface provides a user-friendly tool for building collections, including configuring the import and build commands. Therefore, it is ideal to extend the Librarian Interface to allow the configuration of the Scheduler as well.

Figure 6.19 depicts the Librarian Interface extension to support the scheduling of collection builds. Currently, the Create panel is displaying most of the parameters (*i.e.*, Schedule Options) for the Scheduler. Notice that no explicit options exist for the import and build commands.

This is because the import and build commands are created based on the arguments selected from the Import Options and Build Options panels. Therefore, the user no longer needs to know the exact syntax of the import and build commands.

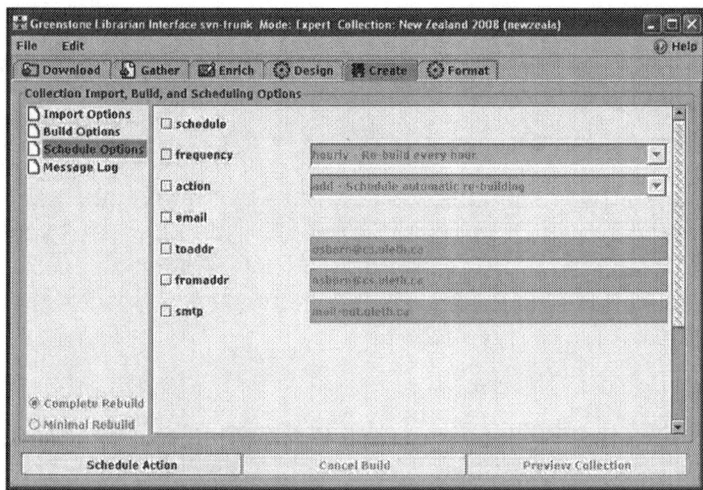

Fig. The Schedule Options Panel.

User Modes

The Librarian Interface has four modes of use—Library Assistant, Librarian, Library Systems Specialist, and Expert—stepwise increasing the functionality available to the user. It was important to determine which modes would have access to the Scheduling Options, and for those modes that were granted access, how much access each would be granted. It was decided that Library Systems Specialists and Experts would be provided access to the Scheduling Options. In addition to determining which options to make available to each user mode, it is also necessary to determine how the Scheduler would interact with the existing import and build functionality in the Librarian Interface.

Mode Level for Options

The Scheduler was first modified so that the passing of command-line arguments conformed with that of other Greenstone commands, such as import and build. This also allowed us to easily specify which user mode could have access to each argument when it is added as a Schedule Option in the Librarian Interface. The Expert user mode is granted full access to all Schedule Options, while Librarian Systems Specialist is only granted limited access to options. This user mode can only specify whether or not to schedule a collection build with the default values—a frequency of hourly, and no sending of e-mail.

Scheduling and Building

Another important decision was how the Scheduler would interact with the collection building functionality of the Librarian Interface. The question asked was, should scheduling be done at the same time as collection building, or be a completely separate task? For Expert mode, the functionality for Scheduling is separate from that of collection building. This is because an expert user may want to configure and manually re-build their collection before scheduling an automatic re-build of it. For Library System Specialist mode, the Scheduling functionality is done at the same time as collection building. If the specialist chooses to schedule, a new scheduled build is created. If the specialist chooses not to schedule, any existing scheduled builds are deleted.

Cron Event Logs

It is important to maintain logs that keep track of the outcome of a scheduled collection build. Both Vixie Cron and Pycron maintain a log that keeps track of the attempted execution of all scheduled tasks. Neither scheduling service keeps track of the success or failure of a scheduled task, nor do they keep track of the output of a task. In addition, to view logs created by Vixie Cron, the user must have root access. Another desirable feature of maintaining logs is the ability to be able to only record output that is considered important, and to disregard all other task output.

For example, if the output from the input and build commands of Greenstone is required, but the output from moving indices and classifiers is not considered important, the log should reflect this. Therefore, the Scheduler is modified in two ways to handle the logging of building script output. The first is to create a custom log for each execution of the automation script. The automation script creates a unique filename every time it is executed by using a timestamp. The second is to specify in the automation script which actions will have its output redirected to the logfile. The actions whose output is to be ignored will have its output redirected to the 'bit bucket'.

E-mail Notification

It is also important than an e-mail notification service be provided, which will inform users of the outcome of their scheduled collection build.

We handle e-mail notification from the Scheduler and Librarian Interface for the following reasons:

- *User Notification:* Whether Cron notifies users about the outcome of a scheduled task depends on the its implementation. For Vixie Cron, the outcome of a task is e-mailed to the owner of the task. Pycron does not send e-mail notification.
- *Flexibility of Notification:* In Vixie Cron it is possible to suppress e-mail notification, either by setting an environment variable to null, or by redirecting all output to a file or the 'bit bucket'. However, this is normally an all-or-nothing event—either all output, or none, is sent by e-mail. Similar to logging, a desirable feature would be to send e-mail that contains only the most important parts of the building process, and ignores other parts of the building process.

- *Greenstone E-mail Support:* Greenstone comes with a Perl e-mail script, that is a wrapper for the Perl sendmail command. The e-mail script is platform-independent. Therefore, it is ideal to use it to provide a uniform way to send e-mail concerning the execution of a scheduled task. In addition, the script does not require the piping of build output directly to it, but instead can send the contents of a file.

Therefore, both the Librarian Interface and the Scheduler are modified so that e-mail notification is handled in a uniform and user-friendly manner across all operating systems. First, options have been added to the Scheduler that are required for the Perl e-mail script—specifically, a flag to specify that e-mail will be sent (–e-mail), the sender (–fromaddr), receiver (–toaddr) and the e-mail server that will be used to send the e-mail (–smtp). Also, the corresponding fields exist in the Schedule Options pane of the Librarian Intcrfacc. In order to assist users in using the e-mail features of scheduling, the Librarian Interface attempts to populate the fields-toaddr,-fromaddr, and-smtp in the Schedule Options pane by consulting the configurations for the Librarian Interface and Greenstone. If suitable values are available from these sources, they are assigned to the appropriate fields. Second, the output from the building script must be captured and re-directed to the Perl e-mail script. The capturing of output already takes place, in the event log. This serves as the file that the e-mail script will send to the user. Also, since, it contains only the output that is considered important, this will be reflected in the e-mail message as well. Finally, the Scheduler is modified so that, if specified, the automation script will send an e-mail message containing the contents of the log to the specified recipient. An added bonus is that if e-mail is not specified, the log can still be consulted by the user if required.

Scheduled Building in Isolation

An important modification to the Scheduler is to ensure that a scheduled build is completed in its entirety without interference from another scheduled build. A build may take a significant amount of time depending on the size of the collection—from seconds for a small one to 33 hours for a collection containing 20 GB of raw text and 50 GB of metadata. To handle this, the automation script for the collection checks for a lock file, which indicates that a collection build is underway. If the file exists, the collection owner is notified via e-mail and information is placed in the event log. Otherwise, a lock file is created before the scheduled build begins, and is removed when the build finishes. This ensures that multiples builds do not occur concurrently.

EXAMPLE: COLLECTING PICTURES WHILE TRAVELLING

We present a simple application of scheduling from the Librarian Interface. In this scenario, we have a traveller who wants to post pictures of their trip in a Greenstone collection for her friends to view. Instead of waiting until the end of the trip, the traveller wants to post her pictures from each day, incrementally adding to the collection on a daily basis. The traveller does not want to worry about obtaining the Librarian Interface to rebuild the collection while traveling. Instead, she simply wants to upload the pictures to the import directory of her collection, and have her collection rebuilt automatically and on a daily basis.

This can be accomplished by setting up a scheduled, automatic rebuild of the collection of travel photos from the Librarian Interface. First, before departing, the traveller runs the Librarian Interface and creates a new collection. Then, the user selects the Create tab to display the collection creation pane. From here, clicking on Schedule Options will display the available options for setting up a scheduled, automatic collection build of the collection of travel pictures.

Figure depicts the available scheduling options, which are displayed with default and derived values as appropriate. Here, the traveller selects schedule, which indicates that she wants to set up a scheduled, automatic build. Also, she selects a frequency of hourly and an action of add.

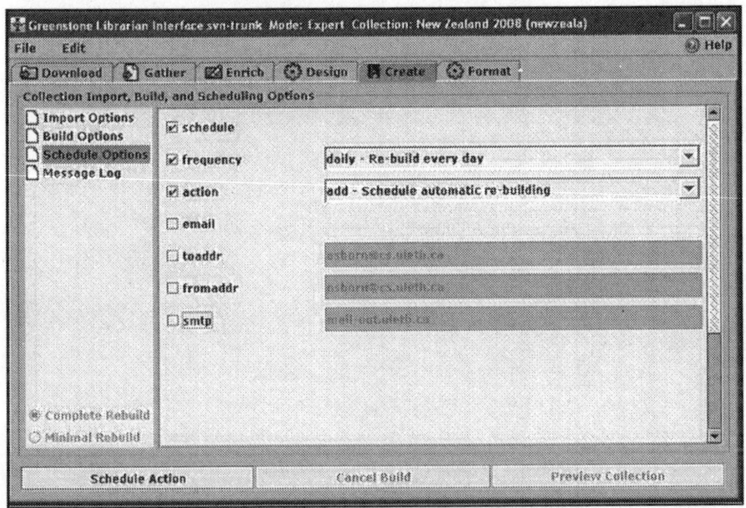

Fig. Build-First Day.

Next, the traveller clicks on Schedule Build. This will set up the building script for the collection of travel pics, as well as the crontab record that will indicate to Cron that the collection is to be rebuilt daily. The collection is now ready to be re-built while the traveller is away. At the end of the first day of travel, she uploads three pictures, which are added to the collection when the collection is re-built automatically overnight.

The updated collection is depicted in Figure. The next day, the traveller uploads three more pictures. When the collection is re-built overnight, these pictures are added to the existing collection.

Fig. Build-Second Day

Fig. Collection Build Scheduling.

Figure depicts the updated collection with the new pictures. Although not shown here, the user can switch to the Import Options and Build Options and select any options that are required for collection importing and building. These options are incorporated into the automatic building script that is created for the collection. In addition, the user can manually build and configure their collection as many times as necessary to confirm the right sequence is being performed, before setting up a scheduled, automatic build.

SECURITY AND DIGITAL LIBRARIES

Security is an important issue in digital library design. Security weaknesses in digital libraries, coupled with attacks or other types of failures, can lead to confidential information being inappropriately accessed, or loss of integrity of the data stored. These in turn can have a damaging effect on the trust of publishers or other content providers, can cause embarrassment or even economic loss to digital library owners, and can even lead to pain and suffering or other serious problems if urgently needed information is unavailable. There are many security requirements to consider because of the variety of different actors working with a digital library. Each of these actors has different security needs.

Thus, a digital library content provider might be concerned with protecting intellectual property rights and the terms of use of content, while a digital library user might be concerned with reliable access to content stored in the digital library. Requirements based on these needs sometimes are in conflict, which can make the security architecture of a digital library even more complex. The design of the security architecture of a digital library must go beyond simply adding one or a few modules to a previously designed system. This is because there may be security holes in pre-existing modules, and because difficulties can arise when attempting to integrate the modules.

The security architecture of a digital library must be designed so that security concerns are handled holistically. A security system designer must view the whole architecture and consider all of the applicable security factors when designing a secure digital library. The nature of a security attack may differ according to the architecture of the digital library; a distributed digital library has more security weaknesses than a centralized digital library. Security attacks can be categorised as physical attacks and logical attacks. A physical attack involves hardware security where keys, locks, cards, and visitor monitoring is used. A logical attack involves an attack on the content or digital library system. We focus on the logical attacks and software security of digital libraries.

SECURITY ISSUES WITH DIGITAL LIBRARIES

According to the DELOS Reference Model there are 6 main concepts in a digital library universe: content, user, functionality, architecture, quality, and policy. Each of these concepts has security issues that affect it.

Content

The content of a digital library includes the information objects that a digital library provides to the users. Some of the security issues involved are integrity and access control. Integrity requires that each object/resource has not been altered or changed by an unauthorised person. Access control encompasses two security requirements. The first is authentication where the user must log into the system while the second is confidentiality, which means that the content of an object is inaccessible by a person unless they have authorisation. Not all digital libraries are free; often content is provided to digital library users for a certain fee, whereupon access control is needed to protect the content.

Further, some content is inappropriate for some users, or targeted to particular user groups; there are a whole host of such other reasons for access control. Logical attacks such as hacking and message tampering can affect the integrity and confidentiality of the content. Improved information access in digital libraries has raised many issues that affect the management of digital libraries. Content Management, or more specifically Digital Rights Management, refers to the protection of content from the different logical security attacks and issues relating to intellectual property rights and authenticity.

Digital Rights Management

DRM provides content protection by encrypting the content and associating it with a digital licence. The licence identifies the user allowed to view the content, lists the content of the product, and states the rights the user has to the resource in a computer readable format using a digital rights expression language (DREL) or extensible Rights Markup Language (XrML) that also describes constraints and conditions. There are 7 technologies used to provide DRM. Table summarises the DRM components and supporting technology.

Each of these components involves mechanisms used to provide DRM:

- *Encryption:* Encryption techniques such as symmetric and asymmetric ciphers can be used to provide access control; public-key encryption is used in payment systems that control how and by whom the content is used. Symmetric ciphers using DES, 3DES, AES, and RC4 algorithms require the use of a shared secret key to encrypt data before it is sent. At the receiver's end the cipher text is decrypted using the same secret key. Symmetric ciphers depend on both the sender and receiver knowing the shared key. Asymmetric ciphers use a pair of keys, public and private, for each of the sender and the receiver. The public keys of both the sender and the receiver are known but the private key is kept secret. If encryption is performed using the public key then only the private key can be used for decryption and vice versa.

- *Passwords:* Stored strings must be matched by users desiring access.
- *Watermarking:* Characters or images are added to reflect ownership. Steganography is used to conceal data inside audio, video, or images. Different watermarking techniques have different aims; some watermarks might be visible while others invisible. Some watermarks are reversible; it depends on the desired use of the watermark and what is being protected.
- *Digital Signature:* Asymmetric encryption can be used. Likewise, hash algorithms such as MD5 and SHA can be used to create a signature.
- *Digital Fingerprint:* Digital fingerprints are a more powerful technique involving digital signatures and watermarking. The creator of the content creates a unique copy of the content marked for each user; the marks are user-specific hence, called fingerprints. Should a user illegally distribute the content, the creator can use search robots to find those copies.
- *Copy Detection Systems:* Search engines also can help locate such copied objects. Copydetecting browsers can protect digital content too.
- *Payment Systems:* Users must divulge personal information to pay for content. Installing payment systems can help protect digital content.

There is no standard mechanism for providing DRM, mainly due to the lack of regulations, however there are various systems and protocols introduced to provide content management and support fair usage policies. There is a tradeoff between security and performance. Nadeem and Javed use a Pentium-4, 2.4 GHz machine running Microsoft Windows XP operating system, encrypt 20527 bytes to 2323398 bytes of data using DES, 3DES, and AES.

For 20527 bytes of data it took 2 seconds to encrypt using the DES algorithm and 4 seconds to encrypt using the AES algorithm. It can be seen that the more complex the encryption algorithm the longer it takes to encrypt the data. In another study, encrypting data with the RSA algorithm using a key size of 1024 took 0.08 milliseconds/operation on an Intel Core 2 1.83 GHz processor under Windows Vista in 32-bit mode, while using a key size of 2048 took 0.16 milliseconds/operation.

User

The User in a digital library refers to 'the various actors entitled to interact with digital libraries'. Digital libraries connect the different actors with the information they have and allow the users to consume old or generate new information. Security issues relating to the users of a digital library intersect with content issues. A main logical security issue relating to users and content is access control. Different access control requirements arise for distributed systems to ensure both confidentiality and authentication:

- Access control must be applied and enforced at a distributed platform level, so should be scalable and available at various levels of granularity.
- Access control models should allow a varied definition of access rights depending on different information and must be dynamic where changes to policies are easily made and easy to manage.
- 'Access control models must allow high-level specification of access rights.'

Digital library users may need to be authenticated before they can access content. Global/universal identification may not suffice. A service provider that provides content based on a non-identity based criteria like age will not benefit from global identification because there is no way to verify the authenticated user's personal information. Usernames and passwords are not efficient ways to provide authentication. One of the most widely used authentication protocols is Kerberos.

It is a client–server model, which secures communication with servers on a local network. Developed at MIT in the 1980s to provide security across a large campus network, it is based on the Needham-Schroeder protocol and has now been standardised and included in many operating systems such as UNIX, Linux, Windows 2000, NT, XP, etc. Kerberos is used as an authentication protocol in cases where attackers monitor network traffic to intercept passwords. It secures communication, provides single sign on and mutual authentication, and does not send a user's password in the clear on an insecure network.

An alternative solution suitable for digital libraries is to represent information about an individual using credentials. Credentials are "abstract objects which contain statements expressing knowledge or information from a definite context." Credentials do not specify direct information about a client and their attributes, they describe the local environment and context in which the requests originate. Digital credentials can be used as a means of authentication in providing DL access control. Two agents can be used to assist in the management: a personal security assistant and a server security assistant, to manage digital credentials using a client/server model. The server must notify the client of the credentials required for the current request. The client then sends its credentials for authentication.

The client must have some trust of the server to give its credentials, which raises privacy issues. The personal security assistant is used to obtain credentials on behalf of the client, store the credentials, parse and interpret the required credentials, and manage the acceptance policies. A server security assistant is available to specify the credential acceptance policies and their usage. There is a tradeoff between flexibility and security that must be considered when choosing an access control model.

Access Matrix Model

This conceptual model specifies the rights that each subject possesses for each object. Actions on objects are allowed or denied based on the access rights specified.

There are 2 implementations of the AMM:

- An Access Control List provides a direct mapping of each object the subjects are allowed to access, and their usage right; and
- A Capability List defines the objects each subject is allowed to access and the usage rights.

Access control lists and capability lists are not suitable for distributed systems. Their limitations lead to multiple problems. ACL provides limited expressibility of policies. Any change in the policies will propagate in the system/ application. Authentication in a system that uses ACL solely is a problem because using username and password in a distributed system is not practical.

In a distributed system, administration of the system should be decentralised by delegation to reduce the overhead. The owner of the object specifies a policy in ACL. If an overall policy is specified by an entity higher than the object owner, then conflicts may occur in the access rights. The number of administrative entities in a distributed system can be very large. Not all the administrators may have trust amongst themselves, resulting in incorrectly defined policies. For example, admin A may trust B but not C, however B may trust C. If A were to define policy for B then it would be implicitly applicable to C, causing problems.

Role-based Access Control

Role-based access control involves policies that regulate information access based on the activities the users perform. Such policies require the definition of roles in the system: "a set of actions and responsibilities associated with a particular working activity". Permissions are assigned to roles instead of individual users. Specifying user authorisation involves 2 steps: first assigning the user to a role, second defining the access control that the role has over certain objects. RBAC is easier to manage and is more extensible than ACL. However RBAC doesn't flexibly handle constraints, where a user with a specific role may need specific permission on an object.

An example of RBAC architecture addressing key limitations is OASIS, for use in distributed systems. Role management in OASIS is decentralised and service specific. OASIS is integrated with an event-based middleware that notifies applications of any environmental changes. Roles are parameterised by applications and services to define their client roles, and to enforce policies for role activation and service invocation within each session. Role membership certificates (RMC) are returned to each user on successful login, to be used as a credential to activate other roles. RBAC is suitable for use with digital libraries because it supports decentralised architectures and varying roles, however RBAC doesn't allow for the definition of different roles in a collaborative group.

Task-based Access Control

The Task-based access control model extends subject/object access control by allowing the definition of domains by task-based contextual information. Steps required to perform the task are used to define access control; the steps are associated with a protection state containing a set of permissions for each state, which change according to the task. TBAC uses dynamic management of permissions. TBAC systems are limited to defining contexts in relation to activities, tasks, or workflow progress. Since, it is implemented by recording usage and validity of permissions, therefore, TBAC requires a central access control module to manage permissions activation and deactivation in a just-in-time fashion.

Team-based Access Control

RBAC doesn't address cases where group members of different roles want to collaborate in a single group. The TMAC model defines collaboration by user context and object context. "User context provides a way of identifying specific users playing a role on a team at any given moment" while object context defines the objects required. TMAC offers the advantages of RBAC along with ability to specify fine-grained control on users and on object instances.

A scalable access control data structure can be used with large collections, applying concepts of team based access control, focusing mainly on the access control data structure, and employing an access control framework called Document Access Control Method (DACM) with a Document Storage System (DocSS). DACM allows the decentralised administration of privileges, the definition of different rule sets to control a single collection, and different delegation patterns as models. Current object access control policies use an array of rules to record the privileges each subject is allowed to each object.

This is impractical to manage in the large data collections found in digital libraries. DACM solves this problem by finding symmetries in a permission function to allow a brief expression without losing important distinctions.

Content-based Access Control

Another approach to access control models involves defining models according to content. This approach is applicable in digital libraries and distributed systems, where the access rights to the user are dynamic and may change with each login. Content-based access control policies are very well suited for digital libraries and distributed systems. Recent research has proposed different models; most use digital credentials for authentication, but vary in the definition/storage of the policy.

An important content-based access control model introduces a contentbased access control system, Digital Library Authorisation System, that utilises the Digital Library Authorisation Model (DLAM). Subject, object, and privilege sets can't be used to define policies in digital libraries mainly because DLs are dynamic with large collections of data and subjects. It defines access control policies based on subject qualifications and characteristics. DLAM provides a means to specify the qualifications and characteristics of subjects. It uses content dependant and independent access control and allows the definition of policies with varied granularity.

Functionality

The concept of functionality encompasses the services that a Digital Library offers to its users. The minimum functions of a Digital Library include adding new objects to the library or searching and browsing the library and other functions relating to DL management. A security attack that can affect the functionality of the Digital Library is a Denial of Service attack, which can affect the performance of the system and prevent users from accessing the system.

Architecture

Digital libraries are complex forms of information systems, interoperable across different libraries and so require an architectural framework mapping content and functionality onto software and hardware components. There are various models for architecture, *e.g.*, client-server, peer-to-peer, and distributed. All these require the protection of the communication channels between 2 parties, where sensitive data might be transferred. Securing the connections involves different layers—Internet, transport, or application layer-depending on the architecture of the system. The distributed model is scalable and flexible.

It is useful when building a digital library with changing content from different sources and offers potential for increased reliability. The security requirements for a distributed digital library are challenging, since, the content and operations are decentralised. Fault tolerance and error recovery are issues that affect a distributed system. Replication is used to increase the availability of the system. While this approach solves problems with denial of service attacks, it complicates the protection of the content because a replica of the content exists. The client-server model doesn't have the same security problems as a general distributed model, however, it presents a major security weakness, the server being a single point of failure. Attacks are concentrated on one server rather than on the multiple replicas of a distributed model.

Quality

The content and behaviour of a Digital Library is characterised and evaluated by quality parameters. Quality is a concept not only used to classify functionality and content, but also used with objects and services. Some of the parameters are automatically measured and are objective while others are considered subjective; some are measured through user evaluations.

Policy

Policy is the concept that represents the different regulations and conditions that govern the interaction between the Digital Library and users. Policy supports both extrinsic and intrinsic interactions and their definition and modification. Examples of security issues relating to policies include providing digital rights management, privacy, and confidentiality of the content and users, defining user behaviour, and collection delivery.

4

Digital Libraries in the Networked Environment in India

USE OF COMPUTERS IN LIBRARY AND PRO-COGNITIVE FUNCTIONS

SYNTACTIC ANALYSIS OF NATURAL LANGUAGE BY COMPUTER

The relevance of automated syntactic analysis to library pro-cognitive systems lies in machine processing, and in eventual machine 'understanding,' of natural language text. There is no thought that syntactic analysis alone - whether by man or machine - is sufficient to provide a useful approximation to understanding. On the other hand, there is no doubt that appreciation of the syntactic structure of natural-language text is a part, and an important part, of the over-all problem. Bobrow surveyed the work that has been done, and is being done, towards automation of syntactic analysis of English.

The efforts to automate syntactic analysis have been, essentially, efforts to implement various theories of grammar through the preparation of computer programmes that operate on natural-language text in the form of strings of encoded alphanumeric characters. The output of a successful syntactic-analysis programme is one or more sets of.assignments of the words of a sentence to grammatical categories plus, for each set of assignments, a representation of the grammatical structure of the sentence.

The grammars that have been used as bases for syntactic-analysis programmes include dependency grammars, phrase-structure grammars with continuous and with discontinuous constituents, predictive grammars, string transformation grammars, and phrase-structure transformational grammars. The main characteristics of, and differences among, these grammars are set forth in Bobrow's report.

Although it is too early to say with assurance which of them is best for our purposes much expert intuition favours the phrase-structure, transformational approach. Many of the programmes that have been successful in making syntactic analyses have depended upon a distinction between 'function words' and 'content words.' The distinction is a simple and familiar one.

Function words are words such as 'and', 'or', 'to', 'from', 'a', 'an', 'the', 'neither', 'nor', 'if', and 'whether'. Content words are words such as 'grammar', 'equivalent', 'structural', 'diagram', 'sentence', 'minimum', 'weekly', 'accept', and 'develop'. There are, of course, many more types of content words than of function words. It is therefore reasonable to store in a computer memory very detailed descriptions of the functions, characteristics, idiomatic uses, and so forth, of the function words. The successful analytic programmes have, in addition, employed dictionaries containing, for each content word, the grammatical categories into which it is normally expected to fall. It is the intention here, not to give a complete summary of Bobrow's report, but rather to relate the idea of syntactic analysis by computer to the over-all picture set forth in Part 1. Perhaps the best way to do that is to show in diagrammatic form some of the analyses that are described in detail by Bobrow.

The notion of 'dependency' gives a direction and a hierarchical structure to syntactic relations. Adjectives depend on nouns, nouns depend on verbs and prepositions, adverbs and auxiliary verbs depend on main verbs, prepositions depend on the words modified by their phrases, and so forth. The system of dependency can be represented diagrammatically in the way illustrated for the sentences, 'The man treats the boy and the girl in the park,'

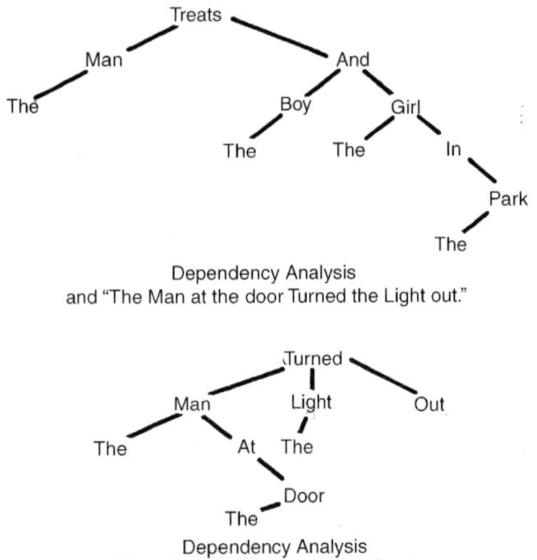

Fig. Dependency Analysis

This second sentence will be used to illustrate other grammars also, in order to display similarities and differences. Computer programmes capable of implementing dependency analysis have been developed or described by Hays of the RAND Corporation, by Kelly of the RAND Corporation, by Gross of M.I.T., by Klein and Simmons of the System Development Corporation, and by several

Russian workers, including Moloshnava and Andreyev. In a phrase-structure analysis that assumes continuous, immediate constituents, t the diagrammatic representation is again treelike, but the nodes of the branching structure are, at all levels except the lowest, syntactic or grammatical categories. At the lowest level, the actual words of the sentence appear. An immediate-constituent analysis of 'The man ate the apple' is shown in the diagram.

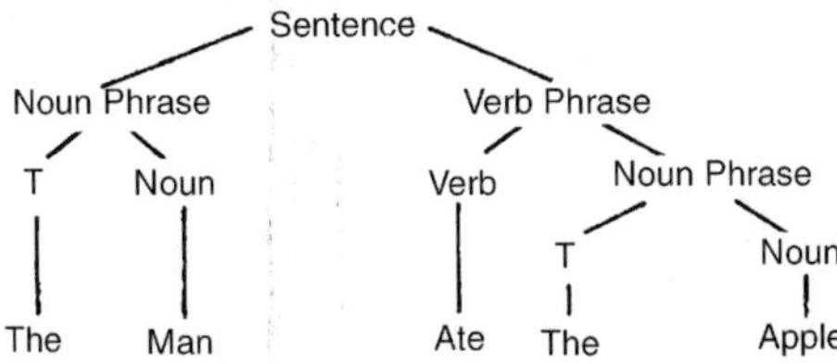

Fig. An Immediate-constituent Analysis of "The Man Ate the Apple"

The analysis starts at the bottom of the diagram with the string of words and proceeds to discover a superstructure consistent with their grammatical class memberships.

However, the analysis may involve trial-and-error differentiation downward from assumed categories to strings of words. The analysis substitutes for 'Sentence' the two category names, 'Noun Phrase' and 'Verb Phrase.' It then substitutes for 'Noun Phrase' the category names 'Definite Article' and 'Noun.'

For 'Verb Phrase' it substitutes 'Verb' and 'Noun Phrase.' It is then in a position to substitute actual words for three of the category names. 'Noun Phrase,' however, has to be passed through one more stage of analysis before the substitution of actual words can be made. The result of the analysis—the diagram—displays the roles of the individual words of the sentence and, in addition, shows how the several roles are interrelated.

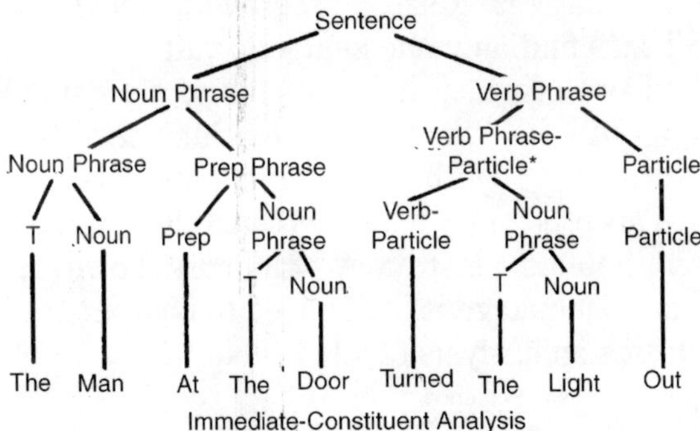

Fig. Immediate-constituent Analysis of 'The Man at the Door turned the Light Out.'

In the foregoing example, the analysis proceeded in a succession of binary branchings. An alternative formulation makes use of multiple branching to produce coordinate structures with fewer levels. Bobrow compares binary structure and coordinate structure in the phrase, 'the old black heavy stone.'

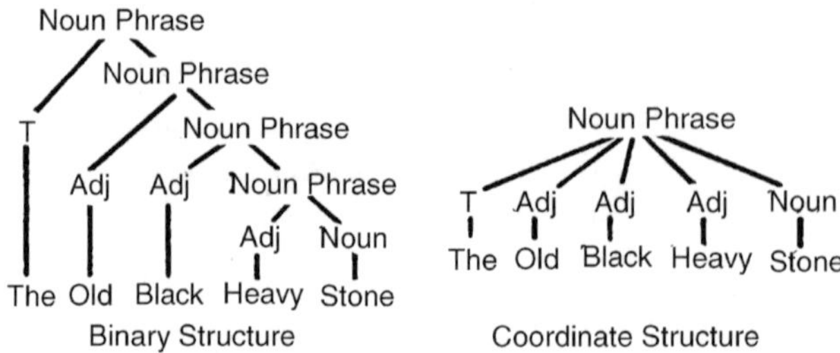

Fig. Binary Structure and Coordinate Structure

Computer programmes capable of making immediate constituent analyses have been developed or described by Robinson of the RAND Corporation, Cocke of the International Business Machines Corporation, and Klein of the System Development Corporation. Kuno and Oettinger of Harvard have developed extensively the technique of predictive analysis advocated by Rhodes of the National Bureau of Standards. Predictive analysis takes advantage of the fact that, once he has heard the beginning of a sentence, the listener can rule out many of the myriad syntactic patterns into which sentences are, a priori, capable of falling. Predictive analyses keep track only of the alternative interpretations that are consistent with the part of the sentence that has already been analysed. At the very beginning, there are usually but few alternatives, for then the interpretations are not differentiated.

In the midcourse of an analysis, there may be many possible ways in which the sentence can go. At the end, however, the analysis should converge upon one pattern of grammatical categories, or, at any rate, upon a set of patterns among which a choice can be made on the basis of semantic interpretation of the sentence itself and of its context. The Kuno Oettinger programmes determine all the alternatives. Related programmes developed by Lindsay of the University of Texas find only one syntactic pattern but provide diagnostic information on the basis of which it is possible to clear up misinterpretation through 'postediting.' A minor problem for machine analysis is introduced by the fact that two words may together fill a grammatical category without being contiguous in text. This problem is not faced squarely by immediate-constituent grammars. In discontinuous-constituent grammars, however, the problem is recognised, and a special linkage is introduced to connect the separated parts. The diagram illustrates an analysis of 'He called her up.'

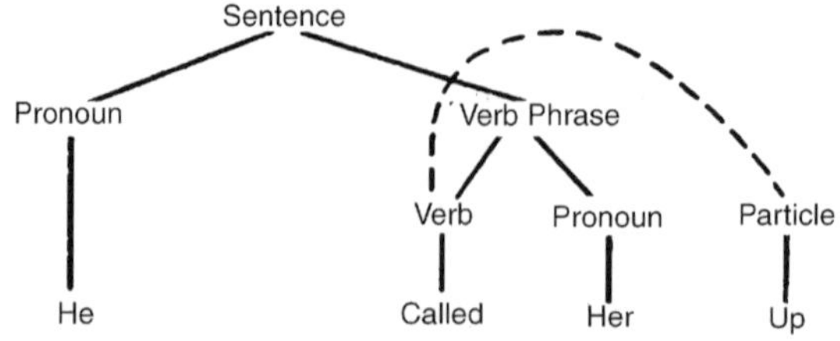

Fig. Discontinous-Constituent Analysis He Called Her Up

The linkage from 'Verb' to 'Particle' connects 'up' to 'called,' from which it has been separated by 'her.' The diagram shows a discontinuous-constituent analysis of the standard sentence, 'The man at the door turned the light out.'

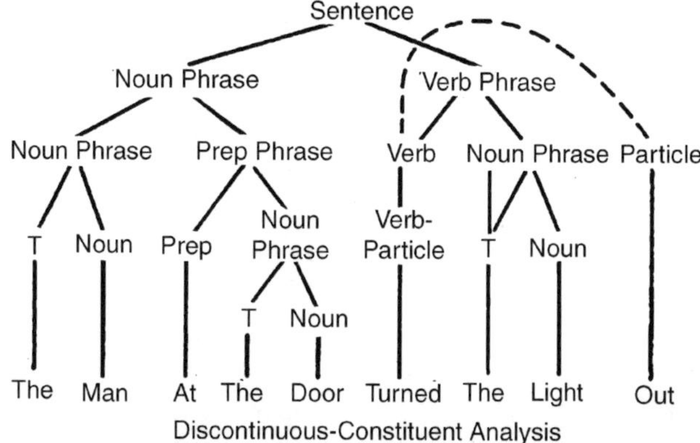

Fig. Discontinous-Constituent Analysis of the Standard Sentence

For the purposes of library pro cognitive systems, the most important problem in this subject area may well be one raised by Chomsky. Chomsky was concerned that two expressions of the same idea, such as 'The man drives the car' and 'The car is driven by the man' do not have similar phrase structures and do not yield similar diagrams when analysed in the ways we have been discussing. Chomsky handled this problem by setting up 'transformation rules' that transform one sentence into another, or combine *n* sentences into one, or subdivide one sentence into *n* sentences.

For example, one transformation takes a sentence from active voice to passive voice. Another transformation combines two single clause sentences into a compound sentence. With transformation rules, one can build up complex syntactic structures from simple ones or analyse complex syntactic structures into simple ones. Bobrow gives an example in which the simple statements are derived from the question, 'What are the airfields in Ohio having runways longer than two miles?' Analysis and synthesis based on such transformations will surely be important for machine-aided organisation of the body of knowledge.

- X's are the airfields
- The airfields are in Ohio
- The airfields have runways
- The runways are long
- Two miles is long

The transformational-grammar approach handles the discontinuous-constituent problem neatly. A transformation changes 'turned the light out' into 'turned out the light.' As the diagram shows, the analysis then proceeds without any difficulty.

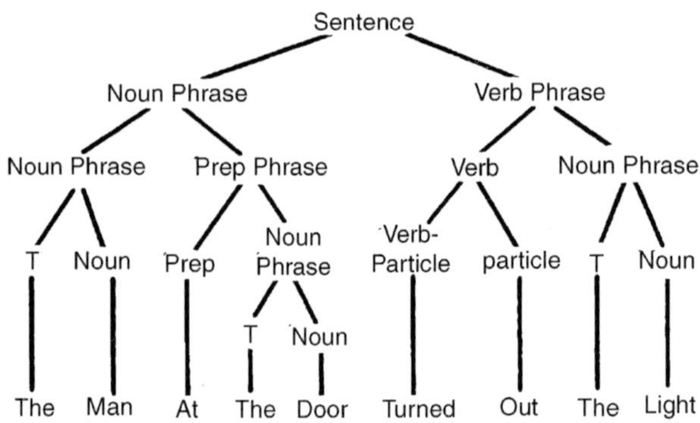

Fig. Intermediate Stage in Chomsky's Transformational Derivation

Walker and Bartlett of the Mitre Corporation are developing a parsing programme based on a transformational grammar. Harris and his associates at the University of Pennsylvania have developed a method of syntactic analysis that is intermediate between constituent analysis and transformational analysis. Although their method does not lend itself to representation by a tree diagram, a rough idea of its approach is conveyed by relating some of its terms to our standard sentence. In the sentence, the 'string center' is . . . man . . . turned out . . . light.' One 'the' is the 'left adjunct' of 'man,' and the other is the 'left adjunct' of 'light'. 'At the door' is the 'right adjunct' of 'man.' This 'string-transformational grammar' has been implemented in the form of computer programmes. The 'Baseball' programme developed by Green and associates at the Lincoln Laboratory - a programme capable of answering questions about the outcomes of the baseball games played in the major leagues during one season - has a methodological kinship to the Pennsylvania work.

From Bobrow's survey, it is clear that automation of syntactic analysis is possible. Indeed, there are several operating syntactic-analysis programmes. It is equally clear, however, that syntactic analysis is only a part - and perhaps, relatively, only a small part - of the over-all problem. The fact is that even the best analysis programmes produce discouragingly many alternative patterns. Selection among the alternatives has to be made on non-syntactic grounds, and there has not been much progress towards automation of that selection.

Furthermore, it is evident that one is a very long way from understanding what is being said when all he knows is the pattern or structure of syntactic categories into which the words of the message fit. The question was raised in Part I, whether it is desirable, in formulating the basic concepts of this field, to separate syntactic and semantic factors into the two insulated bins of a rigid dichotomy, or whether, as subtler and subtler distinctions are made in the process now called syntactic analysis, that process will start to become semantic as well as syntactic. Although we are not in a position to decide, one way or the other, on that question, we have an intuitive feeling that the latter is more promising as a line of development. We should, in this connection, refer to work that we regard as extremely promising, work being carried out by F.B. Thompson and his colleagues.

RESEARCH ON QUANTITATIVE ASPECTS OF FILES AND TEXT

Two studies by Grignetti deal with quantitative aspects of representations of information in digital memories. The first study concerns the average length of representations of descriptions of documents or, in greater generality, the average length of representations of 'terms'. The second concerns the informational measure 'entropy' - or, to look at it the other way around, the redundancy - of English text considered as a string of _ words. Thus both studies bear upon the amount of memory required to store library information: the first with indexes, the second with actual text.

ON THE LENGTH OF A CLASS OF SERIAL FILES

From one point of view, the over-all organisation and concept of a library or of a pro-cognitive system is a more important thing to grasp, or to improve, than is the efficiency of a low-level 'detail' function. On the other hand, a few functions that appear from one point of view to be mere details, to occupy-low levels in the over-all system, are seen from another point of view to be both basic and ubiquitous. One of these functions that looks like a technical detail from one standpoint and like something very basic and general from another is the encoding of elements of information for storage in a digital memory. Let us, for the purposes of this discussion, adopt the point of view from which it seems important. As soon as we do that we may be prepared to examine subcategories, and one of the most conspicuous of these is the subcategory that includes catalogues and indexes.

The study to be summarised deals with such files of information. Perhaps the best schema to keep in mind while thinking about this problem is the schema of an index consisting of the names or numbers of the documents in a collection and, associated with each name or number, a list of terms or descriptors that characterise the corresponding document according to some coordinate indexing system. The problem under consideration is how to encode the terms. The object is to be economical in the use of storage space and, at the same time, to make it easy for a computer to decode the representation and determine the names or numbers of specified documents. One of the most widely used techniques for representing terms is simply to spell them out in full or to record readable abbreviations of them. The direct way to encode such representations for storage in digital memory is to assign a binary code to each character in the character ensemble and to store the binary code patterns.

That technique has the disadvantage of using much more memory space than is necessary. A technique that is more economical of memory space is to number all the terms that may be used and to represent in memory in association with each item, not the corresponding terms themselves, but the numbers that were assigned to them. Since there are sometimes several terms per document, it is important not to let the numbers that represent different terms run together in such a way as to preclude subdivision of the over-all representation into its parts. The encodings of the sets of terms associated with different documents must also be kept separable.

In the past, people have kept codes separable either by using special characters as separators or by adding enough leading zeros to the short codes to make all the codes the same length. The prevailing opinion has been that the use of separators leads to more compact files than the use of fixed-. length codes. The first thing Grignetti did was to analyse that comparison. It turned out that, on the average, and under certain reasonable assumptions, the fixed-length code is actually shorter than the variable length code plus separator. If one thinks about this question with simple, schematic examples in mind, he is likely to doubt this conclusion of Grignetti's and to agree with the prevailing opinion that Grignetti finds incorrect.

However, Grignetti's conclusion becomes quite obvious as soon as attention is focused upon large filing systems in which the list of legal terms is long. Consider, for example, that, of a list of nearly 1000 terms, almost 90 per cent would be represented by three-digit codes. About 9 per cent would require one leading zero, and about 1 per cent would require two leading zeros to bring them up to the 'fixed' length of three digits. In his work on coding efficiency, Grignetti also examined the notion that products of prime numbers might provide the basis for an effective coding system for the purpose we are considering here. In such a system, each term would be assigned a prime number, and the set of terms associated with a particular item would be represented by the product of the prime numbers associated with the members of the set.

Grignetti was able to show conclusively that the prime-number code is an inefficient code, less good than either variant of the elementary system considered in the foregoing paragraphs. The preliminary enquiries just described led Grignetti to look for a truly efficient coding system for terms. He found one. He calls it the 'combinational code.' It is fairly easy to construct a combinational code. First, one has to decide the maximum number of terms that will be associated with an item, say, five. Second, he examines the list of legal terms, numbers the individual terms, and makes up all the possible combinations of term numbers, taken five or fewer at a time. Third, he orders the numbers corresponding to the terms of each combination in a sequence of increasing magnitude. Fourth, he reorders the list of combinations according to a criterion that takes into account primarily the magnitude of the largest number in the subset but also, secondarily, the number of numbers in the subset.

Finally, he assigns integers in increasing sequence to the members of the reordered list. Grignetti gives an analytical procedure for encoding and decoding. He points out that the procedure does not have to be changed, and that existing code numbers do not have to be altered, when new terms are added to the list of legal terms. Finally, he shows that the combinational code is the shortest possible code.

ENTROPY OF WORDS IN PRINTED ENGLISH

Grignetti's interest was attracted to the question of the representational efficiency of direct encodings of the strings of *words* that constitute text by the consideration. That storage of the body of knowledge in processible memories will be an important basis for pro-cognitive systems. In order to estimate the representational efficiency, it is natural to compare determinations of the number of bits required to store a typical segment of text with estimates of the actual information content of the text. The classical estimate of the information measure of a typical word of text is the one made by Shannon in 1951 on the assumption that the frequency of occurrence of word types is sufficiently approximated by Zipf's famous law. Shannon's estimate of the information measure, or entropy, was 11.82 bits per word.

However, Berner using roughly the approximation that Shannon used, calculated that words could be stored, on the average, in 10.76 bits of memory space - with the aid of a compression code that was obviously not optimal. That led Grignetti to examine Shannon's results closely. By a method slightly different from Shannon's, a method that seems straightforward and in which no flaw has been detected, Grignetti found the information measure to be 9.7 or 9.8 bits per word.

From one point of view, the difference, which is only 2 bits per word, does not seem likely to have much practical significance. From another point of view, however, the important question is whether or not further work on encoding of text seems to be intellectually attractive. If it seems attractive, then it is possible, and perhaps likely, that a coding scheme will be found that is highly efficient in use of memory space and, at the same time, economical in respect of processing. On the other hand, if further work is not intellectually attractive, there is not likely to be an increase in either the efficiency of the use of space or the economy of encoding and decoding. Perhaps the 2 bits per word will have a stimulating effect. Clearly, the point on which study should now concentrate is the simplification of encoding and decoding.

A MEASURE OF THE EFFECTIVENESS OF INFORMATION-RETRIEVAL SYSTEMS

To some information-retrieval systems, a particularly simple schema is appropriate. The system is a 'black box' that contains a collection or set of items and that, from time to time, either spontaneously or in response to a request, offers a subset of its contents to one of its subscribers and withholds the complementary subset. An item may be thought of as a document. A subscriber may be thought of as simply a criterion: to the subscriber, an item is either pertinent or not pertinent. If one considers a single item of the collection and focuses his attention upon a particular occasion—a particular request from a subscriber or a particular spontaneous offering by the system.

Note that only two of the relative frequencies are independent, for the sum over the four categories must be unity, and the fraction of the items that meets the subscriber's criterion of pertinence is assumed to be fixed. Note, also, that there has to be some way to ascertain the pertinence or non-pertinence of withheld items. Investigating the problem of evaluation of effectiveness, Swets found that eight of the ten studies that met his criterion of pertinence reduced the analysis to two-by-two contingency tables. However, in none of the studies was advantage taken of the fact that evaluative procedures have been developed for, and found useful in, other fields of application in which performance may be summarised in two-by-two contingency tables. Swets therefore adapted some of the apparatus of statistical decision theory to the information-retrieval context and proposed a measure of merit, a measure that quantifies the ability of the system to maximize the expected value of a retrieval trial, *i.e.*, of an offering or withholding of an individual item on a particular occasion. The measure takes into account the relative frequency and the utility of each of the four categories in the two-by-two table. We shall not review here Swets's explanation of its derivation.

Let it suffice to say that an assumption of normality of distribution is involved, that the measure is based on maximum-likelihood statistics, and that, given the relative frequencies of hits and false drops in a particular sample, one can read the value of the measure from an available table or graph. The measure is simple, convenient, and appropriate. It gives definite meaning to the concept, the 'basic discriminating power' of an information-retrieval system.

The measure clearly separates discriminating power from mere willingness to yield output, thus avoiding a confusion that has been rife these last several years and that appears to be at the root of many informational difficulties. Moreover, the measure brings with it a well-developed system of procedures that facilitate analysis and interpretation of data. We expect Swets's measure to prove useful in evaluation of information systems. The main obstacle may lie in determination of the pertinence of withheld items. That obstacle is wide. It causes trouble for all the approaches to evaluation of performance in retrieval of information from large collections.

LIBRARIES AND QUESTION ANSWERING SYSTEMS

Marill's Report, 'Libraries and Question Answering Systems,' laid the groundwork for subsequent research on question-answering systems. The report consists of three parts:

- Two Concepts of a Library,
- Question-Answering Systems and
- Semantic Nets: Informal Introduction.

The first of the 'two concepts of a library' is a schematisation of a present-day library. In the schema, the library consists of the collection of documents, the 'tag' system, and the retrieval system that makes use of the tags to retrieve desired documents. The contributions that technology can make within this first concept are acceleration of document handling, automation of the process of 'tagging' and improvement of the retrieval process.

Marill argues that this first concept, instrumented on a modest scale, would yield unsatisfactory results, and that, carried to its logical limit, it would be absurd. The second concept of a library is one in which the primary function is to provide not documents but information. The 'system' of the second concept will be able to 'read' and 'comprehend' the documents themselves and not merely their tags. It will have a high capability for organising the information internally. It will be able to accept questions worded in natural English. If it has the requisite information available, it will answer the questions in natural English. Thus Marill advocates a very sophisticated pro-cognitive system. He is concerned that people may believe the goal unreachable because it will be thought to require that inanimate mechanisms 'think.'

Marill refers to the question-answering system called 'Baseball' to forestall that misconception. In his discussion of question-answering systems, Marill defines the primary concepts: the corpus, the question, and the answer. The corpus consists of a set of quantificational schemata and their attendant predicate definitions, one definition for each predicate in the corpus. Thus Marill immediately seizes upon a predicate calculus as the formalism for representation of the information in the body of knowledge. There are two kinds of questions: questions satisfied by yes-no answers, and questions that require sentence answers. Answers, therefore, are also of two types: yes-no answers and sentence answers. The answer to a yes-no question is 'yes' if the question can be deduced from the corpus - if there exists a deduction that has the sentences of the corpus as premises and the question as the last line. The answer is 'no' if the negation of the question can be deduced from the corpus. There is no answer if neither the question nor its negation can be deduced from the corpus.

A sentence qualifies as a sentence answer if the sentence can be deduced from the corpus and if the schema of the sentence is the same as the schema of the question when the question is in statement form. There can be only one yes-no answer, but there can be any number of sentence answers. Marill's treatment of semantic nets is an extension and formalisation of the discussion of relational networks given in Part 1. Marill takes the view that the proper structural analysis of a sentence is given by the quantificational schema of that sentence, as understood in symbolic logic. To this, he adds the view that the meaning of a one-place predicate is identified, ultimately, with the set of objects of which the predicate is true, and the meaning of a two-place predicate is identified with the set of all ordered pairs of objects of which the predicate is true, and so forth. Finally, he adds the notion that the meaning of an object is identified with, first, the set of one-place predicates that are true of the object, and, second, the set of two-place predicates that are true of it and something else, and so forth. The sets with which meanings are identified are extremely large. The machine cannot be required to prove its 'understanding' of a meaning by producing all the members of the sets. Marill maintains that it is enough for the machine to produce a convincingly large sample. The usual representation of a quantificational schema has the form of a string of symbols. Marill views the semantic net as an alternative notation, equivalent to the string notation, but more promising for computer exploitation. To demonstrate the relation between semantic nets and string-form schemata, Marill starts with three simple statements in string notation and transmutes them, by degrees, into diagrams in which lines tie together the several instances of a variable. The elements of a semantic net in Marill's exposition are the following:

- *Rectangles*—which represent the truth functions corresponding to logical operators and their arguments. Each rectangle has one terminal for each argument.
- *Diamonds*—which represent quantifiers. There are two types, corresponding to 'some' and 'all.'
- *A triangle with point down*—which represents 'sentence.' This triangle contains an 'S.'
- *A circle*—which represents a predicate. The circle has as many terminals as there are places in the predicate.
- *A triangle with point up*—which represents an individual.

Mariu gives six rules governing the combination of elements and the formation of semantic nets. The rules are:

- Connecting a predicate to a sentence symbol forms a sentence.
- Inserting a negation rectangle between the sentence symbol and the predicate negates the sentence.
- To connect two sentences, divert their predicates to a two-place truth-function rectangle and connect it to a single sentence-symbol triangle.
- To add a quantifier to a sentence, insert it in the line between the sentence symbol and its nearest neighbour.
- To terminate an unterminated predicate, attach an individual object

to the unused terminal, or connect that terminal to a quantifier that is already in the diagram of the sentence.

- To merge two or more networks into one: for each individual, overlay all the triangles that represent the individual, retaining all the lines that are attached to any of the triangles; associate all the occurrences of the same predicate by connecting them with 'association lines.'

In 'Semantic Nets: An Informal Introduction,' Marill presents diagrams to illustrate the rules and to demonstrate the interpretation of moderately complex semantic nets. Marill's diagrams and discussion make it clear that the semantic net is formally equivalent to the conventional representation of a system of statements in predicate calculus. Marill believes that semantic nets afford a promising path into computer representation and processing of complex systems of relations.

STUDIES OF COMPUTER TECHNIQUES AND PROCEDURES

The following studies are concerned with early steps along the course from present digital-computer system to future pro-cognitive systems. Let us consider the studies in the order of their locations along that course. The first ones were intended merely to make it convenient to carry out some of the functions that are required in research on library and pro-cognitive problems or in the efficient use of large collections of documents. The last ones in the sequence were intended to explore functions that we think will actually be involved in future pro-cognitive systems.

AN 'EXECUTIVE' PROGRAMME TO FACILITATE THE USE OF THE PDP-1 COMPUTER

One of the first needs of the study was a computer programme to facilitate the programming and use of the laboratory's digital computer. The computer is a small but excellent machine, Digital Equipment Corporation PDP-I, specialised to facilitate interaction with users who work 'on line.' The PDP-1 has an oscilloscope display with light pen, several electric typewriters, a set of programmable relays, an analogue-to-digital converter, and an assortment of switches and buttons. Its primary memory is small but it is capable of transferring information rapidly between the primary memory and a secondary drum memory that holds about 90,000 eighteen-bit words. Associated with the computer are two magnetic-tape units. With the computer, it is possible to implement, in a preliminary and schematic way, several of the functions that were described in Part I as functions desirable in a pro-cognitive system. One encounters two main difficulties in trying to do, with the PDP-1 computer, research oriented towards a future period in which information-processing machines will have more advanced capabilities.

First, although the machine is reasonably fast, and although its secondary and tertiary memories make it possible to work with significantly large bodies of information, the machine is not capable of performing deep and complicated operations on really large bodies of text with the speed that would be desired in an operational system. The result is that it may take 30 seconds or a minute to get something that one would like to have almost instantly, that the display flickers on the oscilloscope screen, and so forth. Second, there is not available, at present, on any machine, either a programming language or a man-machine interaction language that makes it easy to do, or possible to do rapidly, many of the things envisioned in the discussion of pro-cognitive systems in Part I of this report. Our approach, during the study, was simply to put up with, and make allowances for, the shortcomings of the hardware system. It was easy to do that in informal experiments conducted by members of the research group; it was not realistic, however, to hope that all the observers of demonstrations would make the necessary allowances, and the shortcomings of the equipment effectively precluded formal experimentation.

Nevertheless, the equipment situation was at least tolerable, in terms of absolute assessment, and it seemed superb when we compared our man-computer interaction situation with any but two or three of all the others with which we were acquainted. The unavailability of highly developed languages and, of course, the interpreter and compiler programmes that would be required to make them useful - was, however, a seriously inhibiting factor. During the period of our study, two good programming-language systems came into being: DECAL, which is a quite elegant and powerful language and compiler of the ALGOL type, suitable for a small computer, and MACRO, which is an ingenious language and assembler system that incorporates several of the features that DECAL lacks and lacks several of the features that DECAL incorporates.

However, neither DECAL nor MACRO was designed for on-line programming, and neither was designed particularly to handle the problems that seem likely to present themselves to users of pro-cognitive systems. Those considerations led to the effort, which was never quite completed, to develop a composite programme oriented and user-oriented system to facilitate our research in man-machine interaction. The system is called 'Exec,' which stands, of course, for 'executive program'– and thus expresses something about the mode of operation: statements of the input language, coming into the computer, are examined by the executive programme, and, depending upon whether or not they fall into the class requiring interpretation, are either interpreted and executed with the aid of a set of subroutines associated with the executive programme or simply executed as machine instructions. Exec was written originally in the symbolic language called 'FRAP' and had, as its main function, simplification of the preparation of programmes and subroutines to be translated and assembled by FRAP.

When DECAL became available, Exec was rewritten in DECAL, and slight modifications were made to facilitate the use of Exec in the preparation of programmes and subroutines to be translated and compiled by DECAL. The original intention - to develop Exec to the point at which it could operate as an on-line language as well as an adjunct to a programming language—was not accomplished. One of the main themes in the work on Exec was to simplify and regularise the 'calling' and 'returning' of subroutines. In most computer-programming systems, and especially in the computer-programming systems that will be required in the implementation of plans of the kind, a computer programme is a complex arrangement of parts. The highest echelon of the structure does little more than represent the chapter headings of the general plan.

The actual work—the detailed processing of data - is handled by subprograms or 'subroutines' that break the task down into successively simpler sub packages at successively lower levels of detail until, finally, there is nothing left for the lowest-echelon subprograms to do but to perform simple, explicitly defined operations upon the few codes or numbers that are supplied to them. In this process of successive delegation of responsibility, the transactions that appear repeatedly are the 'calling' of a lower-echelon subroutine by a higher-echelon subroutine and the 'returning' of control from the lower-echelon subroutine to the higher-echelon subroutine. Calling usually includes transmission of instructions, and also the designation of the arguments upon which the lower-echelon subroutine must operate, from the calling subroutine to the called subroutine.

The transmission of information down the line we shall call 'briefing'. Transmission of results up the line we shall call 'debriefing.' In the conventional way of handling calling and returning, a subroutine eventually returns control to the subroutine that called it, but it may first call one or more lower-echelon subroutines. Fortunately or unfortunately, depending upon one's point of view, there are many different ways in which subroutines can be called and briefed and in which they can return control and do their debriefing. As indicated, one of the main purposes of Exec is to simplify and regularise this whole process.

In order to simplify the process of calling and returning, Exec is interposed between the calling subroutine and the called subroutine at the time of calling and between the called subroutine and the calling subroutine at the time of returning. With each subroutine is associated a compact code, that provides Exec with a description of the needs.of the subroutine. Exec can therefore handle in a systematic, centralised manner several of the functions that would otherwise have to be handled by each subroutine. In taking a burden off the routines, Exec takes a burden off the programmers who prepare them. The arrangements in Exec for calling and returning are set up in such a way that the chain of subroutine calls can be recursive. That is to say, it is possible for subroutine *A* to call subroutine *A*, or for subroutine *A* to call a subroutine *B* which, directly or through one of its minions, called subroutine *A*.

To permit recursive operation, one must handle 'temporary storage' - storage of the scratch-pad jottings made by each subroutine during its operation - in such a way that results written by *B*, for example, do not destroy results that *A* calculated before calling *B* and will need to use after *B* returns control. The functions just described have been implemented in a few programming systems - notably in the systems called IPL and LISP. In IPL and LISP, however, one either works wholly within the system or does not use the system at all. Exec extends the basic programming language and provides the new capabilities and conveniences within the structure of DECAL. In implementing the handling of subroutines, we made use of the technique of the 'pushdown list'. A pushdown list is an arrangement for storing information that resembles the spring-supported tray on which plates are stored in restaurants. If one puts a plate onto the top of the stack, it pushes all the others down, and if one then takes the plate off the top, the others pop up again. Exec, itself, employs one pushdown list.

Another pushdown list is available to the programmer or user through simple commands. He has only to give the name of the entity to be stored into the pushdown list or returned from it and to say whether he wants to push it down or pop it up. In the process of handling a call to a subroutine or a return from a subroutine, Exec examines the subroutine's heading code – determines whether or not, and how, to fulfill each of a number of functions, and then carries out those required. These functions include protecting contents of certain special registers of the processor against destruction during the running of the subroutine, finding the arguments needed by the subroutine and displaying them for its use, accepting the results obtained by the subroutine and communicating them to the calling routine, and protecting the contents of various temporary storage registers and 'flag' registers against modification by the called subroutine.

Exec protects information by putting it into the pushdown list. A second general purpose of Exec is to provide the advantages of generality and the advantages of specificity both at the same time and within the same system. If a computer programme is written in such a way as to make it useful in a particular situation. On the other hand, if the programme is written so that for example, it alphabetises or orders any kind of strings of alphanumeric text in any file or table, then he has to communicate to it, or have the routine that calls it communicate to it, that it should operate on words and that it should alphabetise according to a specified alphabet. In Exec, an effort is made to accommodate very general subroutines and to make it maximally convenient to communicate to them the information required to prepare them for specific applications. This is done by setting up and maintaining a description of the prevailing context of operation. In the terms of the example, his description may contain a specification that the currently prevailing string class is the class of 'words.'

It contains the specification that the *x,* in any subroutine prepared to operate upon 'Table *x,*' should be interpreted as 3. The subroutine, therefore, automatically performs on the operation intended by the programmer, despite the fact that the programmer was thinking in terms of abstractions and not in terms of the particular present task. With arrangements of the kind just suggested, Exec makes it possible to use a subroutine that contains the expression, 'next string,' for example, to operate on the next character, or the next word, or the next sentence, or the next paragraph, or the next section, or the next chapter, and so forth. Exec keeps track of three 'string classes' simultaneously, class *u,* class *v,* and class *w.* At any time, the programmer can set anyone of the string classes to anyone of seven levels. He can write, for example, '*SSCU* word,' meaning to *set* the string class *u* to have the value, *word.* From that time on, until the instruction is superseded, all the subroutines that deal with the string class hierarchy *u* will consider the *u* strings to be words.

The procedure for designating tables is similar to that for designating strings. If the programmer would like to have programmes written in terms of Tables *x, y,* and *z* operate on the contents of Table zones 2, 5, and 7, he writes '*ntox* 2, *ntoy* 5, *ntoz* 7.' * When Exec sees those instructions, it does more than merely substitute 2 for *x,* 5 for *y,* and 7 for *z.* It finds the descriptions, in its file of table descriptions, that characterise the three numbered tables, and it substitutes these descriptions for the pre-previously prevailing descriptions of Tables *x, y,* and *z,* respectively. When a subroutine operates on the contents of the table, it examines the table's description and controls its processing accordingly.

This makes it possible to accommodate diverse formats and conventions. Inasmuch as the adjustments are made 'interpretively' during the running of the programme, the user can change his mind and reprocess something in a slightly different way without having to go through extensive revision and recompilation of his programmes. This is an advantage that the present technique has over the technique, based on the 'communication pool,' that has been developed in connection with the programming of very large computer systems—systems programmed by teams so large as to discourage the effort to enforce the use of a single, standard set of conventions and formats.

The part of Exec that we have been describing is approximately an interpretive communication pool. The third set of functions with which Exec is concerned has to do with the display of alphanumeric information on typewriters and on the oscilloscope screen. Although these are very simple functions, they involve enough detailed programming to be a nuisance unless they are handled in a systematic way. Exec makes it convenient to separate specification of the information to be displayed from specification of the equipment through which it is to be displayed. It uses standard programmes to handle strings that are long enough to be considered messages or texts, but it provides special arrangements to facilitate preparation of labels, headings, and the like.

For example, the programmer can call for the typing of any particular character *x* on whatever typewriter is currently specified to be typewriter *b* simply by writing *'type x.'* If the programmer wants the character to appear upon the screen of oscilloscope *a*, he writes *'scpa x.'* With the aid of Exec, the programmer can define in equally short instructions the size of the print, the vertical position at which the text should begin, and other parameters of the visual display.

Exec's arrangements for displaying capital and lower-case letters on the oscilloscope are primitive, but it is a step in the right direction to have both capital and lower-case letters. At present, a 'lower-case' letter is simply a small capital letter. We settled for that stopgap solution only in the interest of economy. The fourth and final set of functions handled by Exec has to do with display, by the computer, of what the computer is doing. One technique developed for this purpose, a technique called 'Introspection,' because it was developed as a separate project. The arrangements described here are integral to Exec. One of the main causes of difficulty in man-computer interaction is that the computer does not give the man any good clues about what it is doing until it completes a segment of processing and spews forth the results.

When the computer is running, its lights flash so fast that they are scarcely interpretable. It seems important to provide a way of having the computer give a running account of its processing. A part of Exec called the 'Reporting Subsection 'an optional part - is brought into play each time a subroutine is called and each time a subroutine returns control to its caller. When the reporting subsection is brought into action, it examines the list of things that it should do. This list can be changed while Exec and other programmes are running. Ordinarily, the first thing on the list is to give the address, and, if it is available in the directory, also the name, of the subroutine that is being called or that is returning control to its caller. Since the subroutines operate very rapidly, the names and addresses would appear to be presented simultaneously, one on top of another, if they were shown in a fixed location on the screen.

Therefore they are displayed in a format corresponding to that of a conventional outline. If a chain of subroutines is called, each one operating at a level just lower than its caller, the names and addresses appear on successive lines of the display with increasing indentation. Then, as the subroutines return control, each to its caller, the names and addresses are displayed again in such a way as to redisplay the outline pattern from bottom to top. To the display just described can be added, at the option of the operator, a display of the contents of the active registers of the computer. In addition, the operator may see the contents of whatever parts of the computer's memory he wants to examine. He designates the various parts of memory to Exec by typing on the typewriter while the programme is running. He can change his prescription at will. The current version of Exec allows him to specify nine different sectors of memory, either symbolically or in terms of absolute addresses. When he indicates that he wants to see 'the subroutine,' Exec interprets 'the subroutine' to mean the particular subroutine that is being called, or that is returning control to its caller. That will, of course, be one subroutine at one moment and another at another moment. When the operator wishes to examine a table or a programme in detail, he touches the space bar of the typewriter. That causes the system to pause in its progression through the sequence of things to be displayed, and to hold the current display until the operator releases it by touching the tab key. The Reporting Subsection provides a few additional conveniences - minor ones introduced from time to time on an *ad hoc* basis - but the foregoing will suffice to give an idea of the existing arrangement. Let us mention a few of the steps not yet accomplished, however. It seems worth while to connect to the Reporting Subsection the 'Introspection' programmes that will be described later.

It is necessary to complete the arrangements that associate the tables that reside in the primary memory to corresponding structures in secondary and tertiary memory and, in the manner of the Atlas computer system, to arrange it so that information structures are automatically shifted up through the memory hierarchy whenever they are addressed. It is necessary, also, to expand the mechanism that associates symbols with machine addresses. That mechanism is only a simple table-searching system, but it is inherently capable of effecting the translation required to make conveniently readable the reports of 'what is currently going on in the computer.' We found it useful to distinguish, in Exec, between 'intrinsic' and 'extrinsic' subroutines. Exec is highly 'subroutinised' and has the partly hierarchical, partly recursive, structure that we have described as essential for pro-cognitive systems. Each sub-function of Exec that appears to have any likelihood of proving useful in future applications is separated out and set into the form of a subroutine. In the process of writing subroutines to handle substantive problems - subroutines that made use of Exec but were not at first intended to be part of the Exec system - we encountered repeatedly several sets or clusters of functions.

By associating with Exec the subroutines prepared to handle those functions, we were able to build up a system of considerable convenience and power. The part of the system not intrinsic to Exec was too extensive to be held in primary memory at all times. However, it was clearly desirable to bring parts of it into primary memory - coherent clusters of it corresponding to major functions - whenever required in the execution of a programme. The easiest way to accomplish dynamic storage and transfer of subroutines, and to handle the associated bookkeeping, was to take care of it automatically through Exec's ability to examine calling sequences and subroutine headings. We did not make much progress towards that end during the course of the study.

However, we did work with the problem enough to see the great convenience and power that reside in a coherent structure of computer subroutines and a largely automatic arrangement for calling them and transferring information among them. Evidently, the more sophisticated the arrangements, the larger the fraction of the subroutines that will be intrinsic to the arrangements. We visualise a system in a continual process of development, with a set of intrinsic subroutines, a set of extrinsic subroutines, and a continual flow from the extrinsic set to the intrinsic set as more and more functions are brought within the scope and capability of the system.

ON-LINE MAN-COMPUTER COMMUNICATION

'On-Line Man-Computer Communication' by Licklider and Clark discusses several problems in, and several steps towards the improvement of, interaction of men and computers. These include problems and developments in the use of computers as aids in teaching and in learning and as a basis for group cooperation in the planning and design of buildings. The part of the paper that stemmed from the present study was the development of a pair of programmes, referred to earlier as 'Introspection,' that are closely connected with the last described major function of Exec. The two programmes of 'Introspection' were designed to demonstrate that, although present-day computers are opaque and inscrutable, of all the complex organisms and systems in the world, computers are, in principle, the most capable of revealing the intricacies of their internal processes. We consider this to be an important problem calling for much research. Our two programmes constitute only exploratory steps. The two parts of Introspection are 'Programme Graph' and 'Memory Course.' Programme Graph displays, in the form of a graph relating that quantity to time, the contents of any specified register or registers of the computer.

Memory Course displays the progression of control from one memory register to the next during the operation of a programme. With the aid of these two programmes, the operator can see what is happening, as it happens, within the processor and the memory of the computer. These programmes give him at once both a global view and a considerable amount of detail. They let him see relations among parts of the over-all picture. No longer is he constrained, as he has been with conventional procedures, to peek at the contents of one register at a time, and to build up the over-all picture from myriad examinations of microscopic details. To provide a rough impression of the operation of Programme Graph, it may suffice to describe how it operates when it is set to display the contents of the register of the computer that is called the 'programme counter.' The programme counter contains the address of the memory register that contains the instruction that is being executed. In the absence of 'branching' or 'jumping,' control proceeds from one register to the next, and the contents of the programme counter increase by one, each time an instruction is executed. When a 'branch' or 'jump' occurs, the number in the programme counter changes by some integral quantity different from one, and often the increment or decrement is rather large. Programme Graph plots the graph relating the number in the programme counter to the time. The display presents about a thousand individual quantities simultaneously to view. From the graph, it is easy to recognise the upward-sloping line segments that correspond to non-branching, non-jumping stretches of programme.

When the programme 'loops,' as it often does, branching backward and repeating a sequence of instructions over and over, the display shows a saw toothed waveform. When the programme calls a subroutine, the jump to the subroutine, the loops within the subroutine, and the return from the subroutine are all clearly evident. When Programme Graph is used to display the contents of the accumulator, the input-output register, or one of the memory registers, the interpretation of the graph is, of course, quite different. In general, however, its main value lies in its presentation of a large quantity of information in such a way that relations among parts are easy to perceive. The other Introspection programme, Memory Course, displays only the course through memory followed by the programme under study.

It shows that course as a succession of circles connected by a heavy line against a gridlike background representing the primary memory of the computer. The grid upon which the display of Memory Course is shown consists of 4096 dots, arranged in 64 squares of 64 dots each, and representing one bank of memory. A register is represented by a very fine light dot if the instruction and the address it contains are both zero. The dot is a little heavier if the instruction is not zero.

The dot is a little heavier still if the address is not zero. If both the instruction and the address are not zero, the dot is heavy. From the grid, therefore, the user can see which parts of memory are occupied and which are not. In addition, after he has gotten used to the display, he can make out which parts of memory are used to store programmes, and which parts are used to store data. When Memory Course is used to display the 'trajectory' through memory followed by an object programme, the object programme itself is not run in the usual way. Instead, the object programme is operated by Memory Course, which 'traces' the progress of the object programme and displays it on the oscilloscope screen. Each time an instruction is executed, a circle is drawn around the dot that corresponds to the location of the instruction in the computer memory. When a programme 'loop' is traced, the line is set over slightly to one side of the circles it has been connecting. That keeps it from retracing its path backwards and helps it represents the cyclic nature of the course. Memory Course represents loops, as just suggested, by tracing out a closed course. When the programme transfers control to a subroutine, a line jumps out from the dot that corresponds to the call and leads to the dot that corresponds to the beginning of the subroutine.

Thus, Memory Course provides a simple, maplike representation of the programme structure. One can see where the various subroutines are, how long they operate, when they receive their calls, and when they return control to their callers. If an error occurs, either in the computer or in the programme, control is very likely to be transferred to an inappropriate location. If the user knows the structure of his programme, either from having programmed it or from experience operating it, he sees that something unexpected has happened.

He then looks back to the beginning of the unexpected line and determines precisely the location of the register within which the error originated. Having done that, he typically reruns the programme, following its course very carefully as it approaches the critical point. If the error recurs, he reruns the programme once more, this time stopping it at various points ahead of the critical one and using other means to examine the instructions, addresses, and data associated with those points.

A FILE INVERTER

The project to be described next was aimed, like Exec, at increasing the convenience and effectiveness with which the computer could be used in the study of library and pro-cognitive problems. This project, however, had a much sharper focus than Exec. Its aim was simply to implement the operation called 'file inversion.'

A direct file is ordered with respect to its 'items', and usually several terms are associated with each item. An inverse file is ordered with respect to its 'terms,' with several items usually associated with each term. Obviously, both the direct file and the inverse file are aspects of a more general structure consisting of items, terms, and associations between items and terms.

The 'File Inverter' is a computer programme, written in DECAL by Grignetti, that accepts a direct file and produces an inverse file. Since there is no difference in abstract format between a direct file and an inverse file, the programme produces a direct file if it is presented with an inverse one. The file-inverting programme includes a subprogram that alphabetises the entries. If it is used to invert a file consisting of terms associated with alphabetised items, it yields a file of items associated with alphabetised terms.

If the items consist of the bibliographic citations of documents, and if the terms are the key words of the titles of the documents, then the result obtained by applying the file-inverting programme is a kind of 'permuted title index.' Grignetti's programme includes a subprogram that facilitates the selection of key words from titles. The subprogram selects from a string of words all those that do not appear upon a list of words to be excluded. The list of words to be excluded ordinarily contains the 'function' words and, also, words that have been found not to discriminate.

AN AUTOMATED CARD CATALOGUE

Using parts of the file-inverting programme, Grignetti prepared a programme that automates some of the functions involved in using an ordinary card index. The kind of card index towards which the programme is oriented is not precisely the kind used in most libraries. It differs mainly in assuming that each card will contain a series of descriptive terms.

Such card indexes are found more frequently in documentation centers that specialise in laboratory technical reports and reprints than in libraries of books and serials. The 'Automated Card Catalogue' is a DECAL programme for use in exploration of card catalogue problems. The user sits at the computer typewriter and presents his retrieval prescription to the computer in the form of a Boolean function of the terms in which he is interested. A person interested in non-digital simulations of neural processes, particularly including studies made under the heading, 'perception, ' but also other studies in the field of artificial intelligence, might type:

- (Artificial intelligence or perception or neural simulation) and not digital

Using the terms of the Boolean function as retrieval terms, the programme searches a magnetic tape containing the 'card' file. Whenever it finds one of the terms, it looks further within the entry to determine whether or not the function is satisfied. If the function is satisfied, the programme displays the entire contents of the 'card' on the oscilloscope screen for examination by the user. Grignetti's programme makes it convenient for the user to correct his retrieval prescription, to reinitiate a search, to find out just where he stands at any point in his study, and to save 'cards' for future reference.

The programme 'knows' the rules for regular pluralisation and considers the search for a term to be satisfied if either the singular or a calculated regular plural or a given irregular plural of the term is found. In addition, the programme works with a simplified system of spelling, as well as with literal spelling, and is therefore often able to find the desired term on a 'card' even when the term is misspelled in the prescription. In such an instance, it displays, for example,

- Do you mean 'intelligence'?

The user then types y for 'yes' or n for 'no.' The programme remembers this answer and does not bother the user again with the same question. That may be convenient when the user is dealing with names he does not know very well, but it leads to complications that will have to be settled through further programming. Probably it will be better to correct the prescription than to perpetuate the indiscrimination.

A SYSTEM TO FACILIT ATE THE STUDY OF DOCUMENTS

The two programmes described in the preceding sections are related to, and are intended for incorporation into, a system to facilitate the retrieval and study of documents. The 'study' part of the over-all system is described in a report by Bobrow, Kain, Raphael, and Licklider.

The study system, called 'Symbiont' because we hope to develop it into a truly symbiotic partner of the student, displays information to the student via the typewriter or the display screen. It is intended as an exploratory tool, for use mainly by students who are at the same time experimenters, and it does not yet have the perfection or polish required for realistic demonstration or practical application. However, it does make available, in a single, integrated package, several functions that prove quite useful to a student who wants to examine a set of technical documents, take notes on their contents, compare or combine graphs found in different papers, and so forth. Among the functions provided by Symbiont are the following:

- Present for examination a document specified by any sufficiently prescriptive segment of its bibliographic citation.
- Turn pages, forward or backward, in response to the pressing of a key.
- Permit designation of a passage by pointing to the beginning and then the end with a light pen.
- Accept labels from the typewriter and associate them with passages of text.
- Record as a note, and preserve for later inspection, any designated passage.
- Append bibliographic citations to extracted passages.
- Accept retrieval prescriptions from the typewriter.
- Accept from the typewriter coded versions of specifications of such operating characteristics as, 'Consider a neighbourhood to be five consecutive lines of text,' or 'Consider a search to be satisfied when any two of the three elements of the search have been satisfied.'
- Carry out retrieval searches and display passages in which the retrieval prescriptions are satisfied.
- Compose graphs from tabulated data and present the graphs, against labeled coordinate grids, on the oscilloscope screen.
- Set two graphs side by side to facilitate comparison.
- Expand or compress the scales of graphs, under control from the light pen.
- Change the number of grid lines or the calibration numbers associated with the lines, or both together, and recalculate and redisplay the calibration numbers when grid lines are added or deleted.

The search routines used in finding desired passages of text operate with three sets of retrieval terms. The user specifies the terms of each set initially through the typewriter. All the terms of a subset are considered equivalent during the search, and the search is satisfied insofar as that subset is concerned if anyone of the terms is encountered in the text. The user can specify whether he wants to find a passage in which at least one of the terms of one of the sets occurs, or a passage in which at least one of the terms of each of two of the sets occurs, and so forth. Even though this implementation is primitive, it is evident from preliminary experiments with Symbiont that automation of the function of searching for 'ideas' will be a very powerful aid in technical study. Machine aid in manipulating graphs will also be very helpful.

ASSOCIATIVE CHAINING AS AN INFORMATIONRETRIEVAL TECHNIQUE

Most of the information-retrieval systems that have actually been developed, and even most of those that have been subjected to intensive research, retrieve unitary elements of information, such as documents, paragraphs, or sentences. A basic point in Marill's paper is that for many purposes the retrieval of a unitary part of the corpus is inadequate, and that what often is needed is an answer to a question that may have to be derived through deduction from elements of information scattered throughout the corpus.

When the relation between two items is direct, they are said to be connected by a first-order chain. When the relation between two items can be established only through the intermediary agency of a third item, the first two items are said to be connected by a chain of second order, and so forth. In a report on 'Associative Chaining as an Information Retrieval Technique,' Clapp describes the idea of chaining as a general schema, then shows the correspondence between the chaining schema and certain schemata of graph theory, and finally discusses a programme that traces chains of relevance through corpora consisting of files of sentences.

Chaining, as a technique, is particularly simple and easy to discuss when it is separated from the problem of the nature of relevance. In Clapp's work, the two things - the technique and the concept of relevance - are well separated. For purposes of simplicity and convenience, Clapp considers two sentences to be directly associated if they have one or more words in common. Thus, the sentences, 'The cat is black,' and 'Black is a colour,' are directly associated. They have two words in common, 'is' and 'black.' There is no direct, first-order association between the first two of the following sentences, but only a second-order association through the third sentence: 'The cat is black,' 'Feline animals move gracefully,' 'A cat is a feline animal.' It is obvious, even at the outset, that something has to be done to inhibit associations based on the common occurrence of frequently used verbs and function words. In Clapp's approach, however, whatever is done about that is a separate matter from the development of the algorithm that traces out the chains. Clapp's computer programmes are divided into two sets. The first set of programmes facilitates the preparation of a machine-processible file of information units, such as sentences, paragraphs, or documents. It then prepares, from the file, a series of concordances. Finally, with the aid of the concordances, it determines the set of all first order associations.

The second set of programmes operates upon a retrieval prescription plus the set of first-order associations. The retrieval prescription is a set of words drawn from the vocabulary of the corpus.

The first thing that the chaining algorithm does is to find all those elements of the corpus that contain all the words of the prescription. This is what a 'conventional' information retrieval system would do. Then, however, the chaining algorithm goes on to trace higher-ordered chains through the corpus and to retrieve the information elements that are involved in higher-ordered chains up to some cutoff order specified by the operator.

The programme has been tested and demonstrated only with a corpus consisting of sentences. Except for minor considerations having to do with delimiters - the clues that mark stopping points such as ends of sentences or paragraphs - the chaining programmes are not sensitive to the distinctions among sentence, paragraph, document, and so forth, and it is obvious that the chaining operation can be carried out on textual strings of any class. However, pursuing the technique of chaining based on the common occurrence of words beyond a level of the sentence does not seem to offer much promise. It is evident that every book would be directly associated with almost every other book if the criterion were a word in common and it is equally evident that almost no book would be associated with any other book if the criterion were a verbatim paragraph in common. For the technique of chaining, ordinary sentences seem to be approximately the optimal length. Fortunately, the sets of descriptive terms used in coordinate-indexing systems are of approximately the same length as sentences. The notion of association based on inclusion of common terms is quite appropriate for them. It is in that domain that we think it most likely that the chaining technique, and the chaining algorithms developed by Clapp, will find practical application. In his exploration of the relations between graph theory and associative chaining, Clapp developed the chaining schema in considerably more depth than is reflected in this summary. For example, his development uses the number of parallel links as well as the order of the links in the chain of association. Some of his ideas recognise gradations in the strength of association.

That seems important because, intuitively, one thinks of relevance as capable of variation in degree. The next step in the development of the concept of associative chaining, we think, should be an attempt to define the fundamental relatedness or relevance on which the 'association' is based. Associative chaining has a natural connection with the relational networks and with the semantic nets and question-answering systems studied by Marill and Black. The next step may, therefore, take the form of merging the chaining concept with the concepts underlying the relational and semantic nets and the question-answering systems.

TWO QUESTION-ANSWERING SYSTEMS

Marill's short paper on question-answering systems, described earlier, initiated a series of studies that involved a meld of symbolic logic and computer programming. Most of these studies were carried out by Black, who described them in a series of memoranda and a report. The memoranda and the report share with the corpora of the question-answering systems a tight, terse, logical quality that makes them attractive to the logician and difficult for the non-logician to understand. Following is an effort to summarise, without gross distortion, two of the principal accomplishments of the work on question-answering systems in a freer and less formal exposition. One might justify this aim by quoting a paragraph from Black's 'Conclusions on QAS': A string of words cannot be rephrased without significant loss of facts or ideas relevant to some area. However, if we limit ourselves to certain areas, then the string of words can be rephrased without loss of facts or ideas *relative to those areas.* In the final paragraph of the same memorandum Black goes on to say: Before we can rephrase a string of words without significant loss, we must define our interests precisely.

If we are interested in everything, then we cannot rephrase the string at all. Let us say, therefore, that we are interested in assessing the possibility, and also the technical feasibility, of:

- Representing large parts of the body of knowledge, as well as questions relating to the body of knowledge, in a formal language amenable to processing by a computer and
- Developing a system that will, by processing the questions and the stored corpus, deduce and display COrrect answers.

Black's results attest to the possibility of doing those things. However, Black's programmes take a long time to determine the answers to fairly simple questions. That fact suggests that economic feasibility is dependent upon greatly increasing the processing efficiency of the question- answering system or the processing speed of the computer, or both.

The prediction made in Part I that it is unlikely that there will be great increases in speed in the same computers that have a greatly increased memory capacity, may not bear very heavily on this problem. It may be that as suggested, use procedures that are fast, but not very deep, to retrieve parts of the corpus that are rich in statements germane to a particular question, and then turn to deeper and slower procedures for the derivation of the answer from the rich informational ore.

The first of Black's two contributions to be summarised, the memorandum, 'Specific-Question-Answering System,' February 8, 1963, describes Version III of a system written in the LISP language for the IBM 7090 computer. In this system, the corpus consists of statements that are strings of ordinary words, symbols representing variables, and parentheses.

The use of the ordinary words is highly constrained - so constrained that nothing can be said that could not be said equally well in the shorter, but less widely readable, notation seen in books on logic.

The only variables are *Xl, X2, X3, what, when, which,* and *how.* The parentheses have the effect of forcing the system to consider as a unit the string within the parentheses. The 'questions' asked of the Specific-Question-Answering System may be either statements, in which case they are confirmed or denied by the system, or ordinary questions containing the variables, *Xl, X2, X3, what,* and *when,* etc. The answer elicited by a 'yes-no' question is 'yes,' 'no,' or 'no answer.' The answer to any other question is a list of items that constitute a correct and reasonable reply, or 'no answer'.

The system seeks answers to questions by processing the questions and the corpus in a very straightforward, rigourous way.

It looks through the corpus for a statement that is the same as the statement that constitutes the question or that can be transformed into the question by removing a 'not.' If it finds a match, the answer is 'yes'.

If it finds a negated match, the answer is 'no.' If it finds neither, it looks for a conditional statement in the corpus in which the consequent matches the question. If it finds such a statement in the corpus, it undertakes to determine an answer to the subsidiary question, whether or not the premise of the conditional statement is true. Proceeding in this way, it tries every possibility of deriving the question or its negation from the statements of the corpus. The procedure for processing of questions containing variables is a little more complex than the procedure just described.

It is necessary, in seeking an answer to a question containing a variable, to keep track of all the individuals that can be values of the variable. The process amounts, approximately, to determining the list of individuals that meet all the conditions that are imposed upon the variable. The system is capable of answering not only simple, single-variable questions, but also multiple questions, conditional questions, and even questions containing the names of LISP computer programmes.

In the latter case, there is a rigid format that must be followed in giving the name of the programme and its arguments. All the foregoing structures mentioned as acceptable question forms are also acceptable as forms for statements in the corpus. In the corpus, a programme name may occur even in the antecedent of a conditional statement. We mention these things to indicate that the system has the capability of expressing complex relations and of deriving answers to complex questions. To see approximately what the system does, let us consider a few oversimplified examples and one more complex example.

Suppose, first, that the corpus consists merely of two statements:

- Mercury is (a planet) if (Xl is a planet) then (Xl is a planet of the sun)

The question asked of the system, in statement form, is:

- Mercury is a planet of the sun

To that question, the system says, simply:

- Yes

Suppose, for the second example, that the corpus consists of only one sentence:

- Earth is smaller than jupiter

The question asked of the system and the foregoing rudimentary corpus is:

- Jupiter is smaller than earth

The answer given by the system to that question is:

- No Answer

But now suppose that a second statement is added to the corpus. The corpus now consists of the two statements:

- Earth is smaller than jupiter if (XI is smaller than X2) then (X2 is not smaller than XI)

The question is still:

- Jupiter is smaller than earth

The system is now able to determine an answer. It says:

- NO

The question asked of the system and this corpus is:

- What is a major planet

The answer provided by the system is:

- Neptune
- Uranus
- Saturn
- Jupiter

This last example would be more impressive than it is if the corpus contained a large number of irrelevant statements in addition to the statements shown. The presence of irrelevant statements would increase the length of time required by the computer in answering the question, but the computer has the great advantage, in operations of this kind, that it does not tend to forget the relevant facts already found while it is examining the irrelevancies. For a human being, on the other hand, a problem of the present kind that is difficult but nevertheless within one's scope of capability becomes entirely hopeless as soon as a large amount of irrelevant material is introduced. That fact, we believe, is significant in its bearing on the problem men face in drawing answers from the body of knowledge that is now held in libraries and document rooms.

The other paper of Black's that we shall discuss here is 'A Question-Answering System: QAS-5'. This paper describes in detail the operation of a later generation question-answering system, a descendant of the Specific-Question-Answering System that we have been discussing. The main advances made in the interim between the two papers were advances in the handling of quantification and advances achieved by formalising the language approximately in a way suggested earlier by McCarthy. The advance in quantification makes it possible for the system to deal with problems involving 'some' and 'all.'

The formalisation of the language makes it difficult for the uninitiated reader to understand what is being done, but it reveals the flaws and pitfalls to the veteran in a clearer way than the more readable language does, and, moreover, it suggests what to do to correct or avoid them. We consider the formalisation, therefore, to be a step more in a right direction than in a wrong one - a step that must be taken in order to reach a position from which it will be possible to move forward to simultaneous readability and formal effectiveness.

The mode of operation of QAS-5 is similar in basic principle, though somewhat deeper and more complex, to the mode of operation of the Specific-Question-Answering System. Some of the flavour of the method is given by the following protocol:

- Step 1: The system finds the first match for question 1 in statement 6.
- Step 2: The system forms the backward transform of question 1 and statement 6, giving a new conditional (7) - at (desk, *y*), at (*y*, country) at (desk, country).
- Step 3: The system sets up the first antecedent of (7) as a new question (2) - at (desk, *y*).
- Step 4: The system finds the first match for question 2 in statement 2.
- Step 5: The system forms the transform of question 2 and statement 2, giving the answer to question 2 - (I) at (desk, home).

The latter would be read, as one might possibly guess, 'I am at my desk at home.' The problem to which Black's QAS-5 report is wholly dedicated is a problem posed by McCarthy in 1958 and hitherto not solved by any nonhuman system. It is a well known problem in artificial-intelligence and heuristic-programming circles and is called the 'airport problem.'

The problem, stated here informally, is fairly simple: I am at my desk, at home. My car is in my garage, which is also at my home. I want to go to the airport. The airport is in the same county as my home. I can walk from any point that I would call 'at my home' to any other point that I would also call 'at my home,' because, of course, the dimensions of the area subsumed under 'home' are not very great. I can drive from any point in my county to any other point in my county. What should I do? The answer to the question, or the solution to the problem, is said to be:

> I should go from my desk to my garage on foot and get my car, and I should then drive my car from the garage to the airport.

Having stated the problem and given the solution, we should perhaps repeat that, although the answer is obvious to any adult human being who understands English, no one had succeeded in devising a wholly automatic system that would derive the answer from the description of the situation and the statement of the question. Black's report gives a step-by-step account of the procedure used by QAS-5 in solving the problem. In addition, it displays, point by point, the minor differences between the notation suggested by McCarthy and the notation employed by Black. The conclusions that we draw from our experience with question-answering systems are summed up in the assertion that the achievement of Black's programme in solving McCarthy's problem is simultaneously a signal advance in automated question answering and a commonplace performance for a moderate intelligence. In greater detail, the conclusions are:

- Clear progress is being made in bringing logical deduction within the scope of automation.
- In the process of programming a system to accomplish a feat such as the one described, one begins to see how extremely deep and complex are the intellectual processes that one accepts as commonplace and undemanding of intelligence when those processes are carried out by people.
- In the running of such programmes, one begins to sense the magnitude of the gulf that separates a demonstration of the type just described from an economically feasible operating system. As the problems become more complex, and as the corpus becomes larger, the amount of time required for processing goes up steeply. This is a discouraging counterpoise to the pattern of growth of the information-processing technology.
- At the same time, one sees, even at this stage, many ways in which processing can be made more efficient, and one senses that there are - waiting to be discovered ways of formulating the procedure that are much more powerful than the ways thus far employed.

In short, it appears to us that the domain of question-answering systems is an intellectually deep and technologically demanding area for research and development. As suggested, there is an extremely long way to go before useful answers can be deduced from extensive information bases at reasonable cost. On the other hand, it may well be that, in this area, each basic conceptual advance will be a long stride towards the pro-cognitive systems we envision for man's future interaction with the fund of knowledge.

AN APPROACH TO COMPUTER PROCESSING OF NATURAL LANGUAGE

This final project was pursued intensively during the first year of the study, but, for reasons not related to its degree of promise, it lay dormant during the second year. Although the project does not appear to be worth continuing in its present form, the following description may prove useful. The approach selected at the outset - to try to mirror in computer programmes the ontogenetic development of the human ability to generate and understand language - was quite different from the approach, then more popular, based upon syntactic analysis. The approach adopted paid more attention to semantics than to syntax.

However, many of the investigators who earlier had concentrated on syntactic analysis have directed their efforts towards semantic analysis, and what seemed to us at the outset to be an unpopulated field is rapidly becoming crowded. That fact, together with our sharpening awareness of the very great difficulty and even greater extent of the task, account for the negativeness of our thoughts about reactivating 'Ontogeny.' At the beginning of the project, it seemed to us to be a good idea to start with 'baby talk' and to try to recapitulate, as closely as possible, the development of the human language process. Recognising the importance of the 'verbal community' in each individual's development of language process, we set up a situation in which an operator at the typewriter played the role of the verbal community and, acting as stimulator, instructor, reinforce, umpire, and protector, presided over the 'shaping up' of language behaviour in the computer.

It was necessary, of course, to provide the computer with basic structures and capabilities corresponding roughly to those that would be inherited by a human being. It was necessary also to set up some domain of discourse that would be potentially 'meaningful' to the computer, as well as to the operator, and that would provide an analogue to the 'environment' in which human beings behave and with reference to which most of their language - that is not about themselves - is oriented. One part of the internal mechanism - of the system of computer programmes - seems worth describing despite the fact that its nature does not in any direct way determine the nature of the over-all system. This part of the programme is concerned with the representation, in the computer memory, of the words and phrases communicated between the operator and the computer. In the input and output equipment, the words and phrases take the form of strings of characters or character codes.

The codes are the so-called 'concise' codes for alphanumeric characters employed in the PDP-1 computer. Each code is a pattern of six binary digits. Representation of words, phrases, and so forth, as strings of coded characters is inconvenient and uneconomical for many information-processing purposes. In a computing machine that has registers of fixed length, it is inconvenient to have words and phrases of variable length. We were at the outset not so much concerned with economy of representation as with convenience of processing, and we adopted an approach designed mainly for convenience. We represented each word, or phrase, or sentence, or string of any recognised class, by a 36-bit code. The code was made up of a 30-bit main code and 6 bits of auxiliary information, which included designation of the class to which the string belonged. A 36-bit code can be stored conveniently in two consecutive registers of the PDP-l memory. The rule for representing incoming words in the computer memory was the following. If the word consisted of five characters or fewer, the concise-code representation is the computer representation; if, on the other hand, the word contained more than five characters, then the computer representation consists of the concise codes of the first three characters, the six auxiliary bits, and, in addition, a 12-bit 'hash code' calculated by a rather complicated procedure from the concise codes of the remaining characters. This representation is capable of discriminating among about 4000 different words with the same three leading characters.

Because the calculation of the hash code is carried out by a procedure akin to the generation of 'random numbers,' one cannot be entirely sure that two different words will not yield the same code. Nevertheless, he can make the probability of a 'collision' as low as he likes by selecting a sufficiently long representation. In the initial stages of the work, we were not much concerned about accidental confusion of one word with another. Children certainly confuse words. Indeed, we were attracted by the hypothesis that some of the confusions that arise in human communication and thinking are attributable to something like a hash-code process in neural representation. The agent that converts strings of text into hash codes is, of course, a computer programme.

First it divides a string of text into words and determines a code for each word. Then it combines the words into phrases, using punctuation as a guide, and determines a hash code for each phrase from the codes for the words within the phrase. Then it determines a hash code for each sentence from the codes for the phrases within the sentence, and so forth. Thus, for each word, for each phrase, for each sentence, there is a 36-bit representation. After the conversion to this internal code has been effected, and until a stage is reached at which it is necessary to generate a response in the form of a string of alphanumeric characters, all the processing is carried out with the internal 36-bit codes. It is easy to transform alphanumeric text into internal codes. To do that, it is necessary only to apply the transformation programmes that calculate the codes. However, to transform in the other direction - to go from the internal code representation to a string of alphanumeric characters - is another matter. Because information is sometimes lost in the forward transformation, it is not possible simply to calculate the reverse transformation. It is necessary to employ a 'table-searching' procedure. However, it is certainly neither necessary nor desirable to store every string of characters received in order to have it ready to type as a response. If one is to respond in a natural way, he must be able to generate sequences of words that he has never received. Moreover, there are too many strings of words to consider storing them all in a computer memory.

The procedure adopted, therefore, is to associate with each internal word code, but not with the code for any string of any class other than word, its complete concise code, *i.e.*, the string of concise codes corresponding to the characters of the word. The association is achieved in the following way. All the internal codes, for words, phrases, sentences, and so forth, are kept together - along with other information - in a table called the 'Hash Table'. One of the entries in the Hash Table, for each word represented in that table, is the address of the register in the Vocabulary Table in which the corresponding concise-code representation begins. That makes it possible, given the internal code corresponding to a word, to find the corresponding concise code and to have the word typed on the computer typewriter.

For those internally represented strings that are not merely words, there is still another table, called the 'Sub address Table'. The entry in the Hash Table that is associated with a sentence the way the Vocabulary Table address is associated with a word, is the address of a register in the Sub address Table. At that address in the Sub address Table, one finds the beginning of a list of 'sub addresses' that are addresses of registers back in the Hash Table. In those registers in the Hash Table are the entries for strings of the next lower class. With each hash code for a phrase is associated the address of another register in the Sub address Table. Going back to the Sub address Table with that address, one finds addresses of registers in the Hash Table.

Finally, in the designated registers in the Hash Table are addresses of registers in the Vocabulary Table. In the Vocabulary Table, of course, are the concise codes of the words. The procedure just described is implemented by programming, so no effort of thought is involved after the programme has been perfected. The programme runs much more rapidly than the typewriter can type, and there is therefore no observable delay. With the system, one can start out with a 36-bit hash code and wind up with a long typewritten sentence. If the initial code is the code of a paragraph, indeed he winds up with a paragraph. We have checked the system to that level of operation. Obviously, nothing stands in the way of representing an entire book with a 36-bit internal code. However, one cannot uniquely represent the individuals of any set of sise approaching *2n* with hash codes *n* bits in length.

Our selection of 36-bit codes, and our compromise in the direction of readability by man as well as by machine, was conditioned by the fact that we were working with a 'young' language mechanism that would not be expected to develop a very large vocabulary for some time. It is now doubtless evident that a description of computer programmes in ordinary language encounters serious problems of exposition and endurance. We shall, therefore, not describe the entire Ontogeny programme in as great detail. Let us, nevertheless, explain how the system is designed to keep track of the properties of the various words and phrases and the entities and operations for which they stand. The repository for factual information, in Ontogeny, is a table called the 'Property Table.' One of the entries in each section of the Hash Table is the address of a corresponding section in the Property Table. For convenience, the Property Table records the corresponding Hash Table address and also the internal code of the string with which the properties are associated. The properties themselves are represented by internal codes. When it is necessary to determine the meanings of the property codes, one has to find the codes in the Hash Table and go on from there in the way just described. The structure within which properties are represented in the Property Table is a simple hierarchy, an 'outline.'

The rules for listing properties are loose. In the main, they were made up as problems arose, and indeed a certain amount of care was taken *not* to create a sharp, formal, rigid system. Syntactic and semantic properties are mixed indiscriminately. In the basic system, there is not even any distinction between the symbol and the thing for which it stands. That is to say, under 'table' we might record the property of being used mainly as a noun, the property of being used sometimes as a verb, and the property of usually being made of wood. However, the system would be expected to function without great difficulty if, through happenstance, the arrangement were set up as:

We did not reach the point at which programmes actually operated with that kind of irregularity of format, but we did have search programmes that examined the 'next level down' if they did not find a satisfactory property on the level initially assigned.

From the description thus far, it may be evident that the Property Table is, by nature, full of circular definitions. Everything is defined in terms of something else - except for a relatively few primitives that are associated with subroutines. One of the properties of 'move,' for example, is that move is often used as a verb. Another is that, when it is so used, it is to be implemented by executing a subroutine that is capable of taking arguments that answer 'what', 'by whom', 'from where', and 'to where'. Some of the properties of 'pencil' refer to its capability of serving as an argument. A pencil is 'movable', 'takable', 'bringable', and so forth. We are now almost in a position to turn our attention to the procedure through which an incoming message is processed and responded to by the computer. One more part of the system must be described, however, before that can be done conveniently.

This remaining part is the one that has to do with the 'domain of discourse' mentioned earlier. The domain of discourse is a model room equipped with a few items of furniture. The room has a door that can be opened to various degrees, a window that can be opened or closed, a table that can occupy any otherwise unoccupied position within the room, and a chair subject to the same constraint. There are a book and a pencil, to be manipulated, an active agent called 'Comp', and another active agent called 'Oper'. The discourse involves Comp and Oper and is actually carried out by the computer and the operator. The room and its contents are represented in the computer memory, of course, and they are also represented diagrammatically by simple line drawings on the screen of the oscilloscope. When the door is opened, the representation of the door in the computer memory changes, and the schematic door on the oscilloscope screen swings.

The basic subroutines, corresponding to operations in the domain of discourse, are implementations of 'move', 'go', 'carry', 'bring', 'open', 'close', 'put', etc. These subroutines, together with the subroutines that handle the encoding and decoding, the search for properties and the analysis of input messages, were all that we actually prepared and operated. The plan encompassed two additional classes of subroutines. The first of these was to handle the addition, deletion and modification of properties, under the control of input messages. The second was to handle the addition and modification of subroutines, again under the control of input messages. If we had been able to carry through to some accomplishments in the first additional category, we should have been able to increase the verbal capability of the system, but only by adding to its knowledge - to its vocabulary and its fund of facts. If we had been able to move on into the second additional category, we should have had within our grasp the capability of achieving almost unlimited restructuring and reorganisation of the system. But we did not accomplish either of those things, and we mention them here only to indicate that the approach had a higher aspiration than merely to move line diagrams about on the screen of an oscilloscope. Now, at last, we come to the procedure employed in analysing the incoming messages and selecting and directing the actions taken in response to them.

The responses were, as suggested earlier, to move things about in the room, to make replies by way of the typewriter, and - in hope but not in actuality - to add to the internally stored knowledge and to the internally stored behaviour patterns. By knowledge, of course, we mean the contents of the several tables mentioned earlier. By behaviour patterns, we mean the set of subroutines available for use in responding. The problem of interpreting an incoming message is, in the approach we have been describing, to select the appropriate subroutine or patterns of subroutines and to find the arguments that they require under the prevailing circumstances. The selection of subroutines is guided by associating subroutines with verbs. The search is carried out by a part of the programme that examines the internal codes that represent the incoming message and a list of roles that the message segments may play. Records are kept in a matrix during the processing of a message. The rows of the matrix are associated with the words of the incoming message.

The columns of the matrix are associated with the possible roles. In the version of Ontogeny that was carried to the point of demonstration, the processing deals only with words. The first step is to look up each word of the incoming message in the Property Table and place a tally in each cell of the matrix that corresponds to a function that the word can fulfil. When this has been done for all the words of the message, the task becomes one of finding an appropriate and consistent assignment of words to functions and, at the same time, a correspondence between the functions and the argument requirements of a subroutine that goes with the verb. The procedure used to carry out this task starts by 'freesing' the rows and columns of the matrix that contain only a single tally. The next step is to prepare simpler matrix patterns in which each of the words at first associated with two or more roles is assigned to a single role. These simpler matrixes are then considered one at a time.

The subroutines corresponding to the word assigned to the verb category in the first simplified matrix are examined. If one of them has a set of argument requirements that match the roles to which words are assigned, then that subroutine is selected, the arguments are supplied to it, and the response is executed. In an effort to get the system into operation quickly, we satisfied ourselves with the first subroutine that met the requirements. If no subroutine met the requirements of the first assignment pattern, the second assignment pattern was used, and so on. As soon as a suitable subroutine was found, supplied with arguments, and executed, the response was considered accomplished. The programme then simply went into a 'listening' mode and waited for the operator to take the next step.

Towards the end of the work on Ontogeny, we were planning a set of subroutines that would operate on higher-echelon strings than words. With this set of subroutines, there was to be associated a subsystem for keeping track, in a primitive way, of the 'situation.' The system was to be capable of asking, on receipt of a message, 'Am I already familiar with this message in this context?' If so, it was to enquire of itself what response it had previously made and how effective the response had been.

If the result had been sufficiently favourable, then-the system would simply have made the same response again and taken notes on its effect. In the likely event that no record existed of previous experience with the over-all message in the prevailing context, then the projected system would work with lower-echelon segments of the message, hoping to find that one or more of them was already 'understood.' In the absence of usable prior experience at each echelon, the system would drop down to the next-lower echelon until it finally came to words. Failing to understand a word, or failing to understand a phrase given experience with the words of the phrase, it would ask for help. Our experience with Ontogeny left us with five main impressions:

- It seems possible, and even likely, that we could store up enough substantive information in a computer memory to handle the analysis of natural language - semantic as well as syntactic - an analysis capable of supporting 'reasonable' responses, if only the domain of discourse is not very wide.
- It is probably more important to limit the domain of discourse than to limit the length or complexity of the input messages.
- Many so-called semantic properties play roles that are almost indistinguishable from syntactic roles. The distinction between things that are capable of acting with initiative as voluntary agents and things that are not, for example, seems to be approximately as important as the distinction between the active voice and the passive voice of verbs.
- A sympathetic, cooperative, verbal, community is a fundamental essential for the development of a sophisticated verbal mechanism. To develop complex language behaviour in a neutral environment would, we think, take another long-suffering recapitulation of evolution.
- On the other hand, no one seems likely to design or invent a formal system capable of automating sophisticated language behaviour.

The best approach, therefore, seems to us to be somewhere between the extremes - to call for a formal base plus an overlay of experience gained in interaction with the cooperative verbal community.

THE EVOLUTION OF ELECTRONIC PUBLISHING

The scope of the term 'electronic publishing' can be interpreted in many different ways. For example, it could be considered to include all forms of electronic aids to authors, from simple word processing capabilities to actual typesetting and/or mark-up tools as well as networking support to collaborative authorship and electronic communication among authors, editors, referees, and other participants in the publishing process.

Since, 'publishing' implies production and distribution, however, the term refers most obviously to the generation of publications in electronic form or, at least, with the aid of electronics. In this more restricted sense, electronic publishing can be considered to have evolved gradually over a period of about thirty years, the evolution having the following manifestations. Use of computers to generate conventional print-on-paper publications. This development can be traced back to the early 1960s.

The use of electronics to print on paper is not a completely pedestrian application since, it allows new capabilities such as printing on demand and even the production of customised publications tailored to individual needs:

- The distribution of text in electronic form, where the electronic version is the exact equivalent of a paper version and may have been used to generate the paper version. For secondary publications, electronic distribution began early in the 1960s. For primary journals, the development occurred somewhat later. Today there is considerable activity and interest in projects that make electronically accessible the text and/or graphics of journals that are also sold in print-on-paper form. Major projects of this kind include ADONIS, Red Sage, CORE, and TULIP. Moreover, the full text of a significant number of journals is now made accessible online by vendors such as DIALOG.
- Distribution in electronic form only but with the publication being little more than print on paper displayed electronically. Nevertheless, it may have various 'value added' features, including search, data manipulation and alerting capabilities.
- The generation of completely new publications that exploit the true capabilities of electronics. This phase of development can actually be subdivided into:
  - — The presentation of existing text and graphics in innovative ways, and
  - — The production of publications designed *ab initio* to exploit full electronic capabilities.

ELECTRONIC PUBLISHING

For the purposes of this resource guide electronic publishing is defined as:

- Making the content of the journal available online.

This chapter will also address the use of electronic tools to facilitate the processes of, publication, for example online electronic editorial processing.

WHY DO ELECTRONIC PUBLISHING AT ALL

Many journals around the world struggle to attract authors and readers, and frequently suffer from a lack of resources—both human and financial. In addition, research habits are changing and researchers increasingly expect any information to be found online, which means that a journal which cannot be located on the web may be effectively invisible. Online publication can help to address some of these issues. At the same time, many readers still seem to prefer print so you may not feel you can stop producing a print edition as well.

Publishing a journal electronically sounds very attractive. There are a number of good reasons for doing so, but it does have disadvantages too. Before committing yourself and your organisation to the effort and expense involved, it is sensible to look carefully at both the advantages and disadvantages. In the end, the decision will depend on what your main objectives are, so it is important to be clear about why you are publishing, or planning to publish, in the first place: what information you want to disseminate, and to whom. Electronic publishing is often considered to have six advantages over print: international reach, speed, additional capabilities, lower cost, new publishing opportunities and sustainability.

INTERNATIONAL REACH

If a journal is available on the Internet, it is true that readers all over the world can obtain and read your journal; you do not have to arrange for printed copies to be mailed to different parts of the world, which can be both expensive and slow. However, if readers are going to obtain and read your journal they need to know of its existence, and they must want to read the articles you publish. To enable readers to discover your articles/journal, you need to be visible on the main search engines and to encourage use, you really need to carry out some international promotion to raise awareness and trust in your publication.

SPEED OF PUBLICATION

An online journal has a great advantage over a print journal, as it is possible to publish an issue as soon as it is ready, and not wait for it to be printed and bound, then despatched. What is more, you do not need to wait until you have enough articles to make up a complete printed issue. You can, if you wish, publish articles individually as soon as they are ready. These time savings can be very helpful to authors, particularly in fast-moving subjects such as some of the sciences where speed of publication is extremely important. Many of the important processes of publication, however, cannot be speeded up if you want to produce a quality journal. If it is a research journal, you will still need to arrange for peer review to be carried out—and peer review is often the most time-consuming step between submission of an article and its eventual publication.

The transmission of papers to referees, and of their reports to the editorial office, can be done instantly by electronic means, and make some time savings, but the reading, thinking and writing of reports will take exactly the same amount of time. It is also important to recognise that even online publication is not instantaneous; preparing the files correctly, loading them online and maintaining the online service all take time—further time is inevitably introduced if you are working with a third party host.

ADDITIONAL CAPABILITIES

The online environment offers the potential to provide readers with more functionality. One key feature of online publications is the ability to search for articles—at a minimum within one journal, and frequently across multiple journals Another feature commonly added to online journals is that of linking. This refers to the ability to go from one place online to another, at a click of a button—the most common example being the link from a citation within the body of an article to the relevant reference at the end of the article, and from there to the actual article which is being referenced.

Reference linking in scholarly journals is now increasingly being undertaken using DOIs, which are unique identification codes assigned to online articles, and which provide permanent links for the user. This is one of the international standards being developed to assist different systems to communicate and link with each other, to help with visibility and discovery of online material. The methodology of using DOIs in scholarly journals is being managed by an organisation called CrossRef. Electronic publication also makes it possible to include material which you would not include in a print journal, either for space reasons or because the material is difficult, costly or even impossible to print.

Research articles online can be accompanied by the full data-sets from which the results were reached—ideally in a form which readers can manipulate for themselves. Colour illustrations may be prohibitively expensive in a printed journal, but present no such problems in an electronic journal. Moving images, sound, or animations may also be included, although relatively few authors automatically think of providing such material at present and the technical comple-xities may outweigh the benefits. Before introducing any additional features within the online journal, you must consider whether your readers are likely to have the necessary software to make use of the additional material.

It is also worth noting that linking is generally rated very highly by readers, who find it an invaluable way of enhancing their research; however, other additional features are much less highly valued. It may, therefore, not be worth spending a great deal of time and money on these. One final consideration is that the additional capabilities which online publishing can offer may be of particular relevance to you, as the publisher, and not so much use to the user. These may involve the ease with which you can upload your content, and streamline your working practices.

One particularly important new facility which online publishing can provide you with, is a tool to measure and monitor online use. Most commercial hosts will automatically offer sophisticated usage statistics, and most of these will be COUNTER compliant, which is another increasingly important international standard which online publications should comply with.

REDUCED COSTS

It was originally assumed that publishing online introduced immediate cost savings. However, this is only true if the journal is no longer printed at all; continuing to print even a few copies removes most of the cost savings.. If you decide to cease printing altogether, you may save a significant percentage of your total direct costs, although many costs will be unchanged—however, most readers still seem to want print copies. The cost of administering an electronic version will also be considerably lower if you are able to make it available to everyone, free of charge.

Depending on the way the journal is funded, however, you may need to replace subscriptions income by raising author-side charges; this will require an administration system, which will reduce the savings. The costs of publishing a journal can be split into direct costs and indirect costs. Direct costs are those where an invoice is received from an external supplier, and the journal needs to find the money to pay them. Indirect costs are those costs which are covered by the parent organisation, and the journal may be unaware of them. Introducing online publishing may provide an opportunity to reduce direct costs but is likely to increase indirect costs.

NEW PUBLISHING OPPORTUNITIES

It is perfectly possible for an online journal to work in all respects exactly like a print journal. However, the online medium does make possible new ways of doing things—new ways of publishing, new ways of covering costs, and new processes—which may help to address the problems of a struggling journal.

New Ways of Publishing

Publish Often, Print Infrequently

This approach may be particularly attractive if you have difficulty publishing issues on time, whether this is due to lack of funds to pay for printing and distribution, or to a shortage of articles. Online issues would be published regularly and frequently, but you might only produce one, archival, print issue per year. This can help to improve regularity of publication, whilst at the same time saving some of the print and distribution costs.

Article-by-article Publication

This approach may be even more attractive if rapid publication is important to authors in your subject area. Articles would be published online individually, as soon as they are ready. In addition to offering fast publication for authors, this will bring readers back to the online journal frequently, thus increasing usage.

Separate Online and Print Content

Some journals have separated their print and online publications so that they are almost different journals—an example of this is 'electronic long, paper short' used in the British Medical Journal. This model publishes the full article online, but only publishes a shorter version of the article within its print journal.

Some journals include additional sections within their online journal, and some exclude some materials from online version that appear in the print journal. However, if you decide to publish different content in the print and the online publication, this brings extra complexity into the way of dealing with your content, which is likely to increase your editorial costs overall.

New Publishing Processes

Open Peer Review

The Internet makes it easy for readers to comment on papers after they are published by the journal. This may be done once papers have gone through the normal peer review process, or it may precede or even replace it. Some journals then allow authors to modify their articles in the light of feedback. However, this makes for considerable extra complexity, and makes it essential that readers know which version of the article they are actually reading; this approach may not be welcomed in all disciplines, as scholars differ in their willingness to expose their unfinished work to their colleagues, so it is important that you know your reader/author community before making a decision.

Index

You may be able to do without an index if the web site allows searching of the full text of articles, particularly if it also allows searching by specific fields. However, human indexers add considerable value-electronic searching will only find the exact word you are looking for, whereas an indexer can think of synonyms, and will not index irrelevant occurrences of the word. If you can afford it, many publishers believe that a human-compiled index is still worth having.

CHALLENGES

Although publishing online presents many opportunities for journals, it can also present some challenges. Two of the most important challenges are presented here.

PERPETUAL ACCESS AND ARCHIVING

This is an issue which is worrying publishers and libraries the world over. In the print environment, a library which has subscribed to a journal in the past will always have the copies to which it subscribed, even if one day it has to cancel its subscription. However the same may not be true in the electronic environment, where the library does not 'purchase' the online journal, but merely 'rents access' for a specified period of time. Thus the library never holds the content locally, but relies on third-party servers to deliver the content. Many publishers have now changed their agreements with libraries so that the library has perpetual access to any journal issues to which it subscribed; however, this means that the publisher needs to ensure good records and administration of online access to make sure that this works smoothly over time. Print journals are relatively easy to archive but there is no easy way of archiving an electronic-only online journal. Even if the archiving library makes backup files of the journals, these may need to be updated over time as technology changes.

Links to other sites—one of the most attractive features of online journals—may become inactive due to the impermanence of World Wide Web addresses. Some publishers have signed an agreement with archiving organisations to preserve their journals permanently; this has the advantage that they can also provide ongoing access to customers after they have ceased to subscribe, or even in the event of the publisher's own service failing, or of the journal or publisher going out of business.

Much work is going on in various countries to extend their legislation to provide for legal deposit of electronic materials in the same way as is currently required for print. For example, the UK law was updated in 2003, and in 2004 the British Library started a pilot project to test deposit of online journals. Another related consideration is the digitisation and online publishing of your historical print content.

Although it is costly, there are benefits to placing all issues of your journal online so that they can be searched; there is evidence that usage of older issues increases. Some organisations will fund the digitisation on the condition that subsequent access is free.

CITATION AND DEFINITIVE VERSION

Electronic publication gives rise to a whole range of new questions, such as: How do you cite a reference in an electronic-only journal? Or to an article pre-published online? What do you give as the publication date for an article which is published online before the print issue is available? What is the definitive version of the journal—the online or the print? There are more fundamental issues, too, about what counts as 'publication' in an environment of potentially continually updated documents; these are all difficult and, so far, largely unanswered questions.

One issue that has been problematic for journals wishing to move to online-only publication has been the way that these journals are perceived by the research and academic community. In the past they have not always been recognised as credible publications by the relevant authorities when considering tenure and promotion based on publication. Fortunately this attitude is changing, and it has been assisted by the acceptance of online-only publications within indexing services, giving them recognition within the journal publishing community.

Citations can be made far more useful, in online journals, by linking directly to the cited item. This is facilitated by the Digital Object Identifier which provides a much more permanent link than a URL. The DOI/CrossRef system is now being used extensively; it does not in fact require sophisticated publishing although there are charges, these are relatively small.

An illustration of how DOIs may be used in citations can be found on the BMJ web site, in the area called 'Online First' which contains articles that have been accepted, but are not yet published, or assigned an issue. On this web page, the readers are instructed to cite the articles using their DOIs and the date of publication online. In some communities this has become an accepted method of citation, but it is early days and it is still to gain acceptance in many areas of academic publishing and research.

HOSTING ISSUES

Where a journal is published online can affect its success or failure as the online site can help or hinder the journal by the technical facilities and visibility that it offers. The price of online hosting is another important consideration. There are various options open to the journal publisher.

OWN/ORGANISATION WEB SITE

The benefit of publishing your journal on your own web site is that you have complete control over the web site—the design and the 'look and feel' of the site. Although there are, of course, costs associated with this option, no external supplier is involved. However, there are also disadvantages to publishing online this way. These may include a lack of technical skills and support for the journal, and a lack of current awareness of online publishing standards and compliance with new protocols.

In addition maintenance and updating of the web site may not receive enough attention if it competes with the other requirement of the institution's own web site. In addition, the journal may suffer from low visibility, since, it may be difficult to locate within the institution's web site, and visitors will not be attracted to discover it.

COMMERCIAL HOST

Several commercial companies are now hosting scholarly journals on behalf of their publishers. They also frequently provide value-added benefits, for example file conversion, and supply of metadata to abstracting and indexing services, as well as all the benefits of a sophisticated system which is continually being developed.

They are also experienced in dealing with subscribers and access-controlled environments, and ensuring security of the online journal from hackers and unauthorised access.

Against this, there are some disadvantages. The prime one, for a journal with little access to funding, is that they charge for their services, and although most of them offer a price which is reasonable within the budgets of western journals, they may be too costly for journals from the developing world. It should also be remembered that commercial hosts may only provide a hosting service; although they can offer advice on matters relating to online publishing, they are unable to take on the role of a publisher. However, some do offer marketing services—for additional payment—to help increase subscriptions and visibility through promotion.

SUBSCRIPTION AGENTS

Some subscription agents also now offer to host online journals on behalf of publishers. Again, they offer a high level of technical competence and value-added benefits. However they are unlikely to take your online journal unless they feel able to earn sufficient revenue from sales. They will deduct the fee for their hosting from revenues that they obtain, in which case you would not have to find the money up-front. Another potential disadvantage is that they may not be effective at increasing the journal's visibility outside their own customer base.

AGGREGATORS

A number of companies will put your journal content online as part of a large package which they sell in its entirety to libraries.

OTHER ONLINE HOSTS

There are a number of organisations set up specifically to support the online hosting of journals from developing and transitional countries.

Further information about online hosts can be found on the web site of the Association of Learned and Professional Society Publishers, and the International Network for the Availability of Scientific Publications:

- African Journals OnLine (AJOL) is an initiative originally established by INASP, and now managed within South Africa, to host African-published journals. The web site contains abstracts only for most journals, but in addition it has been developed to host full-text journals where required. Currently there is no provision for charging for access but this is likely to be offered in future for journals which require it.
- Bioline is an initiative set up by the Electronic Publishing Trust to host online versions of journals from developing countries around the world. They will convert print journals into electronic format; however, Bioline also supports training to help publishers prepare their own e-files. Bioline only supports journals that are willing to publish under the Open Access model.
- CLACSO provides support for a digital library of social science journals from member institutions within Latin America. Its digital

library site hosts the full text of journals and other publications from the member organisations; the site currently operates under the Open Access model.

- Hrcak is a project of the National and University Library in Zagreb, Croatia, to host Croatian journals online.
- Sabinet is a South African company which hosts and sells African-published journals as a single package–access is thus restricted to subscribers, but this model does provide some revenue to the journals.
- SciElo is another Latin American initiative which hosts full-text, Open Access journals within the biomedical and applied sciences. This platform only accepts journals which are judged to be of high enough quality—so it provides both support for publishers and also quality assurance for users.

MULTIPLE HOSTING

You can–of course–host your journal on multiple web sites, using different hosting services. Although full-text hosting on more than one web site is unusual and probably unnecessary, a common model is for your own web site to host a homepage for the journal, with detailed information about the journal, the editorial board, guides for authors, etc., but to use a commercial host for the full text content. You may, however, wish to consider also including your content in the collection of one aggregators as well.

CHOOSING AN ONLINE HOST

Choosing an online host is an important decision for all journals, and although it is quite possible to change hosts, the decision of which to go with should not be undertaken lightly.

There are many considerations to be taken into account, which are described more fully in a recent publishing Guide Sheet from ALPSP but the first two questions to be asked are:

- What technology and resources do you have within your organisation, and what do you need to buy in from external companies/suppliers.
- How much can you afford to pay for online hosting.

WHAT CHANGES DO YOU HAVE TO MAKE TO YOUR PROCEDURES

Whether you decide to do it all yourself or not, electronic publication will require you to change the way you do things. It is important not to overlook this aspect. You may need to re-examine all your processes—from receipt of submitted manuscripts to final publication—in order to make sure they are as streamlined, and in as logical an order, as possible. In fact, this exercise is often highly beneficial in improving both cost and time-efficiency!

EDITORIAL

The peer review, revision, and editing of articles, as already pointed out, does not become any less important if they are to be published electronically. In addition, editors may need to add electronic links within the article, within the journal, to other publications and to additional material.

The majority of authors may be able to submit their articles in electronic form, and should be encouraged to do so, as this will facilitate the editorial processes.

Electronic editorial processing software is available to manage the entire editorial process from online author submission to article acceptance. These software packages can help to streamline the editorial process, but are not essential to online publishing.

They have several advantages:

- There are no postal delays for authors submitting articles, or for the editorial office, editors and reviewers during the editorial processes, since, everything is managed and held online.
- The systems automate much of the correspondence, which can assist the editorial office.
- Most systems maintain and generate records of article progress, which may be accessible to authors as well as the editorial office. In addition, systems generally provide for a database of reviewers; this assists the editorial team in choosing the most appropriate reviewers for each manuscript.
- Since, the packages operate online, the editors, reviewers, and authors can all access the database and upload or download articles from any Internet connection worldwide, thus facilitating work when they are not in the office.

However these systems also have some disadvantages:

- They require everyone involved in the journal to have online access.
- They only save the time spent in postal delays—they do not reduce the time required to review, correct or finalise the articles.
- They require the authors, reviewers and—especially—the editorial team to be competent in using online systems, since, they are not always very user-friendly.
- They require reviewers and the editorial team to have adequate computer equipment, and either to work entirely online, or to be able to print out articles locally for reviewing, etc.
- Unless the majority of authors, reviewers and editors do make use of the software, such systems can actually increase the workload of the editorial office, who will need to load articles online themselves.
- And of course, most of them also cost money—usually in the form of a software licence fee.

Copyright

It is essential that, when acquiring copyright or the right to publish from your journal contributors—which you should always do—you make sure that you have also secured the electronic rights. It is also important to double-check that you or the author have obtained electronic rights for any other material you wish to include, such as illustrations or quotations from other publications. Examples of appropriate agreements have been produced by ALPSP and INASP.

PRODUCTION

Your methods of production are unlikely to be entirely suitable for publishing in the online environment, and this area of your activities is the one to be most affected by the introduction of online publication. It is sensible to get the articles into electronic form as early as possible; all the subsequent processing should then be done on the electronic version, and both print and electronic version should be output from the same file at the very end of the process. It is highly inefficient to work on a paper version, and then convert it to electronic at the very end.

The first change is that the final articles will need to be in suitable format for online as well as print publication. The most efficient approach is to process all articles in a 'neutral' format from which both print and electronic outputs can be produced. PDF files are adequate for straightforward journals, and of course this does preserve the appearance of the printed page; some systems may require the header information in other formats to enable searching and indexing. For more sophisticated electronic publication, PDF files are not sufficient—HTML or XML will be needed.

To produce appropriate files, you will need either to train staff and purchase appropriate software and computer equipment, or to identify and recruit suitable external suppliers to undertake this work; if it is done in-house, you will need to adapt the existing journal production system to ensure that the correct files are produced. If you decide to introduce additional functionality within the online version, you will also need to introduce production systems to implement this. Illustrations may cause problems if authors cannot supply them electronically, since,—at some point–they need to be converted into digital files for electronic publication. If the authors cannot supply e-files for all artwork, either you or the printer/typesetter/designer need to be able to scan the artwork so that the appropriate e-files can be created for online publication.

The electronic files must be carefully checked for accuracy, as it is surprisingly easy for errors to creep in when they are converted. You will need to devise—and stick rigourously to–a system for naming the electronic files for each article, and for every table or illustration associated with that article; it is sensible to include a version numbering/dating system so that you do not use an earlier version by mistake. When deciding to publish online you need to consider carefully whether your existing staff have the necessary level of skills to undertake the work required, and whether you have the hardware and software needed.

To produce the files required you may need to outsource the work that was previously done by departmental/journal staff, or you may need to change your existing suppliers if they do not have the skills, experience and equipment to provide what you need. Alternatively, the online host may undertake some or all of the file conversion work. If you decide to have different content in the print and online versions you need to ensure that the production set-up takes this into account, and that you are able to manage the administration of different versions.

MARKETING AND PROMOTION

Marketing, in the true sense of discovering what your market wants and then providing it, is every bit as necessary for electronic journals as it is for print journals. Many journals are not sufficiently visible—*i.e.*, not enough people know about them, or are able to discover them—and although publishing online may help, it is vital that some promotional activity is undertaken if online publication is to achieve the goal of making the journal more visible, and thus more used. For any journal—in print or online—conducting market research to identify what readers and authors want is essential.

In addition to talking to as many potential authors and readers and possible, try to carry out systematic surveys by questionnaire. If you see electronic publication as being a way to make your journal more international, your market research should be international too.

This may cost money, but not as much as you could lose if your journal fails. An electronic journal will not sell itself, any more than a print journal. You will need to make sure that those who should be interested in reading it, and writing for it, are aware of its existence. This is not simply a matter of mailing a leaflet.

If you can obtain suitable lists of e-mail addresses, this is much cheaper than a postal mailing; be careful, however, about sending 'promotional' messages to e-mail discussion lists, as this is considered unprofessional, and may generate a strong negative reaction, although straightforward information about journals is welcomed on many lists. You should always check the 'rules' for posting to a listserv with the listserv manager.

In addition, you could involve the editorial team in promoting the journal by, for example:

- Referring to the journal within their e-mail signature;
- Handing out leaflets at relevant meetings, and
- Ensuring that their institutional library is not only aware of the existence of the journal, but also makes it visible to users.

Online publication relies on readers coming to the web site, rather than sending the print journal to their library or their desks. Bringing people back to a web site is particularly important if the journal is published infrequently or irregularly. E-mail alerts are a good way to tell people about the latest issue when it becomes available online, and can be set up manually or you could offer the facility to sign up to an automated alert on the journal's web site.

Linking to and from abstracting and indexing databases, and citation linking using DOI and CrossRef are also important ways to bring readers to your content. To ensure visibility to researchers and librarians you must make sure your journal is covered by the major Internet search engines. Another very important way of ensuring visibility to your community is to make sure your journal is included in secondary databases. The major services used to be resistant to including electronic-only journals, but this is no longer the case.

The one often considered most influential is ISI although their acceptance procedures are quite stringent and the number of journals they include is restricted. However, you cannot include your journal in too many such databases; identify as many as you can which are relevant to the subject matter. You may be asked to provide a free subscription, but this is a very small price to pay. If you can supply 'headers'—bibliographic details and, ideally, abstracts—in electronic form, so much the better; unfortunately, however, there is as yet no standardisation about the format in which they require them.

You should also make sure that your journal is listed in Ulrich's International Periodicals Directory, which is the major reference source for librarians. Some abstracting and indexing databases—such as Medline—require the journal's header information in XML format. If you are unable to obtain these files from your supplier, INASP have a template available for use which simplifies generation of these XML documents. Once a journal is made available online, the process of gathering feedback from readers and authors can be much easier than for a printed title, as the Internet facilitates two-way communications. Online feedback forms, direct links to e-mail addresses, and discussion forums all permit much more effective exchange of information.

SALES

Printed journals need little or nothing in the way of salesmen. Libraries decide which journals they want, and then choose their preferred channel for buying them. However, site licensing of electronic journals does require detailed discussion and negotiation with each customer; this is time-consuming, and if you decide to do it yourself you are likely to need extra staff with the appropriate skills. The alternative is to have someone else, such as a subscription agent, do it for you—but you need to be willing for someone else to negotiate prices on your behalf.

Bear in mind that the price for a single library may represent several subscriptions; if libraries join together to form consortia, this is even more likely to be the case. Selling to library consortia is a particularly difficult and time-consuming process, and the publisher with only a small number of journals can easily get squeezed out.

Initiatives are, however, being developed to help smaller publishers work together to sell a single, larger collection of journals in these circumstances. It may be beneficial to try to work with other publishers, whether internationally or in your own country or region, to overcome these problems. In some countries, the tax situation will be made more complicated if you are selling electronic journals; they may attract tax where printed journals do not. You will need expert local advice on this.

SUBSCRIPTIONS ADMINISTRATION/CUSTOMER SERVICE

If you decide to restrict access in any way you will need to administer this process, providing passwords or other access controls to new users, disabling those which have come to an end, and ensuring that your system can identify authorised users when they try to access the system. All of this will entail even more complicated administration than is required for a printed journal, and will require considerable technical expertise. Customers do not need any help to use print journals; however, the situation is different with electronic journals. Some customers will forget their passwords and you will need to reissue them.

Others will be unable to get access even though apparently using the correct password. Even if you make your journal available free of charge, you will find that some of your customers have technical problems in accessing or using it.

Thus you will need to provide some kind of helpline for customer support, whether on the telephone, on e-mail or both; customers will become very frustrated if help is not available at the exact moment when they need it, so the helpline should ideally be manned full-time during working hours, even if not for 24 hours a day. Of course, if you decide to use an intermediary to provide access to your electronic journal, all of these problems will be taken care of, although naturally at a cost.

WHAT MIGHT IT COST

It is impossible to put precise figures on the cost of publishing a journal electronically; however, it is vitally important to work out your own probable costs in full detail, and not to underestimate either the time or the money that will be required. A summary of the cost differences between print-only, online-only and online-plus-print is given in the table. However, indirect costs should never be ignored!

Item	Print Only	Online Only	Online Plus Print
Editorial costs	Yes	Yes (no change)	Yes (no change)
Copy-preparation costs (*e.g.*, copyediting, typesetting, design and proofing)	Yes	Yes–plus additional costs for e-file preparation	Yes–plus additional costs for e-file preparation
Printing and binding	Yes	No	Yes
Distribution	Yes	No	Yes
Marketing and promotion	Yes	Yes	Yes
Sales	Minimal	Yes–sales and negotiation of licences	Yes–sales and negotiation of licences
Customer support	Minimal	Yes	Yes
Long-term archiving and maintenance costs	Yes (warehousing and some file archiving)	Yes (e-file and online maintenance)	Yes (including print and e-file archiving)
Financial management of subscription/licence payments	Yes (if charge for subscription)	Yes (if still have subscribers to online content)	Yes (if still charge subscription for print–possible additional costs if online subscriptions are sold separately)
Financial management of author charges	Yes (if charge author fees)	Yes (if charge author fees)	Yes (if charge author fees)

TIME

Someone will need to be responsible for thinking through all the questions raised in this document, and making the necessary decisions. This is not a one-time process; your electronic journal will need to be continuously monitored and managed to an even greater extent than a print journal. There will be additional complications to your production processes and new skills and procedures to be learned. If you do it yourself, your subscriptions administration and customer support will also be more labour intensive.

MONEY/PEOPLE

While, taking the 'electronic only' route will save costs on paper, printing, warehousing and despatch, these savings can very easily be offset by new costs.

The areas in which you will incur costs are as follows:

- *Hosting:* Whether you undertake to build and host your own journal web site, or to pay an external provider, you will have start-up and then ongoing costs.

- *Equipment:* You may need to purchase new equip-ment to manage the electronic processes.
- *Online Costs:* You may need to increase your access to the Internet.
- *Staff and Training:* You may need to devote some funds to building skills within existing journal staff, and perhaps to also recruit additional staff.
- *Production Costs:* If you reduce or eliminate print you may make savings on costs such as postage, printing, warehousing and distribution. Further postage savings may be made in the editorial office if you introduce an electronic submission and peer review system. However, you may incur additional costs if you need to outsource more work or to pay for additional services from your existing providers.

It is impossible to give definite guideline costs, as there are so many variables—the number of articles received and published, the number of subscribers, the number of other journals handled by the same system, not to mention local variations in equipment, service and labour costs.

Depending on the accounting principles followed by your organisation in dealing with overheads, your journal's finances may appear to benefit from a reduction in direct third-party costs; some organisations may not allocate a share of internal overhead costs to the journal.

However, it is misleading to ignore these overhead costs altogether in arriving at a realistic appraisal of the journal's financial health. Of course, if you decide to charge for access, some of the additional costs could be offset by increased revenues; however, you need to be realistic in your expectations.

SALES MODELS FOR ONLINE JOURNALS

SELL IT YOURSELF, AND/OR GO THROUGH INTERMEDIARIES

Making the journal available electronically is only half the story. If you rely on subscription revenue, you then need to sell the journal, which includes not only making the sale, but also arranging electronic access and managing whatever access control mechanisms you have selected. In addition, you would be wise to consider the licences which you want your customers to have; unlike print journals, electronic journals provide users with a wide range of possible uses, some of which you may not want to allow.

It is possible to have one or more intermediaries handle online sales for you; many subscription agents are now offering this service, for a fee, for electronic journals. This can make very good sense, as most libraries already deal with sub-scription agents for their printed journals. Furthermore, most subscription agents' systems offer the user the ability to obtain access to all their electronic journals through a single access mechanism; this is obviously preferable for the user, as the alternative is having to use different web sites, with different passwords, for each journal. It is obviously easiest if the agent is also acting as host for your journal; if they are not hosting your journal, you will need to provide them with basic 'header' information for each issue in electronic form so that their users can search these on the subscription agent's site, and from there gain access your journal web site. Taking this route will increase your overall costs, since, you will need to pay the intermediary, but it is very likely also to increase the accessibility, and thus the use, of your journals.

DIFFERENT SUBSCRIPTION SALES MODELS

Singly or 'Bundled'

If you are fortunate enough to publish a number of journals, there may be benefits in selling them as a single package. The evidence shows that usage of titles to which customers did not previously subscribe can be unexpectedly high. If you also publish books or other content related to the journal's subject, an even richer package could be created; you could also include links to material on other sites. Another possibility would be to collaborate with one or more other publishers to create a larger package.

Electronic Version Free to Print Subscribers

You may want to do this either permanently, or for an initial period as a form of promotion. It will require an access control system, and you will need to assign a password or other form of identification to every subscriber. Be careful not to increase the print subscription price too steeply, or subscribers will feel—with some justification—that they are being asked to cover the cost of the electronic version, whether they want it or not; this could lose you print subscribers.

Electronic Version Sales

You may decide to set a separate subscription price for the electronic journal. If there is a parallel print version, it is sensible to consider the relationship of this price to the print subscription. Should it be the same? Or more? Or less? You might want to offer a discount for combined print-plus-electronic subscriptions.

Electronic Version Sold to Print Subscribers for an Extra Charge

A number of publishers are making an additional charge to include the electronic subscription; the supplements range enormously, from 10 per cent to 50 per cent or more. An alternative is to consider the print subscription to be the 'add-on', charging a substantially reduced rate to those who subscribe to the electronic version only.

Individual Subscriptions

The majority of print journal subscription income usually comes from libraries and institutions, but many publishers also sell at a lower price to individuals. You might want to consider offering individual subscriptions to your electronic journals, on one or more of the models. It is indeed arguable that the real benefits of electronic journals are more attractive to the individual reader than they are to the library.

However, you should also bear in mind that if you offer library subscriptions, particularly on the basis of site licences, individuals may already have good access to the electronic journal through their place of work. On the other hand, low-priced individual subscriptions may be the most practical way of permitting users to access the journal when they are not at their place of work. If you offer more than one kind of electronic subscription, and if the privileges or permitted uses differ, remember that your system will need to be able to distinguish the different kinds of subscriber at the point when they access the system.

Member Subscriptions

For those societies and associations which get much of their income from membership subscriptions, and who provide members with their journal free or at a very low cost, electronic journals can present something of a problem. If members see access to their own personal copy of the journal as one of the main benefits of membership, but have access at their own desk through a library subscription at their place of work, there is a risk that they will be inclined to discontinue their membership. Society and association publishers will need to think carefully about this, perhaps offering additional electronic benefits or services only to members.

Annual Subscription or Any-time Start

It is possible to sell a subscription based on either an annual basis or any-time start. With an annual basis, regardless of when the subscriber pays, they will be provided with the journal issues published within the calendar year; this is generally preferred by libraries as it is easiest for them to manage. With an any-time start, customers will receive 12 months' subscription starting from the date of payment. This may be attractive for users, but may also cause complications and additional work for the person who has to manage the subscribers. You may also find it more difficult to work out how much journal revenue to allocate if your organisation's financial year does not coincide with the subscription year.

Site Licences

Universities, companies and other institutional journal subscribers are always very interested in obtaining site-wide access to electronic materials. Access which is only possible from one or more specified computer terminals in the library is very much less attractive than being able to provide it to each faculty or departmental library and office. It is therefore a good idea to work out a licensing policy, and an access system, which permits this. Defining the 'site' may be quite difficult, particularly for a multi-site organisation such as a large company.

Pricing is a particular problem, since, organisations vary greatly in size and in the potential or actual number of users. If you simply have a price based on the print subscription price, then large and small organisations will pay exactly the same, while at the same time none of them will need multiple subscriptions—so you may end up losing revenue. Some method of pricing based on number of users might be more equitable, although it will be more complicated to work out the appropriate price for any given customer.

Although pricing for a set number of 'simultaneous users' has worked well for computer software and databases, it has not proved a popular model for e-journals. Different publishers have looked at the funding of the institution, the total number of faculty and students, or just the numbers in the most relevant department. In most cases, publishers have found it simplest to establish a relatively small number of 'price bands' based on these measures.

Consortium Licences

It is becoming increasingly common for institutions, particularly universities, to band together in order to make better use of their limited budgets, and to share the availability of the materials to which they subscribe. This can be a very effective way of getting your journal content to a much larger community, while still only necessitating a single negotiation. Combined institutions, however, make very powerful negotiators and you need to be careful to make the right pricing decisions and not to allow yourself unintentionally to do business at a loss. It is also difficult for a publisher with only one or a small number of journals to sell to large customers and consortia—and equally difficult for the customer.

The process is no less time-consuming for one journal than for a hundred, and it requires specialist skills and knowledge. Some organisations are trying to act on behalf of many small publishers to overcome this problem. For example the Association of Learned and Professional Society Publishers, in partnership with subscription agent Swets, has established the ALPSP Learned Journals Collection which acts on behalf its smaller member publishers to sell their journals to libraries and consortia throughout the world—it does not, however, offer hosting for online journals. Similarly Project Muse in America, and SABINET in South Africa offer publishers a service both to host their journals and to sell them to libraries.

SINGLE ARTICLE SALES

It is often argued that, since, a reader will only be inter-ested in some articles, it would be better if he or she could buy those articles separately.

While the costs of administering such a system might be prohibitive in the print environment, it is in principle much easier electronically, although the publisher does need a suitable journal system which can provide access to individual articles and collect payment, whether by invoice or by credit card.

One of the problems of this system is that individual readers are often unwilling to pay for articles that they think the library should obtain on their behalf. Publishers have feared that single article sales could reduce the demand for subscriptions, but in fact studies so far do not bear this out—if anything, this seems to tap an additional source of revenue sold in excess of 2000 articles to non-subscribers during 2005, and a survey by ALPSP in 2005 showed approximately 25 per cent of the publishers that offered this service found it was becoming a significant source of revenue). Most commercial hosts and numerous other intermediaries and specialist document suppliers are set up to manage such transactions; the reader needs to be able to pay by credit card online, and the intermediary will retain an amount of the payment to cover its costs.

OPEN ACCESS

The traditional publishing model restricts access to the publication by requiring payment by or on behalf of the reader. However, some argue that in the online environment scholarly information should be free to the reader. It is also possible that Open Access journals will achieve higher visibility and use, since, anyone can read the journal content.

Open Access publishing does remove the cost and complexity of access controls, although it may introduce the requirement for a system to handle author-side payments, and, of course, as with any other electronic publishing model, if the publisher wishes to maintain some form of print version then the costs associated with print will be retained. In general, Open Access simply means 'free access to online research information'. However, there are a number of formal statements which associate various other conditions with this basic idea. It is important to stress that Open Access does not require any specific commercial model—the key point is that the user does not pay to view the material.

There are also various models of Open Access that are designed to minimise any impact on subscription revenue:

- *Delayed Open Access:* Offering free access after a specified period. The length of time after publication which is necessary to avoid loss of subscriptions is likely to vary depending both on the subject area and the frequency of publication of the journal.
- *Short-term Open Access:* Providing free access to articles for a short period after publication, after which they are only available to

subscribers. The argument for this is that this provides immediate impact and raises citation of the articles and visibility, but does not affect subscription revenue, as people are still willing to pay for ongoing access. This may not give sufficient protection, however, for all journals.

- *Selected Open Access:* Some journals make selected articles freely available whilst the rest remain behind an access control system.
- *Hybrid Open Access:* Increasing number of journals are experimenting with Hybrid Open Access. This means that the author can choose to pay the publication charge to make his or her article Open Access immediately on publication. Articles by authors who choose not to pay remain behind the access barrier. Depending on the proportion of articles paid for, the publisher can gradually reduce the subscription/licence price for the remaining content. This model enables a publisher to test the author demand for OA without putting existing subscriptions/licence income at risk; many publishers are currently experimenting along these lines.
- *Partial Open Access:* It is possible to make the journal's primary research content available under an Open Access model, but to make a charge for other value-added content such as editorials and review articles, and/or for additional services. For example, several of BioMedCentral's journals charge subscriptions to cover non-primary material—so does the British Medical Journal.

It is important to remember that the Open Access model only works for online publications. Many Open Access journals still sell a print version on subscription; in addition to covering the costs of printing and distribution, this may also help to defray the journal's other costs.

WHO PAYS FOR OPEN ACCESS

If the user does not pay, any money required to produce the journal needs to come from somewhere else.

Common sources for OA journals include:

- *Funders:* Many journals in developing countries already rely on funders, whose aims may be best satisfied by making the content freely available.
- *Organisations:* Many parent organisations already support their journals 'in kind' by not recharging the cost of accommodation, support services, staff, equipment, etc. Some also provide direct financial support by paying for third-party costs.
- *Government Funding:* Some countries provide support for journals out of government funds, and govern-ments may prefer the funding to be used to ensure greatest access to their content.

- *Author-side Payments:* Some subscription journals, particularly in the USA, already charge authors, although this is becoming less common; some journals in Western Africa, particularly in Nigeria, also charge authors. A number of Western OA journals rely on author-side charges: the authors pay a publication charge on acceptance. A recent study shows that this is in fact a less common funding model for OA journals than it is for subscription journals.

These fees are unlikely to come from the author's own pocket. More likely sources are:

- *Research Funds:* Some research grants already include publication fees, and this may become more common in future.
- *Libraries:* Some publishers encourage institutions to make a single annual payment, in return for which they waive or reduce publication charges for authors based at that institution.

SELF-ARCHIVING

Another way of achieving widespread free access to journal content is for the author to post a freely accessible version of his or her article online. This may be a pre-print or a post-print. It may be deposited on the author's or his or her institution's home page, or in a subject-based or institutional repository. In the last decade the number of online repositories of articles—both subject-based and institution-based—has grown.

Subject-based Repositories

These are most common in disciplines where researchers are accustomed to distributing their work to each other informally before publication, or see a need to make their research available quickly. The longest-established is arXiv, which was established in 1991 and covers some disciplines of physics and related subjects. Initially, publishers in other disciplines often refused to consider for publication articles which had already been posted in such repositories; however, these days most publishers accept this.

Institutional Repositories

A relatively recent development has been the introduction of institutional repositories.

These are similar to the subject-based repositories, but are being developed to preserve the intellectual output of an institution, which often includes theses, working papers., lecture notes and teaching materials. The number of institutional repositories is growing, but the majority contain little content so far and even less in the way of journal articles. The cost to the institution of establishing, maintaining and archiving the repository also has to be taken into account.

Support for Repositories

Some research funders, such as the National Institutes of Health (USA), the Wellcome Trust (UK) and the Research Councils UK, are introducing new rules for the researchers whom they fund, requesting or requiring them to deposit copies of their published articles within subject or institutional repositories either on or at a specified time after publication. In the absence of a specific mandate, few authors have so far complied—it remains to be seen whether making this compulsory will have the desired effect.

Impact on Journals

It is sometimes argued that pre-prints are not a threat to publishers, since, the publisher has added value to the published version. The threat to the business of the journal is even more obvious when the final published articles are posted in repositories; this enables readers to bypass the journal entirely. It seems possible that, if all or most of a journal's content became freely available in this way, subscriptions to that journal might be adversely affected.

If that happens, what will happen to the peer review and quality filtering mechanism currently provided by journals? However, at present many publishers' policies do allow authors to deposit a version in such repositories; there is, though, growing concern about the dangers of this and some publishers are changing their policies, for example to specify a period of time from publication before which the author may not deposit his or her article. Ideally, a research funder's policy should respect these embargoes. publishers only institute them in order to ensure the continuing survival of their journals.

LICENSING CONSIDERATIONS

When you sell a printed journal, it is fairly clear and well understood what your customers are and are not permitted to do with the material. However, in the electronic environ-ment there is much less agreement about what is allowed; abuse is also far more risky for the publisher, since, it is far easier to make a perfect copy of an original item in the electronic environment and distribute it widely. It is therefore sensible to draw up a statement of what customers may and may not do, which they will be asked to accept formally. This should be done whether access is paid for or not. There are different ways of bringing the licence to the attention of the user.

The individual user may be presented with a short summary on screen of what is permitted and forbidden, and you might even want to configure your system so that they have to click on a button marked 'I agree' before they go any further. When a sale is made to an institution, the customer might be asked to sign a more detailed printed licence as part of the sale. The latter approach does allow for a certain amount of negotiation if necessary, although obviously you would wish to design your licence so that it was acceptable to most of your customers without involving both them and you in the time and cost of individual negotiation.

Some of your terms and conditions of use would depend on whether or not the electronic version is free or not, but others would be applicable in any case. You would undoub-tedly want to permit users to search, retrieve, and print articles from the journal; you might or might not also allow them to save individual articles electronically on their own computers. You should think about the best policy on allowing users to re-send articles, particularly electronically, to other people outside the subscribing institution—a number of publishers do allow this on a small-scale, personal basis.

It is unlikely that you would want users to sell articles or redistribute them systematically on a large scale, or to mount all or possibly any of the content on other web sites. While you will probably want a signature or other indication of acceptance of the terms and conditions when a sale is made to an institution or consortium, it is not always easy to enforce these. Within the academic and scientific communities, a culture of trust and honesty generally prevails and evidence of misuse is infrequent.

Some very useful work has been done to produce 'model' licences, or licensing frameworks, which will help you to devise a suitable licence for your own journals. All have been produced in discussion between publishers and customers, and thus try to address the concerns of both.

While you may not wish to use any of them as they stand, without considering carefully the implications of the various alternatives they present, they may save you a great deal of time in working out appropriate wording, and they will also help you to make sure that you don't leave anything out of your licence.

One such example was devised in the UK by a group of university librarians and publishers. The LibLicense site also provides much useful information about licensing and licences. Some publishers have stopped requiring their customers to sign a licence at all—instead, they have a clear statement on the journal site of what is and is not permitted. So far, no problems have been reported with this approach, and of course it saves everyone a great deal of time and expense.

CREATIVE COMMONS

The Creative Commons provides a simple guide to drawing up licences for the Open Access environment. These licences grant the user wide-ranging rights to re-use the content, whilst still protecting the copyright in that content. The copyright owner can select the most appropriate version of the licence. For example, all INASP materials are published under one of the range of Creative Commons licences, which allows re-use for non-commercial purposes, but requires that the re-user must always credit the author.

LIBRARY MANAGEMENT IN INDIA: CHALLENGES AND OPPORTUNITIES

The 1990s have been one of the longest periods of sustained economic growth all over the world since the World War II. This economic growth has impacted all the spheres of human life including higher education. The academic libraries have also grown over a period of time in India and elsewhere. In general, information professionals and librarians have been coping well and addressing the many changes brought about by the electronic information revolution. There are increasing debates, discussions, seminars and other intellectual exercises on academic library management. Efforts are also made to identify the strengths and drawbacks of academic library system with the fond hope of improving the status of academic libraries in the developed and developing nations. The authors have made an attempt to present the salient features of academic libraries in India, focus the relevance of academic libraries in India and discuss the challenges and opportunities for academic libraries in India.

CONCEPT OF KNOWLEDGE MANAGEMENT

Broadly speaking, *Knowledge Management* (KM) is a process of creating, storing, sharing and re-using organisational knowledge to enable an organisation to achieve its goals and objectives of creating knowledgeable professionals and workforce. The advent of the "e-revolution", through the growth of global networks has accelerated the use of *knowledge management* (KM) especially in academic libraries. In the 21st Century KM is increasingly becoming a crucial tool in providing a dynamic and effective service to library users in India and rest of the world. Management gurus, such as Peter Drucker asserted, that for industries and institutions "the most valuable assets of a 21st century institution, whether business or non-business, will be its knowledge workers and their productivity". This affirmation was duly taken up by many academic libraries. Knowledge Management has already been successfully implemented in academic libraries and the policy makers, administrators, scientists and researchers have been actively involved in ensuring knowledge management through academic libraries.

ACADEMIC LIBRARIES IN INDIA

India is well known as the largest democracy in the world. Today there are a total of 237 universities, including 116 general universities, 12 science and technology universities, 7 open universities, 33 agricultural universities, five women's universities, one language universities and 11 medical universities along with 12,600 colleges that provide education in all disciplines. The number of teachers is 3.1 million, and 7.8 million students are enrolled in higher education. Schools of library and information sciences are also established all over the country with a view to create trained information workforce in the country. Indian academic libraries are managed on the basis of tested, tried and trusted principles of management.

INFORMATION AND LIBRARY NETWORK (INFLIBNET)

The University Grants Commission (UGS) has set up an autonomous Inter-University Centre in 1991 called INFLIBNET which is involved in modernizing university libraries in India. It connects the Indian libraries through a nation-wide high-speed data network. It promotes automation of libraries, develops standards, creates union catalogues of serials, theses, books, monographs and non-book materials; provides access to bibliographic information sources; creates database of projects, institutions, specialists; provides training, etc. Almost all academic libraries, especially university libraries, are members of INFLIBNET. It has also developed library automation software called SOUL which is distributed free of cost to its member libraries.

OTHER NETWORKS

Besides INFLIBNET, a number of other national networks and various library networks have also been developed including:

- NICNET (National Informatic Center's network),
- INDONET,
- ERNET (Education and Research Network),
- CALIBNET (Calcutta Library Network),
- DELNET (Developing Library Network), etc.

ADINET is associated with INFLIBNET, DELNET with NIC and MALIBNET with CFTRI. A good number of higher educational institutions are members of these networks. In particular, DELNET has 752 member libraries including 742 from India and 10 from outside which are engaged in compiling union catalogs, creating various databases of experts, providing training to library staff, ILL, online facilities, reference service, assistance in retrospective conversion, etc.

LIBRARY CONSORTIA

Many Indian university and college libraries are not in a position to subscribe to all the required journals and databases mainly due to lack of management support and financial constraints. The libraries are forming consortia in order to facilitate knowledge sharing at a much cheaper rate.

Some special libraries and organizations like:

- The *Indian Institute of Astrophysics* (IIA) Library,
- Inter-university Centre for Astronomy and Astrophysics (IUCAA) Library,
- National Centre for Radio Astrophysics (NCRA) Library,
- Physical Research Laboratory (PRL) Library,

- Raman Research Institute (RRI) Library,
- Tata Institute of Fundamental Research (TIFR) Library,
- Council of Scientific and Industrial Research,
- Department of Atomic Energy, etc., have established consortia to share electronic access to journal literature.

NISCAIR is developing a consortium for CSIR labs for accessing e-journals. Consortia in India are still a new concept that requires proper guidelines and methodologies. The UGC conducted a survey and found that about 142 university libraries had computer and Internet facilities which were interlinked to INFLIBNET. UGC has also launched a major initiative called UGCINFONET which provides high speed Internet connections in order to facilitate electronic access to professional literature including research journals, abstracts, review publications, and databases from all areas in science, technology, social sciences and humanities, and so on. Today, a number of professional journals are available over UGC-INFONET to all universities.

The subscription initiative under UGCInfonet is an important portal for sharing print as well as electronic resources amongst university libraries. INFLIBNET functions as a resource center with an aim to cater to the needs of its members for resources not accessible to them in electronic media or are available in print media.

INDEST CONSORTIUM

The *Indian National Digital Library in Science and Technology* (INDEST) Consortium was established by the *Ministry of Human Resource Development* (MHRD). The ministry provides funds required for the subscription to electronic resources for 38 academic institutions, including the Indian Institute of Sciences, Indian Institute of Technology, Regional Engineering Colleges, Indian Institute of Managements, and about 60 centrally-funded/aided government institutions through the consortium. The INDEST consortium is the most ambitious initiative so far in the area of engineering and technology disciplines. The primary objective of libraries is to organize and provide access to information, and it remains the same although the format and methods have changed drastically.

RELEVANCE OF ACADEMIC LIBRARIES IN INDIA

Academic libraries are the treasure trove of knowledge which cater to the needs of scholars, scientists, technocrats, researchers, students and others who are directly associated with the mainstream of higher education. In this competitive age, the policy makers have to rise to the occasion and create a new generation of knowledge workers. The information personnel of the academic libraries are also called upon to equip themselves with the best tools, techniques, procedures and practices.

The ways in which people communicate, and acquire and share knowledge, will inevitably have an impact on the library, its services, and its staff. The academic libraries play an important role in the academic community by providing necessary forum and resources for faculty and students to do their research and advance their knowledge. In order to effectively meet the growing needs of the clients and achieve success in the management of academic libraries, the academic libraries need to actively address the many challenges for the design and delivery of innovative resources and services. Academic libraries are also required to play the role of scholarly partner in exploring new pathways to knowledge and acting upon this.

It is widely acknowledged that meaningful reference work and research support is absolutely essential to ensure successful dissemination of knowledge to the clients on the basis of meaningful team spirit and work. It is imperative that subject reference workers adapt to the reality of dealing with socially networked clients. Reference interaction has always been a conversation; moving towards reference in the social environment is therefore a natural development that has been shown to be not only practically viable, but also to benefit the community of users in the field of higher education. Academic libraries are required to develop know how and show how systems which are highly essential elements of meaningful academic library management.

CHALLENGES AND OPPORTUNITIES

The vision and mission of academic libraries are changing in India. These academic libraries now take on the key role of providing the competitive advantage to various universities, research and development organizations which play a pivotal role in the process of nation building. Academic libraries are positioning themselves to be the torchbearers and path makers of educational advancement by way of integrating knowledge systems and resources.

These academic libraries are required to do serious introspection on their roles, responsibilities and contributions. Comments and observations are noted very frequently on their strengths and limitations in various national and international forums. The vast literature gleaned from IFLA, ACRL and allied publications on academic libraries aptly reveal the changing roles and responsibilities of information professionals in the modern society. The academic libraries are also called upon to exploit all forms of digital and telecommunication technologies and explore new avenues and possibilities for the enhancement of knowledge resources which are available in different forms and places.

The builders and managers of academic libraries are also required to enrich computer security and authentication techniques which promote information diffusion. The information personnel are also required to enrich their professional competence and leadership qualities which would facilitate meaningful identification, location and evaluation of information resources in order to promote professional excellence among the user community. The "user-centred" paradigm has been adopted in the developed countries to create customizable interfaces and enrich the process of collection development in the academic libraries. The academic libraries really demand a well conceived, designed and maintained systems, practices and operations which would effectively meet the needs of different constituent groups and individual users. The administrators are mainly responsible for creating and sustaining software, hardware, human resources and data bases which would go a long way in promoting research and development in India. The proficiency of *library information science* (LIS) and information skills must be complemented by hardware and software skills for working in an *information technology* (IT) intensive environment.

CONCLUSION

The digital libraries have to be managed on the basis of constant introspection at the individual level and scientific evaluation at the institutional level in this age of knowledge management. Digital libraries in India are called upon to play a crucial and leading role over other types of libraries by transforming their information management skills, techniques, practices and resources. Redefining roles and responsibilities, constructive intervention of the organization leaders in institution building endeavors, positive involvement of information personnel in delivery system and constant evaluation of goods and services will make the Indian academic libraries highly appropriate and resourceful in future.

5

Digital Information Services in the Networked World: An Opportunity for Library Co-operation

The Self-Organising Map (SOM) has been proposed as an alternative interface for exploring Digital Libraries (DL), in addition to conventional search and browsing. With advanced visualisations assisting the user in understanding the contents of the map and its structure, as well as advanced interaction modes as zooming, panning and area selection, the SOM becomes a feasible alternative to classical search and browse interfaces.

Several applications show the SOMs utility for this task. However, there are still shortcomings in helping the user understanding the map there are insufficient methods developed for describing the map to support the user in the analysis of the map contents.

In this paper, we give an overview of existing techniques and applications of SOMs in Digital Libraries, and present recent work in assisting the user in exploring the map by automatically describing maps using advanced labelling and summarisation of map regions. Therewith, the SOM becomes an attractive tool for Information Management.

The Self-Organising Map (SOM):

- Is a popular unsupervised neural network model that provides a mapping from a high-dimensional input space (for example text documents described in a vector space model) to a low, often two-dimensional, output space. The mapping of the SOM is topology preserving – elements close in the input space will also be close in the output space. Due to its interesting properties, the SOM has been used in several applications to automatically organise documents in a Digital Library by their content. Examples are text, as in the SOMLib Digital Library system.
- Or in a map of news texts.
- Or music in the SOMeJB system.

- As a recent example also the Digital Library Management System (DLMS) developed by the DELOS Network of Excellence.
- Reckons the possibilities of using the SOM as an interface to a Digital Library's content, as it offers the user support in analysing and exploring the content. With advanced visualisations and interaction possibilities, the user can exploit the full potential of the SOM. However, we still lack techniques to adequately help the user in analysing the contents of the map. For large maps, containing several tens of thousands documents describing various different topics, it becomes increasingly difficult to quickly analyse the map.

In this paper, we give an overview of existing applications of the Self-Organising Map in Digital Libraries and techniques to explore and interact with the map. Furthermore, we present recent work in making the SOM more usable for Information Management by automatically describing regions in the map through adding semantic labels to the SOM, using clustering methods to identify topical areas and selecting representative labels for those regions. Moreover, we present work on automatically summarising the content of those regions on the SOM.

The remainder of this paper is organised as follows: Section II gives a brief overview of the Self-Organising Map and its application in the context of Digital Libraries. Section III describes our work in labelling and summarising regions, while Section IV presents the experiments conducted. Section V presents conclusions and future work.

SELF-ORGANISING MAP

The Self-Organising Map (SOM) has been successfully used for clustering various kinds of data. It provides a mapping from a high-dimensional input space to a lower-dimensional output space.

In the context of Digital Libraries, the input space is mostly a vector-space model representation of the documents the Digital Library holds, may it be text, images, audio, video, or any other media that can be represented in vectorial form.

Although many different architectures exist, the output space is in many applications organised as a two-dimensional rectangular grid of units, a representation that is easily understandable for users due to its analogy to 2-D maps. Each of the units on the map is assigned a weight vector, which is of the same dimensionality as the vectors in the input space.

During the training process, vectors from the input space are presented to the Self-Organising Map, and the unit with the most similar weight vector to this input vector is determined. The weight vector of this unit, and, to a lesser extent, of the neighbouring units, are adapted towards the input vector, i.e. their distance in the input space is reduced.

At the end of the training process, the output space will be arranged in a way to represent the input space as closely as possible.

For more details on the SOM training process, please refer e.g. to. An important property of the SOM is that the mapping is topology preserving – elements which are located close to each other in the input space will also be closely located in the output space, while dissimilar patterns will be mapped on opposite regions of the map.

The SOM therefore provides a sort of clustering of the data, however, without explicitly assigning data items to clusters. It neither identifies cluster boundaries as opposed to, e.g, the k-Means method.

The generated map can help the user in getting a quick overview of the patterns in the input space. With fitting visualisations highlighting boundaries, it also allows an easier interpretation of the cluster structures and correlations in the content.

A. Self-Organising Maps in Digital Libraries

The Self-Organising Map as an interface to digital document collections has already been proposed in the WEBSOM project., where the contents of a newsgroup collection containing a million of articles was clustered on the map. The application provides the user with a map of the document collection which she can zoom into by pre-defined levels and navigate in.

- On the most detailed zooming level, a list of the documents mapped onto that region of the map is provided. The map itself, and the exact position of the documents on the map, is not available anymore. To add semantic meaning, the map gets automatically labelled by the names of the most dominant corresponding newsgroups, which is a feasible approach when some kind of categorisation is available for the documents. The labels are however not determined by topical clusters, but rather on a unit basis. The SOM as an interface to Digital Libraries has further been demonstrated in the SOMLib Digital Library System
- The SOMLib system utilises the SOM and other techniques to support the user by employing as many concepts as possible which she already knows from a conventional library. Similar to a map of a conventional library, depicting the arrangement of the shelves where books on certain topics are located, the SOM gives the overview over the contents of the Digital Library. Similar to finding related books in the same shelf, once the user has found a specific document of interest, she can find documents that are related in content in the neighbourhood of that document. A symbolic visualisation of bookshelves using the LIBViewer method further supports this metaphor. The SOMLib system utilises a labelling algorithm to

automatically add semantic descriptors to the single map units, without having the need for any category information being available.

- The SOM is used to create a web-based knowledge map of news articles. The application supports hierarchical zooming into the map in pre-defined levels of zoom. However, the map layout changes on different levels of zooming. Besides the map, also a hierarchical list of topics is displayed as an alternative for users who prefer a onedimensional visualisation. uses clustering on the map to apply labels to regions, which are generated based on term and document frequencies, using a tf × idf-based approach.

The focus in this work is on the visualisation, which tries to resemble geographical maps as closely as possible. This is achieved using a separate GIS software system.

The interaction possibilities for the user are limitedzooming is in predefined levels, the labels cannot be changed interactively, and only one type of visualisation is available. Based on the concept of the SOMLib system, a sophisticated desktop client software has been developed, which allows for various ways of user interaction with the Digital Library content.. With zooming and panning functionalities, the user can analyse the content at any desired detail level, from viewing the whole map at once down to viewing single documents.

Tools for selecting rectangular regions or units along a path allow the user to select several documents at once, and open them for example in a text viewer or in an audio application for playlist generation. One important aspect of SOMs as interfaces to Digital Libraries is that they should not be meant to replace traditional query and retrieval techniques, but rather be complementary to it. This approach is presented in., where a Self-Organising Map is integrated into the popular open-source system Greenstone as a new service, based on the existing query services such as search or list browsing.

That way, the user can still use all the basic functionalities provided by Greenstone, but she will also be able to use the wealth of additional information the SOM mapping provides about the documents matching the query results and the whole collection itself.

A screenshot of the system is depicted in Figure, where the left side figures the traditional Greenstone search interface, the lower part the document result listing, and the right part holds the map. The map can be used in two different ways. First, results of the Greenstone search will be highlighted on the map by markers.

The user can immediately see which documents have a topical similarity, as these documents will usually all be located close to each other and form a cluster on the map. This way, distinguishing between different topics found on an ambiguous word as e.g. 'jaguar' becomes easily – the documents referring to the sports car will be clearly separated from those talking about the animal because they appear in a different context together with other words.

Additionally, outliers found via the search become visible as isolated spots on the map. Secondly, the user can explore the map – she can select nodes, upon which the documents lying on that nodes will be added to the result list of the Greenstone search.

This allows the user to retrieve potentially relevant documents for a specific information need, even if they were not initially retrieved by the (usually rather short) query issued. Documents that have been matched both by the map selection and the search result will be marked especially, as they may be of higher importance.

The user can get additional information on the content of the collection by mouse-over popups displaying terms that best describe the documents on a certain node. A small user study suggested that this interface is suitable for Digital Libraries once the user has become a bit familiar with the map.

The SOM has also been used for other types of media besides text. In the SOMeJB project, the concept of the SOMLib system has been extended to audio and music documents.

Similar to the SOMLib system, the SOMeJB arranges musical pieces, described by a set of feature vectors extracted solely from the audio content, into topical clusters by the sound characteristics, as the user is familiar with from a traditional record store. In the PicSOM project., the SOM has been used for Information Retrieval in image databases, incorporating methods of relevance feedback.

III. DESCRIBING THE SELF-ORGANISING MAP REGIONS

In this section we present our work on identifying and describing regions in the mapping generated by the Self- Organising Map. As the SOM does not generate a partition of the map into separate clusters, we utilise another clustering algorithm on the weight vectors of the units to identify the regions.

Applying the LabelSOM method, we create semantic labels for those regions that assist the user in getting a first glance overview of the contents of the map. To further support the analysis phase, we additionally provide summarisation of documents of the regions using Automatic Text Summarisation methods.

Clustering

Clustering is an unsupervised process of finding natural groupings amongst unlabelled objects. The members of a cluster are similar in some way, and are dissimilar to members of other clusters.

To identify topical regions, we are clustering the units of a SOM applying an agglomerative, hierarchical clustering algorithm on the units' weight vectors.

In the beginning of an agglomerative clustering process, every unit lies in its own cluster. In each subsequent step, the two nearest clusters are merged, until finally only one cluster remains. Specifically, we use Ward's linkage (also known as minimum variance clustering) as one of the most performant within the linkage clustering families.

In this algorithm, the distance of each pair of clusters is defined by the increase in the "error sum of squares" (ESS) if the two clusters are to be combined. The ESS of a cluster X of $|X|$ values is defined as:

$$ESS(X) = \sum_{i=1}^{|X|} \left| x_i - \frac{1}{|X|} \sum_{j=1}^{|X|} x_j \right|^2$$

and the distance D between two clucters X and Y is defind by

$$D(X,Y) = ESS(X,Y) - [ESS(X) + ESS(Y)]$$

where XY is the union of clusters X and Y. The result of the Ward's algorithm is a hierarchy of clusters which the user can browse through. Increasing the number of displayed clusters means splitting existing clusters into two new ones, while reducing the number of clusters is achieved by merging two clusters into one.

This is advantageous over a non-hierarchical clustering algorithm, where changing the number of clusters might completely change the layout of clusters, which obviously is not a desired behaviour when we want to allow the user to interactively analyse the map contents by changing the number of clusters.

Moreover, hierarchical clustering allows us to at the same time display multiple layers with a different number of clusters. In contrast to other clustering algorithms, the clusters of a layer with more clusters can never be cut by clusters of a layer with less clusters.

Labelling Units with LabelSOM

To assist the user in interpreting the regions of the SOM, we automatically generate labels for the clusters we identified previously.

The cluster labels are based on the units labels generated by the LabelSOM method, which assigns labels to the units of the SOM describing the features of the data points mapped onto the respective unit.

This is done by utilising the quantisation error qik of the vector elements, which is the sum of the distances for a feature between the unit's weight vector mi and all the input vectors xj 2 Ci, i.e. the vectors mapped onto the unit i.

$$q_{i_k} = \sum_{x_j \in C_i} \sqrt{\left(m_{i_k} - x_{j_k}\right)^2} \quad k = 1...n$$

This means that a low quantisation error characterises a feature that is similar in all input vectors to the weight vector. Thus the assumption is made that this feature describes the unit well. If the input vector however contains features which are non existent and therefore have the value of 0, those attributes often also have a quantisation error of almost 0 for a unit.

Such features are in most cases not appropriate for labelling the unit, since this would describe what the unit does not contain. Therefore, we require a feature to also have a minimum average value, calculated from all the input vectors mapped to the unit.

Labelling Regions

To choose a label for a region, we consider only the unit labels present in that cluster, as the unit labels are already a selection of features describing the contents of each unit. This method is faster in computation than checking all possible features. Depending on the data, it is preferable to choose the region label based upon a low average quantisation error, a high mean value, or a combination of both.

Therefore we offer the user the possibility to interactively assign priority weights for those two measures, to achieve more meaningful labels.

Making use of the properties of the hierarchical clustering as described in Section III-A, we can also display two or more different levels of labels, some being more global, some being more local. In the visualisation of the SOM, the labels are placed in the centroid of the cluster, which may result in some overlapping labels.

To achieve a clear arrangement, the labels can be manually moved on the map, or adjusted in their size and rotation. For some labels, it might also be useful to edit their text, for example if the label text is only a word stem as in our experiment described later in this paper.

Region Summarisation

Even though labelling the map regions assists the user in quickly getting a coarse overview of the topics, labels can still be ambiguous or not conveying enough information. Therefore, we also employ methods from the Automatic Text Summarisation field.

Based on the regions identified from the clustering process, we automatically provide a short summary of the contents of the documents mapped onto those regions, allowing the user to get a deeper insight into the contents.

Automatic Text Summarisation tries to automatically generate a summary of one or more texts to present the main ideas of the contents in a short and compact form. It can in principle be divided into two areas: single and multidocument summarisation.

Single document summarisation deals with providing a summary of a single document, may it be by extraction of the most relevant sentences, or the more sophisticated approach of generating an abstract of the text. Multi-Document summarisation, on the other hand, deals with generating summaries of a whole collection of documents. Simple approaches would just treat each single document separately, generate the summary of it, and then present all the summaries to the user.

This approach of course does not consider redundancy in the extracted sentences. More advanced techniques would treat the whole document collection at once, and extract the sentences which are most important concerning all documents. Redundant sentences are eliminated first by applying a measure for overlapping words, and remove sentences with too high similarity.

Although we also provide summaries of single documents in our application, the main focus is to assist the user in analysing the contents of the Digital Library by providing summaries of the previously identified regions using multidocument summarisation. The application allows the user to select whole regions, or manually any other rectangular shape or units a long a path.

For the chosen documents, the user can choose from several different summarisation algorithms using different weighting schemes to determine the importance of sentences for the summaries, and can also specify the desired length of the summary, measured in per cent of the original sentences.

EXPERIMENTS

The following experiments were performed using the 20 newsgroups data set1, a big benchmark corpus which has become very popular for text experiments in the field of machine learning. The data set consists of newsgroup postings from the 20 newsgroups listed in Table.

Each newsgroup contains 1,000 articles from the year 1993; each text consists of the message body and in addition the 'Subject' and the 'From' header lines.

Table. The 20 Newsgroups Data Set.

alt.atheism	rec.motorcycles	soc.religion.christian
comp.graphics	rec.sport.baseball rec.sport.hockey windows.misc	talk.politics.guns comp.os.ms- talk.politics.mideast
comp.sys.ibm. pc.hardware	sci.crypt	talk.politics.misc
comp.sys.mac. hardware	sci.electronics	talk.religion.misc
comp. windows.x	misc.forsale	sci.med
rec.autos	sci.space	

In our experiments we used a standard bag-of-words indexing approach. Porter's stemming algorithm was applied to remove prefixes and suffixes to obtain word stems. From the remaining word stems, the features for the input vectors were selected according to their document frequency, and the weights are computed using a standard tf $\times$ idf weighting scheme.

This resulted in a 3151 dimensional feature vector for each document, from which the maps were trained. The specific map we will use in the remainder of this paper to illustrate our results is of 75 × 55 units in size.

Cluster Hierarchy Browsing and Labelling Regions

In our application it is possible to explore the clustered SOM interactively: to view the different levels of clustering and to zoom into the map to view the single postings. The user can browse the clustering levels either viewing only the cluster borders, or also highlighting each cluster in a different colour.

The former is shown in Figure, illustrating the steps from one to eight clusters. There is a special cluster in the lower right-hand corner with the a label also used on other clusters – 'god' in the fourth step, and 'gun' in the steps five to seven.

This cluster is, however, not a separate one when viewing the clustering with colours, it becomes apparent that this area is part of the disjoint clusters 'god' and 'gun', respectively, in the upper part of the map. With this interactive exploration of the clusters, the user can gain valuable information about the structure of the documents in the collection.

The upper image in Figure shows nine clusters with larger labels, and in addition 67 clusters with smaller labels.

The two clusters labelled 'david' are in fact one disjointed cluster. As a result of the stemming algorithm, words ending with an y now end with an i, for example the labels 'kei' (containing most of sci.crypt) or 'batteri' (various postings e.g. from sci.electronics or rec.motorcycles). There are also some labels where obviously the suffixes of the original words have been removed, as in the labels 'imag' or 'insur'.

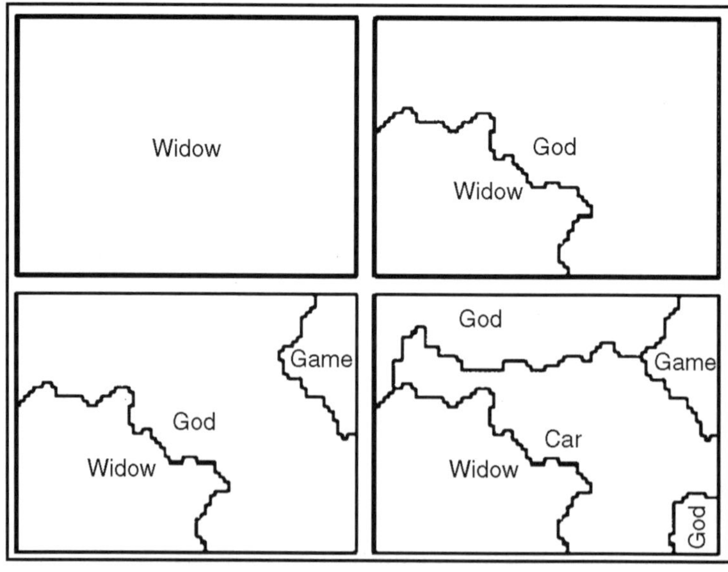

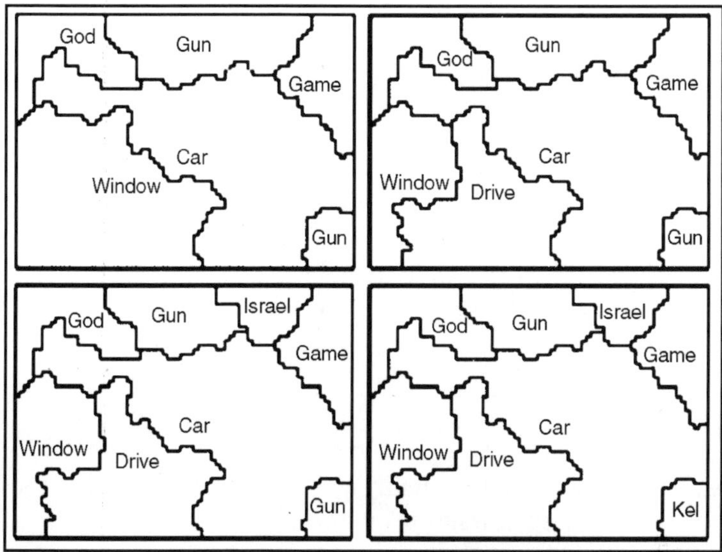

Fig. Clusters With Labels.

The labels were not edited to show the terms based on which the map has been created. In the top right-hand corner is a large cluster labelled 'game' containing most postings from the two sports related newsgroups.

The large cluster next to it labelled 'israel' contains mainly postings from talk.politics.mideast. In the upper left-hand corner there is a cluster labelled 'god' containing all the newsgroups dealing with religion, i.e. alt.atheism, soc.religion.christian and talk.religion.misc.

It is interesting to note, that in contrast to the newsgroup hierarchy, where these groups lie in three different top level hierarchies, they are combined into one cluster here. The large cluster in the middle labelled 'book' contains many of small clusters of which only a few have meaningful labels.

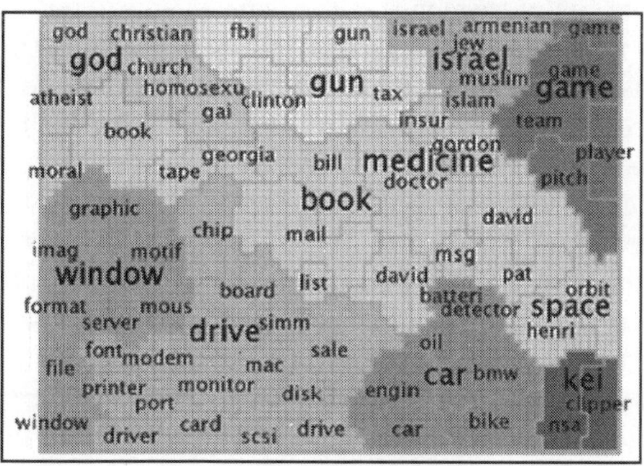

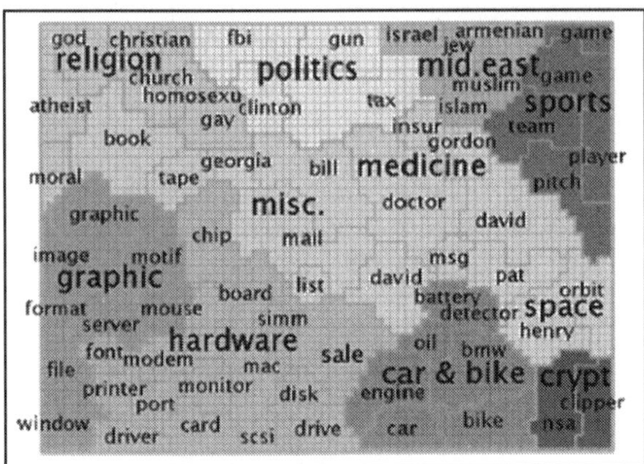

Fig. Nine Coloured and Labelled Clusters and 67 Smaller Clusters with Labels.

The small clusters labelled 'insur' and 'doctor' suggest that they contain postings from the sci.med newsgroup and the cluster label 'orbit' relates to the newsgroup sci.space. The labels containing names such as 'gordon', 'david' or 'bill' do not help in identifying the underlying topics in those areas of the map.

However, names cannot be easily automatically removed, as some common names as Mark or Bill are also a verb or noun respectively. Furthermore names can sometimes be useful labels, for example if they refer to a famous person. The small cluster labelled 'drive' lies in the cluster with the hardware topics but also directly next to the cluster labelled 'car'.

It imples that in this area lies an transition of the word drive being used in the meaning of hard disk drive or in the meaning of to drive a car. To enhance the comprehensibility of the map some labels are manually edited, which is shown in the lower image of Figure: word endings have been added and the labels of the larger areas have been edited to better suit the diverse topics.

For example the cluster automatically labelled 'car' is extended to 'car & bike' to point out both newsgroups contained in this cluster.

The cluster previously labelled 'gun' containing the newsgroups talk.politics.guns and parts of talk.politics.misc and talk.politics.mideast is adapted to 'politics'. The large cluster in the middle is manually described with three labels to point out the various topics inside.

The map thus created can now be used to interactively present the contained information of the Digital Library in an intuitive way.

In this paper we presented the usage of the Self-Organising Map as an interface to Digital Libraries. On top of this well-known approach, we presented recent work on methods to assist the user in interacting with the map. We employ clustering of the SOM to reveal hierarchical structures which can be explored by the user to get a rough overview of the structure of the data on the map.

The clustering identifies regions, which we describe on the one hand very concisely by single descriptive words extracted from the document contents, and secondly by applying automatic text summarisation techniques to generate executive summaries of the contents. All methods are integrated into a single application, that provides additional features such as visualisations and advanced interaction via zooming and panning, and selection of arbitrary regions of the map.

With these tools available, the user can be greatly assisted in analysing the SOM generated from the contents of the Digital Library, and therefore getting a quick overview of the contents of the Digital Library itself, and the structure and relationship of the documents it contains, even if the number of documents is huge and their topics diverse.

DIGITAL INFORMATION PRESERVATION

In this Chapter we discuss long-term digital preservation from an information perspective, rather than the predominant approaches; the Archival and the Technocratic Approach. Our standpoint is that information is at the core of long-term digital preservation. This means that information is the object of preservation in the long term. Information lives longer than people, organizations and tools (software).

The Information Continuum Model provides support for this standpoint. However, we find that there exists no concept to support practical action in preservation from the information perspective. Existing concepts as information object, digital object, preservation object, electronic record, information package and significant properties are context dependent and focus on the object to be preserved, rather than preservation of information.

Consequently, they are not suitable for realizing the information perspective in long-term digital preservation. The concept of Digital Information Preservation Object is therefore introduced and a tentative definition of the concept is presented.

We believe that Gladney is worth to be quoted to begin this paper. He stated, "If all that information is worth creating in the first place, surely some of it is worth saving!" During the last years, the development of digital technologies has been very fast and for the most unpredictable. Consequently, the amount of information created in electronic form is growing exponentially. Records like scholarly studies, multi-media recordings, business, scientific, government and personal records convey information critical to democratic institutions and to human well-being.

Every citizen depends on some information, partly portions unique to him, for practical as well as cultural reasons. According to Runardotter et al., digital information has to be available for the future society by legal, historical and democratic reasons. For instance, archivists have as their mission the preservation of records and its continuing value and the providing access to those records.

At the same time, the development of technologies has created unforeseen problems, such as the obsolescence of hardware and software. There is no information system capable to retain and make the information accessible for more than 30 years.

Constant upgrading of operative systems and software applications in one hand and new storage technologies on other hand are leading to the very difficult access to information.

File formats are experiencing the same problem because what today is standard for some applications or platform shifts or disappears within a decade. The solutions that are today for preservations and foremost to make digital material accessible on long time are insufficient.

Archival inquiry "Archives for Everyone – Now and in the Future", called attention to these great shortcomings and argued that models, methods and platform-independent software for preservation of the digital material are omitted largely.

On one hand, the "problem" with digital preservation is the lack of proven methods to ensure that the digital information will continue to exist On the other hand, the software currently available does not include good tools for saving digital recorded information in the face of rapid hardware and software obsolescence.

It states that digital preservation is suddenly urgent because the needed technology and infrastructure are not in place. The challenges that needed to be addressed include legal, educational, and technical aspects.

Among these challenges only one difficult technical problem impeded digital archiving until recently – how to preserve information through technology changes. Within the practice of preservation, archives are still using methods developed since 1970-1980. These methods cause losing of functionalities of the records when archiving.

Archival science has not developed as rapid as information technology. Information in the digital era demands several kinds of tools for its processing. Nevertheless, there is a lowest common denominator: digital processing.

However, such processing tools are viewed as mediator for digitally recorded information. Digital material that is produced on a certain platform, with a certain application, a certain version and in a certain format, needs to be converted to other platforms, applications and/or formats in order to gain access to information over time.

Another way of retrieving stored information is to emulate the original software (and platform) in which digital material has been produced. In either way, information might be lost and the information retrieved might not be fully reliable.

According to Runardotter et al., the concepts that are fundamental in archival science, such as record, document or archival record, has not the same dignity in systems science. In information systems sciences there are not methods that in the same degree as in archival science deals with long-term, "forever" perspectives.

This has not been detected as an issue in systems science until recently. The transition between paper based mediums to digital media was not preceded by a strategy for long-term digital preservation.

This phenomenon explained in terms of lack of knowledge and experience when handling digital material. Besides, no one could foresee the speed and complexity of the evolution of computers and software.. Information and long-term digital preservation is one of the acutest questions for all kinds of preservation institutions like archives, libraries, local authorities and for society as a whole.

Society and information curators must face the challenge of finding some sustainable solutions to ensure that digital recorded information of today become accessible and understandable in the future. Otherwise, digital material and likewise one part of society's future cultural heritage and history are in danger of disappearing forever. Consequently, legal and democratic demands cannot be fulfilled.

According to Gladney it was stated, that technology has influence in almost every aspect of long-term digital preservation and it is not widely believed these solutions can be achieved solely through technological means.

To find solutions to the problem much research was limited to technical aspects of preservation but our research has taken another view on long-term digital preservation, which puts information in focus. This paper therefore discusses the concept of information as central for long-term digital preservation.

FACING LONG-TERM DIGITAL PRESERVATION

The authors of this paper are connected to the Long-term Digital Preservation Centre (LDP Centre) in Sweden. The major activities of the LDP Centre concern research and systems development within the field of long-term digital preservation.

The LDP Centre has adopted, at this stage, migration as method for preservation. The starting point for digital preservation was the OAIS Reference Model. In this work, the LDP Centre has developed a model for structure for Information Package.

This structure was (and is) intended to be used by archive creating organizations, in order to later deliver digitally recorded information to long-term digital preservation archives. Conceptually, this model consists of a base structure, and other elements. The base structure consists of different sets of metadata according to well-established international metadata standards used in archiving.

These standards are Metadata Encoding & Transmission Standard (METS, covering technical and provenience metadata), Encoded Archival Context (EAC, covering archival metadata about the creator of the information), Encoded Archival Description (EAD, covering structural metadata) and PREservation Metadata Implementation Strategies (PREMIS, covering technical and process metadata).

We found out that the existing models for structuring information about the object to be preserved, produces problems in implementation. As we can realise from the descriptions above, these structures are used as "wrappers" carrying metadata sometimes overlapping one another.

Consequently, dealing with all these structures causes both intellectual complications and technical implementation difficulties. We, at the LDP Centre, have experienced that all these structures have some kind of inherent philosophy which focuses on special features or attributes of digital material. Here we did three significant observations.

- The used structures do not focus specifically on information.
- Using several structures sometimes causes an intelle-ctual "mess" due to their inherent philosophies (such as ontological confusion).
- The used structures are inherited from the archival world and, as we see, they support legislative (or authority) records more than digitally recorded information in general.

We also found out that putting a lot of efforts on these structures, made us loss focus on that we believe is important to preserve, to be precise information. It is obvious that technical or other aspects of the digital material to be preserved are Ó÷üëéï: kika i boken! indeed important to deal with, but those are just means of preserving information while the digital "technology is a live".

We do not know how long this technology and its tools are going to be a part of our society. Perhaps in just some years from now a new informational paradigm will occur. Another issue concerns the fact it was archival institutions that early experienced the need of digital preservation, it was obvious that the first efforts on preservation started from archival work practices.

Consequently (archival) metadata standards were developed in order to support digital preservation. The archival inheritance spokes for the principle of provenience as one of the stone corners in long-term digital preservation, because this principle supports authenticity and trustworth-iness of any kind of digitally recorded information.

Consequently today's "solutions", based on the Archival and/or the Technocratic Approach, supports preservation only in a (relatively) short-term. To approach a solution concerning the question about how to preserve information through technology changes and surpassing the archival inheritance, the LDP Centre's research activities has taken a new view on long-term digital preservation, which puts information in focus.

This includes the development of a detached *Digital Information Preservation Object* that is independent of technology and deals with the question of provenience in a new way. Such preservation object might be transferred between different technologies.

This is viewed as the main key to a viable solution for long-term digital preservation. Such view demands a higher level perspective of information and its continuing value without neglecting the constant changing technical aspects of digital preservation.

Developing the Information Approach

This paper is a result of two research activities, literature review and interaction in the developing R&D team at the LDP Centre. The literature review was carried out with the purpose of developing a definition of Digital Information Preservation Object and the interaction helped to gather data about the developed structure through seminars, (informal) "interviews" and systems development meetings.

There is a large quantity of literature about the concept of information. But in comparison, the amount of literature in the field of long-term digital preservation is relatively small.

The process of critical selection of relevant literature was based upon parameters such as "well known writers", "established perspectives and/or schools", in order to address the key sources, key theories and definitions of the topic. Since our intention was to provide a broad view on the subject, the initial literature review made it clear that several research projects have shown its own approaches to what we call Digital Information Preservation Object.

The development of the base structure, were a joint task of the entire LDP Centre. Everyone (at some extent) was involved in its development and several research observations were made during these activities.

The resemblance with Action Research as research method is purely unintentional. Nevertheless, adopting Action Research as a research method in this work will underpin the scientific value of the paper. Some words about Action Research are then necessary.

Action Research, as research method, is suitable in order to describe the origins of the gathered data (the structure developed by the LDP Centre). Further, some of the parts of the named structure were and still are being developed in joint seminars between system developers and researchers at the LDP Centre. This implies that a social context is set up.

This team interacts together in order to find improvements to already existing drafts. Together, the team define problems, co-generate relevant knowledge, learn and take actions. This "socio-technical" unit, is relatively smali (nine persons) self-managing and "posses the skills and authority to control the operation of their technology" and appropriate to carry out Action Research a low-system level. In our work, we tackle questions like: what are the elements of the Information

Approach? what properties/characteristics constitute a definition of the notion Digital Information Preservation Object? Since the LDP Centre intends to develop a general preservation model in which Digital Information Preservation Object is the mediator for preservation, this paper will have influence for further research as well as for what methods, models and techniques that will be developed and used. Furthermore, our result will influence the development of the information systems intended to serve long-term digital preservation.

About Information

The term information is used with different meanings by different groups and in different contexts and there is no well-defined definition of the terms "data" and "information". A common and short definition is that information is interpreted data. Hence, data is signs used to represent information, or signs which carries with them the possibility to compose and/or decompose the text, photo, music etc. from which it is derived.

Thus, retrieving the source provides access to information and we can start reading/viewing/listening but also interpreting and analysing the information existing in the source.

This results in the creation of knowledge, that is, we learn from information. The central idea is that data become information by a process of interpretation. The infological equation states that I = i (D, S, t) where *I* represent the information we can get through the interpretation process *i*, which is operating on data *D*, together with our pre-knowledge *S*, during a certain time *t*. Langefors [ibid.] states that "One of the central insights from infology is that data or texts do not "contain" information (knowledge) but will only, at best, represent the information to those who have the requisite 'pre-knowledge'" and he also means that the infological equation is a representation of this.

Dealing with information systems require a broad view of information, since using a computer implicitly involves information services of some kind, that is, we get service by being informed by data. According to Langefors it is necessary to define information as knowledge, since "information is knowledge and not physical signs".

He regards information as knowledge structured in such a way that it is communicated. Because of this it can also be stored, which leads to information being stored knowledge. Checkland & Holwell provides the view that information is a service that supports decision making within organizations. Data are facts and a starting point for mental processes.

They introduce the concept of "capta", which is the result of selection of certain data (we pay attention to, create some new category or get surprised by the data). In other words, data that catches our interest transforms to capta, a consciousness of something.

This signifies that turning data into information is done through a mental process and during that process the data changes shape, and will ultimately lead to knowledge. Once we have selected, paid attention to or created some data, or turned it into capta, we relate it to other things or put it in a context, we attribute meaning to it, and by this we once again convert it, this time to information.

This can be done individually or collectively and this process, selection and conversion of data into meaningful information can lead to larger structures of related information, or what we call knowledge. The interpretation process emphasizes is implicit in this reasoning.

This is line with our claim – that information is not equated with knowledge. Just like data must be interpreted in order to become information, so must information be interpreted and analysed in order to be knowledge. Information is never the knowledge itself, the knowledge is within the knower.

We agree with Langefors with his notion that in order to understand information people must have pre-knowledge. This we see as knowledge that consists of the ability to assimilate the information, but also to have an understanding of the information content, or the subject in focus.

If these abilities are found, new knowledge is created the moment someone (individually or in a group) thinks of an issue. When people's ideas, or knowledge, are being shaped and transferred to a media they are made available for others to share. Hence, the knowledge has now once again become information and exists physically (or digitally), available for people who need it in order to learn and increase their knowledge of something, for example within an organization.

Information Continuum Perspective

Runardotter et al., put information in a long-term digital preservation context that is a new circular view of the information life cycle. Information lives longer than people, organizations and tools. The authors manifested that information is a living concept and is in progress during constant ongoing process.

The fact is that people, organizations and tools are replaced over time. Further, they observed the phenomenon that information never dies provided that it is preserved and used. The statement is based on that information is constantly shaped and reshaped, evolving through time, picking up further information or losing some parts and in that way information is all the time under reconstruction.

To keep information alive demands a set of ongoing activities, both organizational and technical. The idea of living spiral is also supported by the Records Continuum Model and Information Continuum Model. According these models information and records continues to evolve in space/time and therefore are no end products..

The Records Continuum Model is widely known about and discussed in the archival profession, unlike the Information Continuum Model discussion of which is only just beginning to be opened up. The named models are founded on Giddens' structuration theory.

This theory of time/space distanciation has been translated into a "rhythm" for information processing derived from the processes of creating information, capturing it as recorded information, organising it and bringing it together within the plural domains of competition.

Each item of information once created, may or may not be recorded, stored and managed in ways that can benefit individuals, groups, communities, and can push that information out into the plural domains of the further reaches of space/time.

The continua (the dimesions of the model) in the Information Continuum Model are collectively meant to focus analytical attention on the nature of recorded information as an allocative resource, something to be shared and to be used within our activities.

The continua in the Records Continuum Model collectively are meant to focus analytical attention on the nature of recorded information as an authoritative resource, something to be relied upon not because of its content but because of the way, it has been created and maintained with some continuing contact to the original specificities of its occurrence.

According to Upward, information (and its reconstituted products) outwardly spiral from the original act of creation of a document. This idea is also derived from Giddens' theory of structuration. In the Information Continuum Model, information is derived from a principle source (for example, an information object such as an interview), and becomes transformed through the agency of people and technologies for different purposes.

Information Objects are both embedded in the "context of the action in which they are part, and are recursively involved". Information artefacts, as records and outcomes of action, become disembedded and reused in other contexts, for example, a research interview is "unitised" and its parts are reconstituted via different technologies or processes as evidence for particular research and theoretical constructions in academic production.

The interview, or any data, is therefore moved space/time, and is reconstituted, reused, re-embedded according to particular human or machine agency (human speech is transformed by agency of speech recognition software into text), or human agency makes particular interpretive decisions about how ambiguous sounds should be transcribed in transcription. The interview data (or its constituent parts) become pluralized with the production of different knowledge artefacts: theory, the application of theory and the development of scholarly and practical publications. Its pluralisation can also lead to it being used in other forms of action, such as social action, lobbying, or policymaking.

The incorporation of the time/space dimension is also important for several reasons. First, it recognises that information object have a changing historical life, and in addition, the reconstruction of time and space through modernity, and particularly through the agency of ICTs, gives information objects new potentiality.

We could use Giddens own "words" and transform these to our vocabulary of Information Continuum. Giddens "structure" equals to rules and resources organized as properties of systems.

Systems equal to reproduced relations between actors or collectivities organized as social practices. Finally structuration equals to the continuity or transformation of structures, and therefore the reproduction of systems.

The dynamic of structuration is crucial in our view. "Social practices evolve over time and space and must replicate even to stay the same" (the essence of long-term digital preservation). The term of continuity (i.e. continuum) promotes the reproduction of systems (i.e. memory traces, organized social practices) by means of digitally recorded information and its continuing value. Information is seen as an (allocative) resource, something to be shared and to be used within our activities.

In the long-term gaining access to digitally recorded information (through longterm digital preservation activities) will tell us what sorts of things were out there in the world. We could summarize our view in simple words as "Digital preservation will ensure, through the continuing value of information, that social systems will be reproduced as memory tracks of human activities".

Predominant Approaches in Long-term Digital Preservation

In our research we could observe that there are two predominant approaches trying to define the object of preservation. The first is closely related to Archival (including Records Management) and the second is a technical (or merely a technocratic) perspective. We could also observe the lack of an approach based on Information (and/or Information Continuum) perspective.

The Object of Preservation in the Archival Approach

A definition of Preservation Object is given by Dollar as "Preservation Objects are those to be archived. These objects are physically compound by set of files in maybe different formats. The objects logically are compound by data – the content for instance birth date of a person, and metadata – that should describe the context when the birth date of a particular person was used".

The Records concept opens another view on the object of preservation. Preservation is a key characteristic for records, which is followed by their creation purpose to be re-used. The preservation also makes the record a vital component in the memory of organizations, individuals and in some cases of society. A record is more than just information, it suppose to be trustworthy i.e. being able to serve as evidence, and support accountability. The time for preservation could vary from days or months up to hundreds of years. The International Standards Organization definition of records is: "Information created, received, and maintained as evidence and information by an organizations or person, in pursuance of legal obligations or in transaction of business."

In the Guide for Managing Electronic Records of the International Council on Archives, from an archival perspective, a similar definition of record is given as "recorded information produced or received in the initiation, conduct or completion of an institutional or individual activity and that comprises content, context and structure sufficient to provide evidence of the activity."

Records can occur in different forms and representations.

They are usually represented as logically delimited information objects, for example, as distinct documents. But increasingly we find records in the form of distributed objects, such as relational databases and compound documents.

According to Thomassen a record has four characteristics, which make the record unique in relation to other types of information:

- Records serve as evidence over actions and transactions
- Records support accountability
- Records are related to processes, i.e. information that is generated by and linked to some work processes
- Records are going to be preserved, some even for eternity.

Cox stated that the evidential value of a record can only exist if the content, structure and context are preserved. The context is the link between different records that belongs together, and also to the process where the record was created. According to Dollar the electronic record is more of a logical entity, where integral parts can be managed at different places within an information system, or even in different information systems.

The question "What is a record" has been one of the fundamental issues in debates and discussions in archiving and digital preservation over the past twenty years. Attempts to arrive at general definition of an *electronic record* were made in the last decade by several research projects and have by now being replaced by more constructive approach to define properties and functionalities of electronic records that need to be preserved in a given context.

An electronic record can be understood as a package or a set of technical properties and possibilities, and of administrative context where some of these technical possibilities were put to use. In contrast, one approach in Digital Libraries that might have a significant difference is proposed by Nichols.

In this approach the concept of "artifact" is central an defined as "a physical object produced at some time in the past, and attesting to a given set of practices, thinking, and ways of viewing the world, but whose importance will be defined by present and foreseeable future needs and use. The value of the artifact is strongly influenced, but not completely determined by, the document/object's features that are unique". An artifact is then an object with a set of values such as Evidential, aesthetic,

Associational, Market and Exhibition value. An artifact is of value to the extent that it testifies to the information being original, faithful, fixed, or stable. Although, this approach do not mention the term record but "artefact", we interpret this approach to be similar to the Archival Approach.

The definitions of records are to some extent usable in our perspective. Nevertheless the usage of terms as "legal obligations" or "accountability" or "evidential" are strongly connected to Records Management and Archiving. Information is important but not central. We perceive the evidentiallity of records as the major focus of Archiving and Records Management and less focus is given to records as informational source. Thomassen gives emphasis in the need of preservation of records in order to be reused as memory traces.

This encompasses our Continuum perspective which is beyond of just records. The "big difference" is that our perspective is turning the precedence of information in relation to Archiving. Another difference is that our perspective deals with any kind of digitally recorded information as evidence of human activities not just with records as legal evidence.

The Object of Preservation in the Technocratic Approach

A definition of Digital Object is given by Blanchi & Petrone as "a unique identified data abstraction that encapsulates content and access policies while providing a high-level, self-describing, type definition. Digital Objects are described trough the use of an abstract typing mechanism that we refer to as content type".

The concept of Information Package of the OAIS Reference Model states that data is interpreted using its Representation Information (described in metadata), which produces information, that an information object consists of not only data content, but also the information necessary to interpret that content. In order to successfully preserve such a generic Information Object, it is critical for an Open

Archival Information System (OAIS) to clearly identify and understand the Data Object and its associated Representation Information, which together forms what, is called an Information Package.

The PREMIS data model describes intellectual entities, objects, rights, agents and events. Objects, according to PREMIS, can be bitstreams, files or representations (digital objects "instantiation or embodying an intellectual entity") Further, in scientific material the notion Preservation Object can be compared to the approach of Persistent Object articulated by the US National Archives (NARA) in cooperation with the San Diego Supercomputing Centre (SDSC).

The persistent object method presumes that all records can be represented as objects with their specific characteristics and behaviour.

The concept of Significant Properties, proposed by the National Library of Australia (NLA), are functions or characteristics of an object that are essential to its meaning. Preservation of digital objects, in this approach, in some cases will necessitate changes in look, feel, functionality or content if the object is to remain usable at all. Although significant properties may be seen as individual and specific to a given object, most digital archives try to create classes of objects based on common properties.

In the Cedars project, Significant Properties were associated with the Underlying Abstract Form (UAF) of an object. Therefore, objects with the same UAF have the same significant properties. Conversely, if significant properties varied, than objects that were otherwise similar could have different UAFs.

The PREMIS working group, following on the work of OAIS, Cedars and NLA, defined Significant Properties as those "characteristics of a particular object subjectively determined to be important to maintain through preservation actions", noting that "Significant properties may be objective technical characteristics subjectively considered to be particularly important, or subjectively determined characteristics".

Further, the FEDORA architecture describes a content container abstraction, the Digital Object, and the nature of Repositories that provide access to these containers.

They conceptualize a Digital Object as having:

- A structural kernel, which encapsulates content as opaque byte stream packages
- An interface, or behaviour, layer that gives contextual meaning to the data in the Digital Object.

One useful metaphor for a Digital Object is that of a cell. A similar approach is given by Saidis et al. as Digital Object Prototypes (DOPs) which provides the Digital Library (DL) designer with the ability to model diverse types of digital objects in a uniform manner while offering digital object type conformance.

They described a Digital Object that has constituent components, that is to say files, metadata, behaviours and relationships. The derived digital object typing information – that is, which components constitute each different type of object and how each object behaves – is not realized in a manner suitable for effective use by higher level Digital Library application logic including DL modules and services.

A DOP is a digital object type definition that provides a detailed specification of its constituent parts and behaviours. Digital objects are conceived as instances of their respective prototypes.

The approach to Digital Libraries proposed by Arms et al. described the "digital object" in a slightly different manner. The main building blocks in this approach are: "digital objects", which are used to manage digital material in a networked environment; "handles", which identify digital objects and other network resources; and "repositories", in which digital objects are stored.

From a computing view, the digital library is built up from simple components, notably digital objects. A digital object is a way of structuring information in digital form, some of which may be metadata, and includes a unique identifier, called a handle. First lets have a look to the terms and concepts used by this approach.

Very common are the terms of "data abstraction", "data", "bitstreams", "files", "instantiation", "characteristics and behaviour", "functions", "functionality", "objective technical characteristics", "structural kernel", "encapsulates opaque byte stream packages", "interface", "metadata", "behaviours and relationships", "manage digital material in a networked environment", "stored". Looking to the ontology of this approach is quite obvious that the terms utilized comes from computer science in general and at some extent from Object Oriented terminology.

This spokes for data management through information systems making data central. The term object is also important being conceptualization of data (such as files, bitstreams, etc.) having some behaviour (its functionality or implemented functions in as information system). No emphasis is made on information neither on its contents as traces of human activities.

Towards a Definition of Digital Information Preservation Object

Every other approach to define a the object of preservation has focused from different perspectives of preservation and from different characteristics of the digital object using its own ontology. Furthermore, we found that a) there is no existing or established definition of Digital Information Preservation Object, b) existing concepts are context dependent and focuses specifically on object to be preserved. After our study we came to conclusions that research carried out so far do not handle

Digital Information Preservation Object from Information Continuum perspective and do not contribute with any definition of the notion Digital Information Preservation Object. However, the studied research results merely focus on the structure and physical nature of the digital object. Their described abstractions are conceptualizations of the underlying physical level. Nevertheless, although these approaches support our activities to some extent, the definitions provided by these approaches are not suitable for our view, hence; we experienced the emergence of an own definition of Digital Information Preservation Object that specifically focuses on information.

However, this study gave us insights to take another perspective. To define the notion of Digital Information Preservation Object it is needed to take a standpoint. We cannot begin the definition from structure of the object; nonetheless, we will begin definition from a global view. If we start from the structure, we are viewing an object as a delimited entity at structural level, since our focus is on information, not the object itself.

We want to distinguish the conventional view to the object that is a construction, a container or a carrier to hold together the elements (depending on level of conceptualization) from the view that is to see an object from continuum perspective. An object there is a piece or pieces of information that reflects human action in a social context in the continuum.

There is an important remark before we provide our tentative definition of Digital Information Preservation Object (DIPO). We need to state that any for any object is to say that its analysis is made depending on the level of abstraction adopted and due a set of variables at that specific level.

The Structure developed at the LDP Centre and the descriptions in section are (technical) conceptualizations of "digital (physical) objects"; they concentrate their efforts in describing or defining (at a very low level) the object to preserve regardless of its continuing information value. Our intention (or level of abstraction) lay merely in the general level or, so to say, we try to define DIPO at an "ethereal" level; we want to define the "thing" DIPO.

We take stand in the philosophy of Dooyeweerd who stated that Meaning rather than Existence is the primary property in created reality. In our perspective, this view encompasses the Information Continuum

Model perspective in which put the continuing value of information (i.e. its reconstruction of human social actions) as the meaning (*raison d'être*) of the DIPO. The DIPO is a recorded result of human's action in form of information pieces. This information is categorized in an information type from social context. These information pieces can have relationships to other information pieces either within its own physical carrier or toward other objects.

The vital characteristic of the information object from continuum perspective is that new object can be created through the combination of information pieces that can be a piece of other objects. In that way, the information will be reused in another context and reproducing human social actions. It means that information can be related to processes (that is generated by, and linked to work processes). Furthermore, the information in the object must serve as evidence over actions and transactions as well. The natural question that arises, should be what is this definition good for? Having a definition of DIPO and a clear perspective of the continuum, long-term digital preservation issues might be easier to tackle. Something we observe is that there is a need of a uniform "aspectual abstraction" of the Digital Information Preservation Object.

This level should be based in deep philosophical foundations that should cover several aspects of the object (i.e. its attributes, characteristics or properties), such as physical aspects: decay of materials, biotic: pests eating it the storage material, lingual: language changes over long term, social: social and cultural connotations and meanings change over long-term, juridical: legal matters of e.g. long-term ownership, for instance after someone has died, pistic: the religious or faith, moral ethical, normative contexts that can change, probably slowly (over centuries), so this might provide a better degree of harmony over the preservation period than earlier aspects.

6

Some Aspects in the Economics of Information

The starting point for a study of economic models of the digital library such as this must be an understanding of the meaning of the term 'digital library'. Numerous definitions of the term have been proposed. They vary considerably with regard to their proximity to the concept of a traditional library. The latter classifies, catalogues, and provides access to quality-controlled information resources. It also offers related services and tends to restrict access to a well-defined user group.

The term digital library is used less precisely and may refer to anything from a limited list of hotlinks to the entire content of the Internet. The only common factor in these definitions is the idea of digitisation.

A study of economic models of the digital library requires a definition. Although the UK Electronic Libraries Programme (eLib) and the US Digital Libraries Programme have done a great deal to progress the concept of digital library and, latterly, the hybrid library, a clear and universal concept is still lacking.

Before an economic model of a digital library could be tested, not only would a clear definition be required but considerable progress should have been made towards development and implementation. Such progress has been made with regard to specific digital library resources and services.

Thus, with a view to exploring economic models of the digital library in a systematic and useful manner this study focuses on models of specific digital library resources and services. It takes as a starting point the different areas of the eLib programme.

This chapter will review and compare economic models of the academic digital library. Until now, empirical testing of economic models of digital libraries has been limited. Economic issues tend to be tested after solutions have been found to the more pressing technical, cultural and legal issues because no library manager or user would consider paying for a service that had not been shown to be technically sound, legal and useful to its target audience. The pace of development of different elements of the digital library has varied over the last two decades.

This document will include models of aspects of the academic digital library that are sufficiently developed to be modelled. As electronic alternatives to traditional library services are developed, shifts occur in the roles and activities undertaken by different stakeholder in the academic information delivery chain.

Consequently, there have been sometimes unanticipated changes in the apportionment of costs and benefits to those stakeholders. Many roles are still fluid and change will continue until effective models are established.

There will be no attempt here to predict the future. This report evaluates and compares only models that have been proposed or tested. A useful economic model of the digital library must accurately represent all stakeholders in the academic information delivery chain, their relationships to the supply and delivery of digital resources, and the associated costs and benefits. The principal stakeholders involved in digital libraries are:

- Academics as authors; · academics as editors and referees;
- End users (inc. academics as researchers, students, and clinical, professional and industrial users of electronic academic information);
- Academics as teachers and recommenders of texts;
- HE librarians;
- HE computing support departments;
- Publishers of both primary and secondary literature (commercial, not for profit, University presses, etc.) and other electronic content suppliers (such as museums);
- Booksellers;
- Funding bodies;
- Subscription agents;
- National libraries;
- Document suppliers such as the British Library Document Supply Centre (BLDSC);
- Reproduction rights organisations;
- Intermediaries such as the National Electronic Site Licence Initiative (NESLI) and Higher Education Resources ONdemand (HERON);
- Internet service providers and other aggregators and distributors (including companies such as CatchWord and Ingenta which provide Internet publishing for publishers);
- The Higher Education Digitisation Service (HEDS).

These stakeholders are both individuals and organisations of both present and future generations. Some groups have a more direct stake than others.

Arguably, the most important are academics as authors; academics as users of scholarly information; academics as teachers; HE libraries and librarians;

publishers; and information brokers (including subscription agents and document supply agencies).

Economics of Digital Library Services

When considering the economics of digital libraries it can be tempting to focus on financial factors that are directly related to digital library services, for example the price of resources and infrastructure. It is important, however, to be aware of other economic factors.

These include the cost of downloading bandwidth-hungry images and time spent filtering information in an environment where the signal-to-noise ratio is minuscule. While the authors acknowledge the importance of these factors it was beyond the scope of this project to determine their economic impact.

Electronic Journals and Electronic Individual Article Supply

The Serials Crisis

Much of the incentive for the development of electronic journals and electronic individual article supply (eIAS) services has arisen from the financial pressure on libraries caused by:

- Budget restrictions;
- An explosion in scholarly information;
- The fact that, over the last two decades, journal prices have consistently increased well above the general rate of inflation.

Librarians have become increasingly critical of publishers, focusing on journal subscription prices as the significant factor in the serials crisis. It may be argued that this single contributing factor is over emphasised in discussion of the serials crisis. The problems faced by academic libraries as a result of budget restrictions is significant.

The explosion in scholarly information is not only a key factor but one driven from within HE. However, library budget cuts are one element of a larger problem facing the HE sector which cannot be addressed within the scope of this study.

Furthermore, attempts to address the problems associated with the scholarly information explosion tend to focus more on alternative and cheaper formats for publication than on reducing the quantity of published research output. Librarians continue to focus on journal subscription prices and they appear to have legitimate cause for complaint.

There is evidence that the market for commercial journals is anti-competitive and at the very least, does not show much price elasticity. Furthermore, rationalisation, in the form of mergers, has occurred and although users may expect this trend to drive prices down, it has resulted instead in significant price rises.

Publication Costs

The advent of electronic publishing has been hailed by some as an opportunity to overcome these problems. It is argued that electronic publication is much cheaper than publication of hard copy. Proponents of this argument maintain that the cost to print and distribute a journal represents a significant proportion of the total publication cost.

Content is received and refereed free of charge and typically, the author assigns copyright to the publisher who is then free to package the material in any appropriate format and distribute it for a fee.

In an electronic environment, the cost of distributing content is negligible and thus, the total publication cost for an electronic journal should be significantly lower than it is for a print journal. Publishers, among others, argue that fixed costs (or first-copy costs) represent at least 70% of journal production costs and thus that a change in delivery medium could save at most 30% of total costs.

Furthermore, libraries expect publishers to supply electronic journals in multiple formats and end users expect additional functionality from electronic journals, for example multimedia elements, hot links to references, links from abstracting and indexing services or from OPACs to full text.

Clearly, to succeed, any move to replace print journals with electronic journals must be supported by end users and those users will not invest time and effort in learning to use electronic journals unless there appears to be clear advantage in doing so; added functionality, or speed of delivery are examples. However, additional features require time and personnel with expensive skills which adds to production costs.

It is argued that this makes electronic journals at least as expensive to produce as print. A publisher distributing an electronic journal for a fee must also meet the additional cost of controlling access. This is likely to be small if a well-established system such as ATHENS is used (http://www.athens.ac.uk). ATHENS is a JISC-supported service which provides a single password to HE users for accessing new datasets and services within the UK HE community and manages password accounts for the service suppliers. However, although ATHENS is clearly valuable to the HE community, its use may not be consistent with a publisher's commitment to supply statistics on usage to libraries.

Another consideration is that libraries consider it important, having paid for a subscription to a journal, that the volume is still available to their users even if they cancel the subscription at a later date. A publisher can fulfil this requirement by supplying the basic journal content on a portable medium such as a CDROM or by granting permission to the library to create and/or archive a digital copy.

If a publisher itself were to guarantee online access in perpetuity it must migrate such content to new technologies when current technologies become obsolete. These additional costs make it less likely that electronic journals will be cheaper to produce than print journals. To date, publishers have found electronic publishing to be even more expensive than anticipated (Albert Prior, personal communication, 8 February 1999).

The Relationship Between Cost and Price

On balance, it seems that the additional costs associated with publishing a new valueadded product outweigh the costs of reproduction and distribution that are saved. Nevertheless, the argument that journals are overpriced remains valid.

It is important that journals are priced at a level sufficient to recover costs. In a print environment this has never been a problem. On the contrary, commercial journal publishers make large profits, and are sometimes more profitable than companies like Microsoft. Correlation between cost and price is not strong.

As an example, Odlyzko cites the 'three most prestigious maths journals' which are published by a commercial publisher, a university and a scholarly society respectively. Prices vary by a factor of seven, suggesting that first-copy costs are not the primary factor determining price.

Journals are priced according to what the market will bear and, until recently, the market has been relatively inelastic; academic journals are considered to be 'must have' items and one cannot easily be substituted for another should the latter become too expensive. Thus, profit margins in print commercial academic journal publishing generally fall within the range 40–60%.

When compared with, for example, school text publishing at approximately 12–15%, database publishing at approximately 18–20%, or fiction publishing at approximately 5%, it is clear that commercial publishers of print journals have continued to extract large profits despite the financial pressures facing libraries.

There is a clear need for academic libraries to demonstrate to publishers that the demand for scholarly journals is not inelastic. However, while there are no alternatives to the 'must have' material offered by publishers it is very difficult for libraries to do so.

Non-commercial Electronic Journal Publication in Higher Education

As a solution to the serials crisis various stakeholders within the HE sector have proposed that academics bypass commercial companies and publish electronic journals themselves.

There has also been an initiative in the US called the Scholarly Publishing and Academic Resources Coalition (SPARC) which aims to facilitate origination and publication of affordable journals which compete with expensive commercial journals.

SPARC will support sympathetic publishers by guaranteeing a market for their journals. Alternative journal publication models such as these often focus on cost savings gained by:

- Automating the editorial function;
- Dispensing with desk editorial work such as marking up and proof reading; and of course,
- Distributing the material electronically.

Whether costs are reduced or not, a viable economic model must include a costrecovery mechanism. Furthermore, that mechanism should be transparent as users and contributors will consider a publication to be unstable if it has no apparent means of recovering costs.

The additional costs associated with charging subscription fees (e.g. maintaining accounts and restricting access) combined with the 'gift culture' of the Internet that effectively requires most content to be available free of charge, make it difficult to recover costs directly from users.

An alternative to the traditional subscription model recovers costs from authors in the form of page charges and makes journals available to users free of charge. An important element of this model is that page charges should be levied at a rate acceptable to authors as a fee for widespread distribution of their papers; Harnad and Hemus suggest 'dozens rather than hundreds of dollars per page ... $400 for a 20-page article'.

Clearly, papers that are refereed and then rejected must also be paid for by the model. Variations on this model would recover costs by charging only for submission and/or acceptance. In common with the models of others who propose to bypass publishers, Harnad's model and variations of it require a reduction in publishing costs when compared with print journals.

The Institute of Physics Publishing Publishing (IoPP) and Deutsche Physikalische Gesellschaft (DPG) have recently launched a new pure electronic journal, the *New Journal of Physics*, that is based on this type of model (http://www.njp.org/).

The journal was started after widespread international consultation with librarians and physicists. It is available on the Internet free of charge to users. Authors are required to pay $500 on acceptance of their papers. A discount is available for IoP or DPG members.

Authors are invited to submit only articles of 'outstanding scientific quality; likely to be widely read and highly cited'. Presumably, this criterion is intended to keep the rejection rate low so that the publication fee can cover the costs of papers that are refereed and rejected. The rejection rate of papers in science disciplines tends to be much lower than in social sciences at rates of around 10–30%.

This initiative suggests that IoPP and DPG consider it viable that the *New Journal of Physics* be financed by author acceptance fees of only $500. A journal consisting of, say, 120 papers would be produced for only $60 000. If a journal produced at this cost were to adopt subscription as a price mechanism it could recover costs by selling 1000 subscriptions for only $60 or 500 subscriptions for only $120. Either rate would be very cheap for a physics journal.

This comparison suggests either that:

- Those publishers who claim that 'no-frills' electronic publishing is almost as expensive as print publishing are wrong;
- That the cost of journal production in either format bears no relation to the subscription price and that many commercial publishers are determined to maintain high margins.

Economic Characteristics of the Academic Information Delivery Chain

Authors and Editors

Among these models, there are undoubtedly some that accurately represent the economics of publishing electronic journals at reduced cost. However, the journals produced would almost certainly not incorporate the additional functionality demanded by users as it would be too costly to do so.

The incentive for authors to submit their papers to these 'bargain basement' publications and for academics to leave the editorial boards of quality commercial journals to sit on the boards of these journals is unclear.

The importance of academics in their capacity as authors and editors must be recognised if a useful economic model of electronic journals is to be developed. Authors are not simply content originators; they drive the information explosion by seeking the most prestigious outlets for their increasing quantities of journal articles.

Both authors and editors then apply pressure to ensure that their institutional libraries hold the journals to which they are affiliated either as authors or as editors. Thus, academics as authors and editors effectively represent demand in this 'market'.

Libraries

The economic model of electronic journal publication proposed by Andrew Odlyzko identifies library costs as the significant element in the 'serials crisis'. Odlyzko argues that a system-wide perspective reveals that the serials crisis is a library cost crisis.

Libraries have focused on subscription prices as a visible problem which contributes to library budget crises but, in fact, for every $1 spent on journal acquisition, $2 is spent on processing, storing and handling print journals.

Furthermore, if publishers were to include many library functions in their delivery systems, libraries subscribing to their electronic journals would save so much in operating costs that they could afford to pay subscription fees at or above their current levels.

Comparative cost–benefit analyses of a hard-copy journal collection and access to an electronic archive, conducted at the University of Michigan supports Odlyzko's arguments that holding a traditional journal collection is an inefficient use of library resources.

However, the cost to publishers of compensating for the relative lack of information skills among end users when compared with librarians is not insignificant. 'Ease and relevance of retrieval is directly proportional to the work put into the data beforehand', and that work represents additional cost.

One reason why publishers have found electronic publishing to be more expensive than anticipated is that they have included in their systems some functions that, in a print environment, were undertaken by other information professionals (Albert Prior, personal communication, 8 February 1999).

A controversial element in Odlyzko's model is his explanation of how publishers will make available in digital form archives of previously published volumes. Odlyzko claims that digitisation costs are small (as low as $0.60 per page) and suggests that publishers digitise their back runs and make them available to libraries.

This, he says, would be a one-off investment for a publisher migrating to the digital environment. Experience of projects in the UK electronic libraries programme (eLib) indicates that creation of accurate, searchable digital text is much more expensive than Odlyzko suggests.

Furthermore, the cost of this activity would not be recovered quickly. The cost of digitising journal archives is a major market entry problem for existing commercial publishers of academic journals (David Worlock, personal communciation, 9 February 1999).

Odlyzko acknowledges that costs vary significantly depending on what level of functionality is required. He claims that the last 20% of functionality accounts for 80% of the costs. Reports suggests that, for users, a primary interest in electronic journals arises from the added functionality of the new medium.

Odlyzko's model requires users to differentiate essential functions from those that are nice to have. At present this distinction is likely to be arbitrary. The SuperJournal project found use of electronic journals to be 'an essential pre-condition for answering the question of what readers really want'. Until exploitation of functionality has been developed and explored, it will be difficult for anyone to identify the essential functions of electronic journals in the 21st century.

Users

A system-wide view of the costs and benefits of producing and delivering journal articles must acknowledge the costs and benefits to users. Some of these are referred to above, for example additional functionality is an added benefit as is access to users' desktops; time taken to visit the library is directly related to use of library resources. However, the time that it takes to identify high-quality information and to download it to the desktop is a cost as is time spent learning to use a new interface.

This is demonstrated by the fact that users will not invest time learning to use a new system unless a critical mass of material is available using that system. All of these factors will affect users' uptake of electronic journals but many of them are fluid and are difficult to quantify.

Pricing Mechanisms

The pricing mechanism in traditional journal publishing (annual subscription per title) creates a very low-risk market for journal publishers. The consumer base is widespread and payment is made in advance. In an electronic environment, it is unnecessary to bundle articles into issues before distributing them; it is possible to distribute individual articles on-demand at very low cost to the publisher.

It is possible also to reconfigure bundles to better meet the needs of researchers in specific disciplines and subject areas, e.g. to include in a bundle articles from a variety of journals which may be published by a range of different publishers.

Bundling

For electronic journals, a very low-risk pricing mechanism from the publishers' point of view is a site licence arrangement whereby a publisher's entire list is licensed to one or more institutions as a single product.

This is known as bundling. This not only guarantees payment in advance; it also secures payment for low-use journals which subscribing institutions might otherwise cancel. The UK Pilot Site Licence Initiative (PSLI) is a high-profile example which used bundling as a pricing mechanism.

Pricing schemes adopted by publishers participating in the PSLI varied but all represented some form of bundling. Several of the publishers effectively extracted more revenue by offering as a single product all of the titles on their lists. Institutions valued these titles differently; i.e. on a single subscription basis institutions A and B would have subscribed to different titles but during the PSLI both institutions paid for a collection of titles which included their selected journals among others.

The PSLI represented an opportunity to introduce electronic journals to large numbers of users throughout the UK. However, its value as a means of testing the pricing mechanisms and pricing levels was limited. Not only were the costs subsidised by the JISC but publishers were not necessarily testing realistic pricing models.

The Institute of Physics Publishing, for example, made electronic copy of its journals available free of charge to institutions that subscribed to hard copy of those titles.

An IoPP representative at that time described this pricing strategy as unrealistic and said that charges would be introduced. The PSLI was criticised for propping up the 'serials crisis'; not only did it mask the effect of rising subscription prices, it also sustained circulation levels of high-cost, low-use journals that many libraries would otherwise have cancelled. For the duration of the initiative, use of PSLI journals was limited; the PSLI resources were used heavily at only six institutions.

It was possible however, to identify 'core' materials that were heavily used and a large number of titles that were used only occasionally. HEFCE suggested that, in future, institutions may use these data to negotiate different rates of discount on titles published by a single publisher. If institutions succeed in these negotiations, one of the benefits of a bundled site licence may be lost to those publishers.

When the PSLI ended, the National Electronic Site Licence Initiative (NESLI) was established. NESLI is a service rather than a project. It was established with JISC funds but the cost of content provided to institutions is not subsidised and NESLI must become self financing.

NESLI will attempt to address the issues raised by the PSLI with a view to meeting the needs of libraries and end users in the UK HE community. A model licence has been developed with a view to agreeing standard terms with publishers.

Not all publishers will agree to all of these terms, but the journals of those that do will be offered through a seamless interface which allows users to access the journals of a range of publishers. The variety of proprietary systems required to access PSLI journals proved to be frustrating for users.

The formal launch of the NESLI service is expected in October 1999. Institutions will also be granted ownership of the electronic copy of journals to which they subscribe; i.e. access will not be withdrawn when subscriptions are cancelled.

Other issues being explored include the facility to subscribe to subject-based clusters of journals from a variety of publishers, the facility to link to NESLI journal articles from library OPAC entries, and supply of useful management information in the form of statistics on 'hits' at various levels including table of contents, abstracts and full text.

An important difference between NESLI and the PSLI is that the latter tied the price of electronic copy of journals to the price of hard copy offering subscriptions only to parallel publications. NESLI aims to offer access to the electronic format alone if publishers are willing and institutions wish to subscribe on those terms.

Thus, if Odlyzko is correct and the 'serials crisis' is largely related to the cost of handling and storing print journals, NESLI will enable libraries significantly to reduce the costs associated with journal subscriptions.

Price Differentiation

As well as facilitating sale of products in bundles that vary in size and content from an article to a publishers' entire list, the electronic environment facilitates price differentiation, i.e. varying the price of information with willingness to pay. An example of the potential for price differentiation was identified by researchers working on the ACORN project at Loughborough University.

It was suggested that if charges for journal articles from the electronic reserve service were introduced, they may be escalated towards the exam period. This would effectively reduce the load at peak times by charging a higher rate to students who cram for exams.

Price differentiation can be implemented only if differences in user types are easily observable. In a print environment, it is possible to differentiate between different types of journal subscriber, for example professional vs. educational or library vs. individual.

However, it is very difficult to observe user characteristics beyond this, e.g. to observe the quantity of articles read by any researcher or their relative use of tables of contents, abstracts, and full-text articles. In an electronic environment, it is feasible to observe different types of use.

Thus, it should be possible to differentiate between users based on the quality and quantity of the information that they require or for which they are willing to pay. For example, some users may be willing to pay for additional functionality such as hotlinks to all citations in a paper, while others would be willing to forgo this facility to access the text at a cheaper rate.

It is increasingly common for authors to publish the text of their research papers on the Internet despite publishers' attempts to protect their exclusive right to publish. It has been predicted that when publishers have to cede exclusivity on individual papers, they will begin to trade in added value, for example retrieval services tailored to individual needs.

PEAK: Exploring bundling and price Differentiation

The PEAK project at the University of Michigan is a collaborative venture with Elsevier Science which aims to test three different pricing models for electronic journals. The models are based on the economic theory on bundling and on price differentiation.. It is argued that:

- 'Non-linear pricing is facilitated by lower transaction costs for fine-grained purchases and feasible direct usage monitoring' by publishers or libraries;

- That bundling can extract revenue from those who value content differently. A key research objective of PEAK is generalisability to other user populations.

The number of possible dimensions which can be manipulated when defining a bundle is very large, for example, the 'article component (abstract, references, text etc.); time limit on usage (unlimited, per use, per year etc.); and usage rights (read only, read and print etc.)'.

To infer anything from data gathered during PEAK, it was necessary that the variables be limited. Only three different pricing mechanisms are being tested. These are described below.

- The electronic journal is supplied on the same terms as a traditional print subscription, i.e. articles are made available on an issue-by-issue basis to all authorised users at a subscribing university.
- The Institution pays in advance for a specific number of articles and may then access articles from any of the 1100 titles available from Elsevier in electronic form. The fee paid is $5.46 per article. If the institution has used these 'vouchers' and wishes to purchase more it must pay for them at the higher rate of $7. Thus, Elsevier and the institution share the risk. Note that both the reduced voucher price of $5.46 and the higher rate of $7 are very low and when converted at the current exchange rate ($1.571/£1 on 19 May 1999) both are cheaper than the price of an interlibrary loan request from the British Library (£4.95).
- Articles are ordered as required and are paid for either by the institution or by individual users within institutions. Articles are more expensive to order in this way than they are in model.

When an individual has ordered an article through PEAK, it is made available to all users at that individual's institution and use of that article is then monitored. On average, each article has been accessed 2.5 times.

The three pricing mechanisms operated by PEAK are effectively two-part tariff schemes as institutions are required to pay $25K to the University of Michigan to join PEAK and then they incur fees for journals and/or articles.

Although there are three discrete pricing schemes, participating institutions need not restrict themselves to one. They may, for example, subscribe to 'core journals' and buy vouchers for additional provision.

Ten institutions are participating in the PEAK project. Very few results have been reported by PEAK researchers but initial results indicate that the traditional subscription is the least popular pricing model. The PEAK project is due to end in August 1999.

Electronic Individual Article Supply

One of the pricing mechanisms being tested by PEAK is electronic individual article supply (eIAS). This mechanism effectively disintegrates the traditional product and increases the publisher's risk. The publisher is no longer paid in advance for a package of around 120 articles to be delivered in 6 or 12 issues throughout the year. The publisher can no longer focus marketing effort on the 120-article bundle and its identifiable market; each article must sell on its own merits and thus is an individual product.

The eIAS model characterises access or 'just-in-time' provision as an alternative to holdings or 'just-in-case' provision. Users can benefit from access to a much wider range of titles than the institution could afford if it maintained journal subscriptions.

Furthermore, comparison of the costs of access and holdings models indicate that the former is economically efficient for libraries and is popular with end users. However, to date, the scale of comparative studies conducted has been limited; there may be economies or diseconomies of scale inherent in a large-scale access model which are not yet evident.

IAS in those studies was not a seamless process whereby the end user searched, identified and received articles directly from the supplier and had them delivered electronically to her desktop. Although end users had access to the OPACs of collaborating universities and thus were able to identify the location of requested items, orders were made via librarians at the borrowing and lending libraries and documents were supplied in hard copy by post or courier.

To date, access models have tended to rely on library privilege whereby libraries are legally permitted, without paying a copyright fee, to supply an individual with a single copy of a document for the purposes of research or private study.

However, users must sign a print request before they receive their copy of the requested document. Thus, the process whereby the end user searches, identifies and receives the required resource is necessarily interrupted and this interruption represents a significant additional library administration cost.

Furthermore, widespread adoption of an access model which relies on library privilege would undermine the economic incentive to publish as libraries would cancel journal subscriptions thus reducing subscription bases and publishers would receive no alternative revenue from article supply. Publishers are unlikely to comply with library requests for permission to fulfil ILL requests electronically.

Alternative copyright-cleared sources of individual articles in electronic form are available. It is difficult to assess their relative costs and benefits when compared with subscription, however, as services offering copyright-cleared articles tend to operate complex price differentiation policies. These policies can be based on several of the following variables: the country from which a request originates; the type of user; the number of requests; the type of delivery; and the speed of delivery.

Most services offer at least two alternative payment mechanisms, including, most commonly, pay-as-you-go schemes based on credit card payment and payment in advance based on deposit accounts or pre-paid forms. One drawback of pricing electronic articles individually is that the facility to hotlink to citations is less attractive when every link incurs an additional fee.

It is worth noting that JISC has agreed in principle to provide sums to help launch an eIAS service in the UK under JISC/PA auspices, but the details of the Tender call have yet to be concluded.

Scholarly Communication and the Market

A recent eLib supporting study compared different models for pricing electronic scholarly journal articles including those based on bundling, price differentiation and IAS. Fishwick *et al.* consider the current academic information delivery chain to be inefficient due to a number of distortions in the supply–demand chain. Among these are that:

- Authors represent a principal source of demand for publication but make no contribution to publication costs;
- Those consuming the information, i.e. the readers, seldom pay for it, preferring instead to obtain it from libraries;
- Much of the journal publication work is undertaken by editors and referees without payment, or with minimal honoraria.

Fishwick *et al.* propose an alternative model which introduces 'normal' market feedback mechanisms into the academic information delivery chain with a view to overcoming the serials crisis and developing an efficient market for scholarly articles.

The most efficient pricing mechanism would be determined by the market; a number of alternatives would be available in the first instance. Publication would be funded by authors and users both of whom contribute to demand. The publisher would receive usage-based payment at a level sufficient to sustain the model.

Editors and referees would be paid to encourage efficiency, and authors would receive royalties to encourage them to submit for publication only material of the highest quality.

Papers would then be available individually or in customised bundles from the publisher database. Included in the system would be a mechanism to support authors who cannot afford to pay a submission fee. Furthermore, payment by authors would facilitate publication of papers that may be important scientifically but are unlikely to be popular among readers at their time of publication.

The current system for selecting papers to be published in a journal, peer review, assesses them based primarily on quality rather than wholly on their likely popularity at the time of publication. The contents of a journal issue will contain a selection of papers, some of which will be widely read at the time of publication and some of which will attract very few readers. In economic terms the former subsidise the latter.

When the journal is disaggregated and electronic copy of each article sold ondemand this cross-subsidisation will end and publishers may find it difficult to recover the publication costs of lesser-read papers.

The authors of the study acknowledge that publication of such papers may not be guaranteed, and suggest that public support be available to ensure that all important developments are recorded through publication; the merit of all papers would continue to be gauged by peer review. The basic product would be unsophisticated electronic text.

Additional functionality would be available for a higher fee. An important element of this model, it is claimed, would be generation of management data based on usage which would be useful to library managers and publishers. This type of feedback is most useful if users are required to prioritise between materials that are available to them. Thus, it is argued that access should be rationed, even to material obtained by site licence.

Printing and additional functionality are approached in the same way, i.e. it is suggested that if users are required to pay for prints they will filter before, rather than after they print. This argument suggests that end users waste resources by gathering information that they do not really need.

Time, for any student or researcher, is a scarce resource and it takes time to gather information. If end users do need all of the information that they acquire, it may be argued that rationing would prejudice their ability to work effectively.

Fishwick *et al.*'s model incorporates elements from many different economic models including Harnad's model. However, in spirit, the model is the antithesis of Harnad's.

Harnad argues convincingly that scholarly communication differs from other types of publication in that it is not a commercial market. Authors of journal articles are not motivated by the promise of royalty payments; they want their papers to be distributed as widely as possible and, in the past, have often paid to acquire offprints so that they could contribute to this dissemination process.

This view is reinforced by a recent study of what authors want from publication. Fishwick's argument that structural problems in the current system preclude the introduction of an efficient system that would benefit all stakeholders is compelling but uncomfortable for those who consider scholarly communication necessarily to be qualitatively different from trade commodities.

Whether or not the principle of introducing normal market economics into the scholarly communication chain is valid, certain elements of the model proposed by Fishwick *et al.* are problematic:

- Like many other HE proponents of alternative models for scholarly communication, Fishwick *et al.* claim that print and distribution represent the most significant costs in the journal production process and thus, that distribution in an electronic environment should be significantly cheaper. This would be an important factor in maintaining authors' publication fees at an affordable level. The proportion that print and distribution contribute to publication costs is a contentious issue. However, it may be less important than many authors suggest as publication costs may well be low even though current prices are very high.
- The basic product proposed by Fishwick *et al.* is unsophisticated electronic text. It may be difficult to persuade authors and editors to abandon print journals in favour of such a 'bargain basement' publication. However, if submission fees are introduced, and thus submission in high-quality journals is expensive, those authors not in receipt of large research grants may find that they cannot afford to publish in a high-quality publication.

Thus, the result could be a two-tier system whereby research that is not grant funded is published in the Fishwick *et al.* alternative system and grant-funded research is published in a more sophisticated format.

This problem could be overcome only if all authors, including those in receipt of large grants, are prepared to publish in and thus to support 'alternative' journals that are cost effective for HE such as those proposed by SPARC.

This would require a massive attitude shift among important authors. At present authors publish in the most prestigious journals because to do so carries more weight with regard to research assessment and tenure awards. Authors would have to be persuaded of the utilitarian benefits of publishing in 'alternative' cost-effective journals. It is difficult to imagine how such an attitude shift would come about.

International co-operative agreements resulting in HE policy directives may solve the problem but co-operation at a national level let alone at that level is notoriously difficult to achieve. Because this model differs radically from that proposed by Harnad and his ilk, it was also evaluated in the research reported later in this report.

THE MODELS

A variety of different approaches to publishing cost effective electronic journals have been proposed in recent years. Many have common characteristics. Four models will be tested here. The second models non-commercial production of a journal that is available for use free of charge on the Internet as described by Harnad. The third is a non-commercial journal funded by users by a combination of subscription and eIAS.

The fourth is an alternative non-commercial journal model proposed by the authors which differs from the third model only in that costs are recovered through a combination of a modest submission fee and sales of subscriptions and individual articles. None of these models assumes that the production process will be conducted entirely by academics or other stakeholders who have neither experience nor expertise in publishing.

User studies show that professional design is important to user acceptance. Journal production and related tasks such as marketing are undertaken more efficiently by publishing professionals; this is reflected in the models. Tasks that can be automated effectively are automatic in all of the models.

The Conservation Ecology (CE) project has demonstrated that all administrative tasks in the editorial process can be automated and, in an international enterprise, that an automated system can be more effective as it is not constrained by a time zone. Furthermore, the cost of copy editing *Conservation Ecology* is much cheaper than the equivalent cost in a print environment because the bulk of formatting is done automatically1.

Conservation Ecology is published by two permanent employees, a parttime production editor and a part-time systems administrator. All versions of each manuscript are archived by the software. Metadata can be amended at minimal cost as standards change by using a formatting template.

The whole process can be decentralised because all actors in the chain can access files remotely from any networked PC throughout the world. There is no reason why any of the models described here should differ from the others with regard to exploitation of this type of system so editorial costs for each of the models will be based on the CE model.

Variables in the Models

All evidence to date suggests that people prefer not to read at length on screen. They may use the electronic medium to search and identify resources and they will read small portions of text on screen but having established that they wish to read a substantial amount of text such as a journal paper, users obtain a print.

Often electronic journals are not even published in a format suited for reading on screen; electronic versions of journals published in parallel print and electronic form tend to be made available in PDF, a format that is cheap to produce in a parallel production process but is designed to be printed.

The models explored here will be used to examine the economic implications for users and/or their institutions of tending to print or read on screen. One variable with a very significant impact on costs for electronic journal production is the degree of functionality required by users. Most of the models described here require a reduction in production costs. This implies a lack of additional functionality. It has been suggested that users not only want additional functionality but are unwilling to learn to use new systems unless there are clear functional advantages.

However, despite their expressed interest in additional functionality, in practice end users are most interested in content, browsing (including linking), and printing. Odlyzko asserts that cost-effective journal production requires users to discriminate between those functions that they need and those that they would like.

However, although it is claimed that added functionality will significantly increase journal production costs there are no published data which differentiate the costs of different functional elements. Odlyzko estimates that the last 20% of functionality will incur 80% of the total cost but does not attempt to apply this with reference to different functions.

Variations in electronic journal production costs should be explored but it is beyond the scope of this project to do so. Generally, it is assumed that scholarly journal articles have a limited audience. This characteristic contributes to the expense of publishing such articles.

First copy costs are inevitably spread across a relatively small number of potential users. However, some recent work has suggested that the market for journal articles can be expanded. Odlyzko forecasts increasing use of journal articles by pressure groups. This is plausible given the recent shift in political activity among ordinary citizens towards single-issue politics. Researchers at Project Muse found that institutions that had not subscribed to John Hopkins University Press titles in print did subscribe to journals in electronic form.

MONOGRAPHS AND TEXTS

For the purposes of this report, a monograph is defined as a low-volume work intended for library purchase and use as a resource by researchers. The market for monographs is 'global and export driven'. In contrast, a textbook is defined as being intended to be used as a teaching resource and for student use. If successful, a textbook may be reprinted or new editions may be issued.

Textbooks usually depend on the home market; they are 'developed or adapted in the local market'. However, the distinction between textbooks and monographs is not always clear cut. In any case, it is difficult for publishers accurately to predict the size of the market for a work.

Some works commissioned as textbooks sell so few copies that perhaps they should be categorised as monographs and some commissioned as monographs are far more successful than anticipated and may reasonably be categorised as textbooks. There may be a greater rationale for supplying a textbook in electronic form than for a monograph.

The former is likely to be required by large numbers of students at the same time, while the latter is likely to be consulted by individuals and demand is unlikely to be concentrated to specific time periods. As people do not like to read more than a small amount of text on screen, a monograph in electronic form is unlikely to meet user needs. It would be too expensive, both financially and in time, to print the work.

However, if a textbook were required by all students in a large undergraduate class it may be viable as an electronic product as all students in the class could access it at any time, perhaps from their residences, and select those parts that they wished to print. Experience on the ELINOR project suggests that students do not use electronic text in this way; they use it to identify useful materials which they then borrow from the library shelves.

This experience may however, have been due to design, screen resolution and similar factors. As these factors are constantly improving, so a similar experiment run today may generate different results.

Developments towards electronic books for individual use that are portable and facilitate book marking, annotation etc. in the form of Rocket eBook and other similar tools while important, are not library developments and will not be explored in this study.

Monographs

The obvious advantage of digital publishing of monographs is that there is no requirement to invest in inventory (David Worlock, personal communication, 11 February 1999). Nevertheless, digital publication requires investment in first copy costs and, as in most publishing ventures, these represent the most significant proportion of monograph publishing costs. Developments in digital publication of monographs is at a very early stage.

The experience of University presses in the US is that if monographs are made available free of charge over the Internet, sales of hard copy increase 2–3-fold. This is attributed to the reluctance of users to read on screen or to spend time and money downloading and printing substantial quantities of text which are available in a more convenient format from booksellers.

These early projects have explored the market for digital analogues of print monographs. Studies with journal users suggests that it is inadequate simply to deliver in a digital environment material which has been designed for print; to be useful, digital resources should be designed for the medium.

Those publishers attempting to explore the utility of the digital environment for monograph publishing have come to question its suitability and suggest that this environment may change the very nature of the format. For example, use of open review pre-publication may, ultimately, result in a new format: a hybrid between a journal and a monograph.

Publishers are aware that for digital monographs to succeed added value is likely to be important. However, they argue that any additional functionality will increase the cost, and therefore, the price of monographs. In recent years, 'monograph publishing has almost disappeared in many disciplines because short print runs and library budget problems have made it untenable'. Any increase in cost and price is likely to exacerbate rather than alleviate this problem.

Texts

Publishers have used digital technology to offer university and college teachers the facility to customise texts. For example, Wiley's custom publishing service offers teachers the facility to select chapters from a CD-ROM database of large general texts in a specific subject.

Chapters must be drawn from a minimum of two titles and the teacher must order a minimum of 30 copies. The material is collated, bound and delivered to the campus bookseller for sale to students.

Perhaps custom publishing by the publisher precludes alternative means for students of obtaining the information. Thus, by adapting to the market, Wiley is more likely to maintain its customer share and profitability. Furthermore, when texts represent good value, students may be more prepared to buy them and become less reliant on library provision for core materials. Developments at Wiley use digital technology for production but not for delivery and thus this experiment has limited relevance to the digital library.

There is no evidence to date to suggest that texts are being produced for electronic delivery. Development work in this area suggests that, as yet, there is no market for digital texts. The Internet can, however, be used effectively to facilitate sale of peripheral products such as self-marking tests for certification of professional skills such as nursing. Such tests are also delivered free as an value-added supplement to a print publication, i.e. effectively as an incentive to buy/use the associated text.

As with journals, publishers are working with academics to explore ways of utilising the digital medium for teaching. A good example is ChemConnections, a Wiley collaboration with the University of California and Beloit College which is grant-funded by the National Science Foundation.

ChemConnections comprises a number of modules which can be used over a period of weeks for teaching on a variety of different areas of chemistry. Evidence to date suggests that, as yet, publishers are only exploring the utility of the medium for both text and monograph publishing.

Economic modelling is likely to be explored much later in the development cycle, after products have been shown to be sufficiently useful that libraries and/or academic departments would pay for them. At that time, publishers expect developments such as the digital object identifier (DOI) to be important in facilitating commercial transactions. '

As yet use of metadata by monograph publishers is inconsistent and ad-hoc. Given the embryonic state of electronic monograph publishing it is likely that a more consolidated approach to charging models will emerge in the future'. No economic model for producing and delivering electronic texts has been published. Therefore, this area is not the subject of a modelling exercise here.

ELECTRONIC DATASETS

The economic model for electronic reference works is better established than for most other areas of the digital library. A database or dataset consisting of a number of databases is generally supplied on licence either on CD-ROM or online. Where both formats are available the price tends to be similar.

Negotiation of licence terms can be undertaken by institutions individually or by consortia. Economic factors related to licence negotiation are covered below in the section on licensing.

In the UK, the Combined Higher Education Software Team (CHEST) negotiates with dataset suppliers on behalf of the JISC to secure favourable access terms for UK Higher Education Institutions (HEIs) and to standardise terms and conditions of use wherever possible.

Standardised terms reduce costs for all parties including individual institutions which must adhere to those terms. Networked access to these commercially supplied datasets from one of JISC's data centres (BIDS, EDINA, and MIDAS) is then offered to the HE community.

Each individual institution can choose which of the available datasets it wishes to pay for and, for an annual fee, it obtains a site licence. Institutions then supply end users with access to these datasets free at the point of use.

CHEST licences are usually agreed for five years so institutions subscribing to a dataset commit to take it until the end of the CHEST agreement. The five-year commitment has been cited by several institutions as a reason for not taking JISC datasets.

The price of a dataset is obviously important to institutions when deciding whether or not to subscribe but it is not the only factor. Some JISC datasets are made available to the community free of charge but uptake is still not universal. One reason may be that use of datasets by end users can increase demand for journals and ILLs, and thus increase pressure on the workload of library staff.

Another is that even a 'free' dataset involves the HEI in some opportunity costs. An economic advantage to institutions of supplying datasets to end users is a reduction in mediated online searching. Furthermore, as more datasets become available online rather than on CD-ROM, technical support and maintenance costs are reduced. The current annual subscription with a minimum commitment, usually of five years, does not suit many UK HEIs, especially smaller institutions.

A recent survey of attitudes to pricing of JISC-funded databases found that institutions would like the option of usage-based payment. There was also a call to render prices more equitable by allowing a number of small institutions to subscribe as a consortium which would pay at the same rate as a large institution; institution size would be based on student numbers. It is difficult to model provision of datasets to the UK HE community as:

- The term dataset covers a wide range of different types and volumes of content;
- The contribution of the JISC and the terms that it demands from suppliers are unclear. As this is not a controversial area and economic relationships are established and work effectively it is not modelled and explored here.

Bibliography

Ajay Kumar Srivastav and Rajesh Kumar Singh: *Glossary of Library Information Communication and Technological Terms and Acronyms*, Shree Pub, 2007.

Ajit Singh Siwatch: *Encyclopedic Dictionary of Library and Information Science, Vols. I to III*, Shree Publishers, 2010.

Amjad Ali: *Ane's Encyclopedic Dictionary of Library and Information Science*, Ane Books India, 2006.

B. Rajasree and P. Aravinda: *Glossary of Library and Information Science*, Anmol.

B.S. Aggarwal: *Issues in Library Information Science*, Oxford Book Company, 2007 .

Bhupendra Narayan Singh: *Encyclopaedia of Library and Information Science in the Digital Age Vols. I to III*, Anmol Pub, 2011.

Bikika Laloo Tariang: *Essays on Library and Information Science Education*, Ess Ess Publications, 2012.

C K Sharma; Rakesh Kumar and Akhil Kumar Singh: *Library and Information Science (3 Vols-Set)*, Atlantic, 2008.

C Lal and K Kumar: *Descriptive Questions in Library and Information Science*, Ess Ess Pub, 2010.

C.D. harma: *Advances in Library and Information Science Vol. 1: Computer Applications*, Scientific, 1995.

C.K. Sharma: *Encyclopaedic Dictionary of Library Information Science and Network*, JBD, 2002.

C.R. Karisiddappa: *Current Studies in Library and Information Science,* Manak, 1994.

Cherian Mathew: *Dynamics of Library and Information Science*, Cyber Tech Publicaitons, 2011.

D.B. Patil and M.M. Kooganuramath: *Library and Information Science*, APH, 2011.

I.M. Goswami: *Encyclopaedia of Library and Information Science (5 Vols-Set)*, Commonwealth, 1997.

Jogender Singh Burman: *Encyclopaedic Survey of Library and Information Science : Principles and Practices (5 Vols-Set)*, Rajat

Publication, 2006.

K.A. Isaac: *Glimpses of Library and Information Science*, Ess Ess, 2001.

Kundan Godia: *Electronic Services in Library and Information Science*, Adhyayan, 2007.

L.S. Ramaiah: *Images and Perceptions in Library and Information Science*, Ess Ess, 1998.

Mahendra Kumar Seth: *A Guide to Library and Information Science Jobs*, Abhijeet Publications, 2006.

Manisha Dawra: *Encyclopaedia of Modern Library and Information Science (5 Vols-Set)*, Rajat Pub, 2003.

P.P. Rawat, O.P. Gupta and V. Venkatappaiah: *Current Developments in Library and Information Science : Papers presented in honour of Prof. P.N. Kaula on his 71st Birthday*, Reliance, 1998.

Punit Ralhan: *Advancement in Library and Information Science*, Oxford Book Company, 2009 .

Raghunath Pandey and M.N. Velayudhan Pillai: *History of Library and Information Science*, Jnanada Prakashan, 2011.

Santosh Patel: *Library Information : Preservation and Access*, Authors Press, 2003.

Shyama Balakrishnan and P.K. Paliwal: *Library Information Procedure*, Anmol, 2001.

Tariq Ashraf and Sanjay Kumar Jha: *Handbook of UGC Net for Library and Information Science*, Synergy Books India, 2014.

Vrushali Dandavate: *Application of Six Sigma in Library and Information Science*, Ajay Khatri and Pradip Umdale, Ess Ess

Publications, 2013.

Y.L. Chopra and Mamta Chopra: *Challenges Before Library and Information Science in New Millennium,* Ess Ess, 2001.

Index